Khans and Shahs

Khans and Shahs

A History of the Bakhtiyari Tribe in Iran

GENE R. GARTHWAITE

I.B. TAURIS

LONDON · NEW YORK

Paperback edition published in 2009 by I.B.Tauris & Co Ltd
6 Salem Road, London W2 4BU
175 Fifth Avenue, New York NY 10010
www.ibtauris.com

Distributed in the United States and Canada Exclusively by Palgrave Macmillan
175 Fifth Avenue, New York NY 10010

First published in 1983 by Cambridge University Press

ISBN: 978 1 84885 096 5

A full CIP record for this book is available from the British Library
A full CIP record is available from the Library of Congress

Library of Congress Catalog Card Number: available

Printed and bound in India by Thomson Press India Ltd

TO COLE, EMMA, DYLAN, AND ABIGAIL

Contents

Note on transliteration
The *International Journal of Middle East Studies* system, without diacritics, is generally
followed except for Persian or Arabic words commonly used in English. The *izafah* is not
indicated.

Acknowledgments

When members of the Bakhtiyari families opened up their collection of documents for my research, I had no intention of publishing either their texts or photographs of them; I personally took the photographs for my own study purposes. Subsequently, I decided to include them in this monograph, and planned to return to Iran to rephotograph the documents to be included and to examine them once again more carefully. The revolution has made that impossible; some of the originals have been lost and possibly even destroyed. I apologize for the absence of more technical descriptions and the poor quality of the photographs.

This book simply would not have been possible without the interest, generosity, and hospitality of the Bakhtiyari, especially Suhrab Asʻad, Gudarz Bakhtiyari, Malikshah Zafar-Bakhtiyari, Sarhang Abu al-Fath Uzhan, and Muhandis ʻAli Asghar Bakhtiyar. For assistance in Iran I also wish to thank Iraj Afshar, David Stronach and the British Institute of Persian Studies, Maheen and Ismat Moulavi, Franklin Burroughs, Javad and Surayya Gorji, and the Dr Abol-Ghassem and Helen Bakhtiyar families.

My interest in Iran's social history goes back to 1959–60, when we were members of the University of Chicago's Iranian Prehistoric Project, and I would like to express my gratitude to Bob and Linda Braidwood and Patty Jo and Red Watson, whose encouragement dates back to that year in Kermanshah. Special thanks are due to the late G.E. von Grunebaum, Amin Banani, Hasan Kamshad, and, particularly, Nikki Keddie for their guidance and assistance from the time when I first began my dissertation on the Bakhtiyari.

I am also indebted to those who have read this manuscript either in part at various stages or in its entirety, and who have offered much helpful advice and encouragement: Mustafa Ansari, Lois Beck, Connie Cronin, Dale Eickelman, Ernest Gellner, Bill Irons, Nikki Keddie, Roger Savory, and Richard Tapper. And in this regard I owe special thanks to Jean-Pierre Digard.

I should also like to thank Ann K.S. Lambton, who graciously checked my readings and translations of many of the documents at an early stage. When I finally finished my transcriptions, translations, and notes Alexander Morton carefully, critically, and generously checked them all; I owe a special debt of gratitude to Mr Morton for catching many of my errors and for expanding my understanding.

I would be remiss not to thank my colleagues at Dartmouth College, especially Michael Ermarth, John Major, Marysa Navarro, and Charles Wood; and Gail Patten, who typed, and retyped, the manuscript with her customary accuracy and good cheer. I should also thank Sony Lipton for proofreading and Henry T. Wright for the photograph of the Dasht Gul pools.

Finally, my research has been funded by the G.E. von Grunebaum Center for Near Eastern Studies at U.C.L.A., Dartmouth College, the Social Science Research Council, the National Geographic Society, the American Philosophical Society, the American Council of Learned Societies, and the National Endowment for the Humanities (Translation Grant No. 34994-79-447); I express my appreciation to them.

Preface to the paperback edition

It was late spring 1992 and in Bazoft, a valley deep in the Bakhtiyari Zagros mountains, I signalled to the driver of the jeep to stop at a random group of black tents. We stopped at one of them and were welcomed. After the briefest introduction, I was asked if I was Japanese and when I replied no I was American, the immediate question was about the Rodney King incident and rioting in Los Angeles. My Bakhtiyari hosts had no television, but they did have radios and, moreover, they had relatives who lived in California.

In the mid-1960s the Bazoft valley was remote, but 30 years later modern, asphalted roads had made it easily accessible. These same roads had transformed the formidable Bakhtiyari migration of many weeks into a day trip in which, with ease, families transported their flocks and belongings by truck from the winter to summer pastures. Education, military service and Iran's economic growth, especially in the cities, had brought the Bakhtiyari more outside opportunities and this had resulted in a shortage of shepherds. These newly urbanized Bakhtiyari returned for family celebrations or to help out seasonally. Being Bakhtiyari is changing.

In rethinking *Khans and Shahs* (1983) I am reminded of the importance of the essential bases of history – sources and contexts, including time. Given the political sensitivity of the Bakhtiyari in the Pahlavi period, I was denied access to that region until after the 1979 Revolution. Travelling through that region for the first time in 1992, my earlier notions and ideas were clarified; moreover, I was struck by the extraordinary changes from the government policies of the early 1980s. These observations reinforced my understanding of Bakhtiyari and Iranian history acquired from written sources.

While "revolution" has long lost any specific meaning and is used to describe rapid change as well as a process, it nonetheless results in all kinds of unexpected changes. In popular usage, revolution has come to mean dramatic shifts in power and in the elites exercising that power. The Iranian revolution of 1978–9 saw the overthrow of the Pahlavi dynasty and the establishment of the Islamic Republic of Iran, which resulted in new elites, new policies and institutions that subsequently included a cultural revolution. On the other hand, the 1979 revolution could not have taken place without the Pahlavis', particularly Riza Shah's, centralizing policies and the formation of the modern nation-state. It was this evolutionary revolution that set in train the profound changes to the Bakhtiyari – and not only Bakhtiyari elites – and ended their military and political roles, along with those of Iran's other great tribal confederations.

The revolution also brought to an end a decade-long period of research, especially among British and American scholars, which has yet to be re-established. My own research on the Bakhtiyari was suspended with the expectation that it would be quickly resumed. *Khans and Shahs* ended with the sad note that the whereabouts of the documents upon which it was based were unknown, and with the certainty that a number of them were destroyed and dispersed in the upheaval of the revolution. Furthermore, with the passage of time it became increasingly difficult to re-establish contact with Bakhtiyari families. Death and exile of many of those who had graciously opened their family records to me have taken their toll. The Ilkhani and Hajji Ilkhani families, the two most important of the elite families, had originally allowed me access to family documents on condition I stopped in 1921, for the late Pahlavi period still contained pitfalls for them. Consequently, in *Khans and Shahs* (1983) I only provided a summary overview of post-1921 Bakhtiyari history. Stephanie Cronin helps fill in the details in that time period in her *Tribal Politics in Iran: Rural Conflict and the New State, 1921–1941* (2007), and several anthropological studies cover the late 1960s and 1970s, most notably Jean-Pierre Digard's *Technique des nomads baxtyâri d'Iran* (1981).

In 1992, my thinking moved back and forth across the twentieth century and through the cliché of continuity and discontinuity to arrive at some conclusions that reconciled texts with what I was seeing for the first time. Importantly, central to Bakhtiyari history are four interacting factors. These are the geographic and administrative region; the pastoral nomads particularly associated with it; social and political leadership, historically the elite families' surviving written sources; and the Iranian government. The tribespeople or nomads have experienced different patterns of twentieth-century change from their elite leadership. Increasingly, and beginning with the Constitutional Revolution of 1905–9, the elite leadership assumed national political, economic and government roles as they moved from the Bakhtiyari to Tehran, and to a lesser extent to Isfahan. Even after Riza Shah destroyed the power of the khans in the Bakhtiyari and imprisoned and executed leading khans in the early 1930s, they continued to serve a patronage role between the government and tribespeople until after the 1979 revolution when that role was institutionalized and brought under direct government control in the Organization for the Nomadic Peoples of Iran. The Islamic republican government has attempted to suppress even the historical memory of that earlier leadership – for a time the title *"khan"* (the common male honorific) was not even used in the Bakhtiyari. Similarly, tribesmen with close ties to the *khavanin-i buzurg* (lit. the great or elite khans) benefited economically and likewise moved out of the Bakhtiyari, but the majority of tribespeople continued pastoral nomadism, even while the Pahlavis were incorporating them into their wider policies and even though attempts at forced settlement failed. Later, other government policies on education and economic development had a more gradual, if more profound impact that increasingly afforded the Bakhtiyari people opportunities in Khuzistan, Isfahan and other regions.

These observations reinforce key generalizations that continue to be important. Pastoral nomads depend on a range of strategies and options for survival; second, pastoral nomads require security so that they can plan and exercise those options; third, nomads function within a specific social framework – their own and that of a larger society – that cannot be ignored; fourth, until recently planners who have been frustrated in the failure of the agricultural sector to meet economic goals and who, in many cases, regard pastoral nomads as primitive and out of place in a modern society, have designed the policies that affect pastoral nomads and agriculturalists; and fifth, policies always have significant unexpected consequences.

As I drove through Chahar Mahall/Bakhtiyari, the present administrative nomenclature for the traditional Bakhtiyari summer pasture region (the winter one is still largely in Khuzistan province), I realized from the extraordinary geographical complexity and richness of that region that it constitutes an ecosystem. To the east is the drop-off to the central Iranian plateau and Isfahan; to the north is the Zayandah River and the province of Luristan, access to which the massive mountains of the Kuh Rang watershed limit; to the west – essentially on a northwest to southeast diagonal that follows the Zagros mountains and the Karun River – is Khuzistan, the uplands of which include the Bakhtiyari *garmsir* (winter pastures); and to the south are Boir Ahmad, Kuh Giluyah and Fars. The enclosed region includes vast and rugged mountain ranges, narrow valleys and broad plains. The climate is varied and the area is well watered, which allows for a broad range of plants, shrubs and trees. While agriculture, which pastoral nomads also practise, is typically based on wheat, barley, arboriculture, viniculture and truck farming, rice culture is possible in deep and narrow valleys. This region also includes a far greater variety of people, cultures and societies, as well as of cities, towns, villages and nomadic encampments than I expected.

Despite the diversity of Chahar Mahall/Bakhtiyari, there is a unity in the physical geography that encourages human interaction. This can be seen most graphically in the Bakhtiyari migration that follows trails and roads from Khuzistan through narrow passes to Chahar Mahall. These trails have since become highways that link Khuzistan to Isfahan and to other parts of Iran. Variety and unity can also be seen in the relationships established between pastoral nomads, agriculturalists and the market communities in Chahar Mahall/Bakhtiyari. The interaction between pastoral nomadism and agriculture is complementary but it can also be a source of friction. Settlements may have increased recently – one has only to look at the phenomenal growth of Shahr-i Kurd and other towns even since the revolution – but I suspect that we have underestimated agriculturalists and towns in this region historically.

A related observation, and one to which I shall return, is the importance of options for pastoral nomads. Pastoral nomads have no or little control over critical factors such as changes in the weather or government policies. Precipitation is critical for agriculture and for pastures. Changes in land usage in the last two decades have resulted in increased competition between pastoralists and agriculturalists for scarce resources. Consequently, vulnerability and competition have resulted in increased diversification. One nomad, for example, possessed 1000 head of sheep and goats, agricultural lands and trucks that he used in trade to Khuzistan. He also had four sons, two with him in the *sardsir* (summer pastures) to manage flocks, one who was in the military and another at university. Indeed, the shortage of shepherds has become a chronic problem. This pattern has several variations, including sons who worked in Kuwait or in Iranian urban centres, who would return to help out periodically; resources could be shifted if setbacks or losses were to be anticipated.

Again, in moving through Chahar Mahall/Bakhtiyari and talking to nomads and agriculturalists, I became aware of a number of their qualities. Their self-respect and sense of dignity, their skills and expertise as pastoralists or agriculturalists, and the importance of the underlying social structure immediately struck me. Even from the most casual observation I became aware of their responsiveness to changes in the market. This can be seen in the nomads' and agriculturalists' greatly increased number of flocks, and in the expansion of arable land through either irrigation or extending fields to higher elevations. One can also see that new fields are being cleared of rocks, arable land is being expanded through terracing, and numerous new orchards are being planted.

It is no surprise to hear pastoral nomads ask a stranger what his *tayafah*

– a tribal level or clan designation – might be, but I was struck by how often settled, even urbanized, Bakhtiyari asked the same question. I understood for the first time what the long lists of *tayafah*s in nineteenth- and early twentieth-century written sources signify. The names of the *tayafah* – and subgroups such as *mal* (camping unit) or *tirah* (clan) – are codes that represent and relate the individual to the world, structure social and economic activity, and permit shared responsibility and support – even in cities, outside the Bakhtiyari and pastoral nomadic context. The individual becomes identifiable and new relationships can be established on the basis of *tayafah* without having to go back to yet another starting point. *Tayafah*s, thus, establish a kind of moral solidarity in the face of uncertainty, whether that uncertainty is in the pastoral nomadic sector or in an urban setting.

One last point here relates to the observations I made regarding appropriate technology and administration. The period since the revolution has seen construction of roads and small-scale irrigation projects – leaving aside the massive Kuh Rang Dam, irrigation system and power project in Chahar Mahall – the provision of veterinary services for animals, education and health care for the human population, research on animals and plants, and the administrative structure provided by the Organization for the Nomadic Peoples of Iran. Such modest inputs and projects have had a significant impact on the well-being of the Bakhtiyari and people of Chahar Mahall/Bakhtiyari and have facilitated production and trade by reinforcing indigenous practice and values.

I cannot conclude this section on my observations without noting their impact on my understanding of Bakhtiyari history. The geographical limits of Chahar Mahall/Bakhtiyari were made even clearer to me and resolved several historical problems. I had long suspected that the origin of power of the family of Husain Quli Khan, the first Ilkhani of the Bakhtiyari and generally known by that title, came from their large land-holdings in Chahar Mahall, which are identified in eighteenth-century documents, especially in the rich agricultural area of Mizdij. Estates there and in Khuzistan were to be linked with the Bakhtiyari pastoral nomads through Husain Quli Khan Ilkhani for the first time. Similarly, his conflict with Mu'tamid al-Daulah, governor of Fars, over Falard at the southeast corner of Chahar Mahall – currently part of the province of Chahar Mahall/Bakhtiyari – was a critical one for the Qajars. Had Ilkhani succeeded in controlling Falard, he would have had a base from which to expand his power to encompass Boir Ahmad-Kuh Giluyah and to threaten Fars.

Significant changes have occurred in the Bakhtiyari since Ilkhani's execution in 1299/1882, and he would hardly recognize today's even more complex social and political structures. Long before his death, Iran's integration into the expanding world market and the resulting commercialization of production had affected Iran's pastoral nomads. Subsequent large-scale transformations have had significant economic and political ramifications. The Qajars began tentative centralization of the state, which the Pahlavis would consolidate. Along with the consolidation of state power and more recent state changes, has come the problem of shrinking resources and competition for them. In addition, industrialization and urbanization have affected the nomads.

In a variety of ways nomads have responded to world markets, commercialization, the rise of the state, the development of the nation-state with its new identities, the consolidation of state power, shrinking resources, industrialization and urbanization. New opportunities for economic investment, employment and capital accumulation affect social stratification and the responses nomads make. We should remember too that some policies and factors facilitate while others hinder pastoral nomadism. Iran's pastoral nomads do not live in isolation, in fact they never have; they participate in and are affected by all the changes in the larger Iranian society and culture.

I would like to go back in time to address what it was like to be Bakhtiyari from the vantage point of 1862, 1921 and 1962 before returning to 1992 and the present. In AD 1862 Nasir al-Din Shah awarded Husain Quli Khan the title and office of "*Nazim* of the Bakhtiyari". The firman that made that award was the earliest extant document to recognize the Bakhtiyari as an administrative and political unit. Then in AD 1867 Nasir al-Din Shah, through another firman, granted the title of "*Ilkhani*" to Husain Quli Khan. This firman provided the first documentary evidence of the Bakhtiyari office of *ilkhani* and confirmed the hierarchical structure of the Bakhtiyari when it called on other Bakhtiyari leaders to recognize the suzerainty of Husain Quli Khan. In effect, the central government recognized a single Bakhtiyari confederation. The modern Bakhtiyari identity that encompasses *tayafah* ones, dates from this period when Ilkhani unified his power and the Bakhtiyari.

In these two firmans the Qajars acknowledged Husain Quli Khan's success in establishing and consolidating his power over the Bakhtiyari. Nasir al-Din Shah and his governors apparently hoped to use Husain Quli Khan to maintain order, provide cavalry and remit taxes. In effect, the government sought greater efficiency through a single administrator of a unified Bakhtiyari; and it was more efficient. For example, from 1867 until Ilkhani's execution in 1882, general order prevailed and the Bakhtiyari economy, despite the severe drought of the 1870s, improved.

Later, after the Karun River had been opened to commerce in 1888, the

Iranian government and Bakhtiyari leaders agreed to employ Lynch Brothers to develop the Bakhtiyari Road in 1897. This road linked for the first time the Persian Gulf and Khuzistan with Isfahan and the central Iranian plateau through the Bakhtiyari. (The current highway between Isfahan and Khuzistan follows the original Bakhtiyari Road, which is sometimes referred to as the Lynch Road.) Horses and mules became important not only as pack animals for the new road and internal trade, but also for export to India and Africa. Before his death, Ilkhani had sought to improve animal bloodlines.

Subsequently, and even more importantly, in 1905 these same Bakhtiyari leaders signed an agreement to allow the first oil exploration and development to take place in the Bakhtiyari *garmsir*. Like the road agreement, the various oil agreements could not have gone ahead without Bakhtiyari unity and government (now British) support for that unity. Bakhtiyari commoners were employed as workmen in the fields and as guards on the pipeline. The khans were given oil shares and income and, in turn, they reinvested much of their capital in the Bakhtiyari, Chahar Mahall and Khuzistan, which affected the lives of ordinary Bakhtiyari.

On the other hand, even before Husain Quli Khan's death, Qajar recognition of his consolidation of power posed a threat to them and their rule. This was an unexpected but feared consequence of Bakhtiyari unification under an ambitious *ilkhani* who could rally armed and mounted forces. The Qajars faced similar challenges from their recognition of comparable tribal confederation leaders. In the case of the Bakhtiyari, the confederation was weakened for only a short period after Ilkhani's death. From the time of the Constitutional Revolution – specifically the victory of the constitutionalists under Bakhtiyari leadership in putting down the 1909 attempted coup – until the middle of the 1930s, the Bakhtiyari elite khans played powerful national roles (and could effectively challenge the central government).

The year 1921 marked the rise to power of Reza Khan, subsequently shah in 1926, and the establishment of the modern nation-state. After reuniting Iran, the new Pahlavi ruler sought to centralize, industrialize and Westernize the resultant nation-state and to provide a new identity for its people. Great tribal confederations, like the Bakhtiyari, were perceived as not only a military and political threat to the government and national unity – particularly because of their British ties – but also as anachronistic in the modern era. Pastoral nomads were not found in the West and government policy sought to turn those in Iran into settled farmers and industrial workers. Furthermore, tribal and other identities were seen as competing with new Iranian nationalist ones and attempts were made to remove them. Urban antagonism towards Iran's tribes may have been intensified in this period over the issue of identity and the various tribes' relationships with nationalism. From an urban perspective, pastoral nomads were now not only rustics, whose loyalties to the nation were questioned, but also uncivilized. In addition, the educational and cultural reforms implemented in cities widened the urban–rural and pastoral–nomadic gap.

Throughout the 1920s and early 1930s Reza Shah went through a sequence of co-opting tribal leaders, disarming the tribes, imprisoning or executing their leaders, imposing military administration over tribal areas and finally adopting forced settlement policies. No government inputs were provided and the economic impact of what were essentially political and military policies was not considered. The government showed no understanding of pastoral nomadism let alone concern for the costs to pastoralists. Drought and the imposition of new taxes and compulsory military service exacerbated the impact of such consequential changes.

The tribes never again successfully challenged the centralization of the nation-state and the political and economic power of the tribal leaders was greatly weakened. Even before 1941 and the abdication of Riza Shah, pastoral nomads resisted forced settlement and many returned to nomadism. What the government achieved was at a great cost to pastoral nomads in terms of human and animal life and to that sector of the economy. There were unexpected consequences for Iran's economy as a whole, which in the 1920s and 1930s was still predominantly agricultural. The effects of these dislocations in terms of reduced income to the state, decreased amounts of capital and shortages of essential foods affected Iranians long after 1941.

The first phase of land reform was initiated in 1962. The initial goal was to redistribute land to peasant landholders with a view eventually to increasing agricultural production and raising the rural standard of living. The initial phase and aspects of subsequent ones may have taken into account economic and social factors and could have been positive. Successive additions, however, were made to what was styled the "White Revolution"; and these were increasingly based on political decisions. Additions to the White Revolution included nationalization of pasture and forest lands, which ultimately had a major impact on pastoral nomads and increased competition between nomads and agriculturalists. Repeated and basic changes to land reform *per se* and to the government's role in agriculture led to increased vulnerability on the part of food producers. This uncertainty, more than any other factor, resulted in the failure to meet agricultural planning goals. It also fed the rural flight to cities, which then resulted in the weakening of the rural social order and the loss of critical skills.

Not only did changes in the government's land and agricultural policies increase uncertainty, but its decision to subsidize food imports to offset declining food production also added to the problem. Three factors in particular led to the decision to subsidize food imports to meet the increased demand of a growing population and a rising standard of living in urban areas. The first was frustration at the agricultural sector's failure to meet its planning goals. The second was the shah's hubris and increased sense of power from the mid-1960s onwards. And third, increased oil revenues made it possible to implement food subsidies as well as many other policies. The government also had a political incentive to subsidize food imports. It was anxious about rural–urban migration and all the changes wrought by industrialization and modernization, for which a labour force was required. Subsidized food imports would meet increased demand, keep prices low and maintain social and political stability.

The attractions of urban life and increasing migration to urban centres, where peasants and tribespeople sought greater economic security through better jobs and higher incomes, further exacerbated the uncertainty. It has been argued that the government and planners deliberately encouraged rural–urban migration because the mechanization of agriculture would make it more efficient and those displaced would provide a labour force for the economy's rapidly expanding industrial and service sectors.

The erosion of rural society and the loss of valuable skills were among the unexpected consequences of these land reforms and agricultural policies. Despite criticisms about the productivity of Iranian peasants and pastoral nomads, when all the factors that make up Iran's agricultural sector are taken into account they were remarkably skillful and sophisticated. The government's changing policies and failure to provide adequate inputs, except to agribusinesses, heightened rural insecurity and economic vulnerability, with the result that the agrarian structure and its supporting social system disintegrated. With subsidies for food imports, agricultural and pastoral production simply became unprofitable. The government's policies not only resulted in rural flight but also led to major urban problems and a worsening of political and economic conditions, which ultimately brought about the Islamic revolution.

Many factors undermined Iran's economy and social base. Iran exported oil on the world market and, to give but one example, the income derived from it paid for cheaper imported food. Furthermore, the state's industrial policy undercut the agricultural sector. One response by those who were impoverished was to migrate to the cities; another was to increase the number of dependants able to produce more food or income. This, in turn, resulted in intensification of land use and competition for rural resources. A cycle was created that increased urbanization and the commercialization of agriculture, yet also led to the destruction of rural society – a process commonly seen in the West.

Given such changes, what does Bakhtiyari mean? This takes us back to 1992. Part of the answer lies in those who remain pastoral nomadic in that by sustaining their economic viability they are able to maintain the necessary social and economic bases in the face of continued change. Without that viability, pastoral nomadism would become increasingly marginalized and the Bakhtiyari as a pastoral nomadic cultural artefact would not be "Bakhtiyari" except in memory. On the other hand, because of the profound changes that have taken place, large numbers of Bakhtiyari no longer function as pastoralists and base their futures on the education and opportunities available in urban contexts. Despite significant changes in the twentieth century, traditional values and identities have persisted in pastoral nomadic society because their basic economic and social units have been remarkably flexible and responsive to change. Nevertheless, and despite emigration, a Bakhtiyari memory and history has persisted. It can be seen in the continued use of the Bakhtiyari dialect and oral tradition, in a sense of place and even in the migratory cycle between pastures; it can be seen in lineages, family alliances and marriage patterns, as well as in the material culture, including dress, carpets, lion funerary monuments, cultural associations and publications.

Interestingly, although Bakhtiyari, even if far removed from the region and from pastoral nomadism, identify themselves as such, there has been no Bakhtiyari nationalist movement. In terms of national identity, Bakhtiyari readily identify as Iranian – a precedence that goes back at least to the Constitutional Revolution and Hajji 'Ali Quli Khan Sardar As'ad's role in it as an Iranian nationalist leader. The most recent Bakhtiyari to play a major governmental role was Shapur Bakhtiyar – appointed prime minister by Muhammad Riza Shah's in the last days before the fall of the monarchy – and who owed the appointment not to being a member of an elite tribal family but to his impeccable nationalist credentials. Also, despite their strong identification with a region and its economy, there has been no demand for Bakhtiyari autonomy within the Iranian state. Tribal structures continue at the basic socio-economic level among Bakhtiyari who still practise pastoral nomadism and they continue culturally for those who do not. A distinct Bakhtiyari identity persists, even among those who are sedentarized and urbanized, but at a level of representation that is acceptable to the Islamic Republic. This identity is comparable to a regional, even nostalgic, cultural identity that poses no potential threat to their national identity and loyalty – in other words, Bakhtiyari adaptation continues.

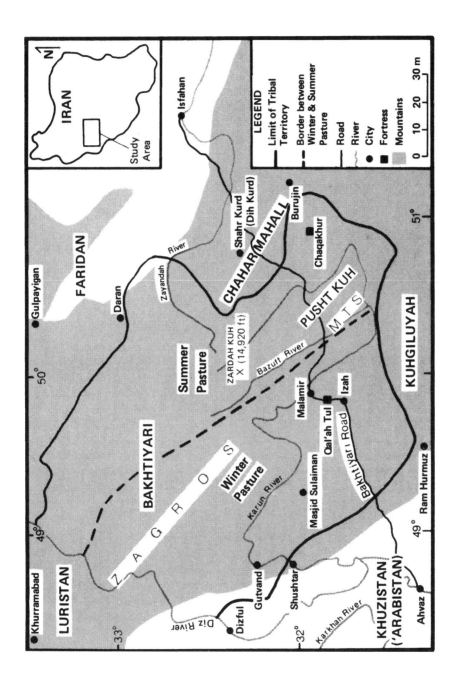

LEGEND

Limit of Tribal Territory

Border between Winter & Summer Pasture

Road

River

● City

■ Fortress

Mountains

0 10 20 30 m

IRAN

Study Area

N

Isfahan

Gulpayigan

FARIDAN

Daran

Zayandah River

Shahr Kurd (Dih Kurd)

CHAHAR MAHALL

Burujin

Chaqakhur

PUSHT KUH

M T S

ZARDAH KUH X (14,920 ft)

Bazuft River

51°

50°

Khurramabad

LURISTAN

BAKHTIYARI

Summer Pasture

Z A G R O S

Winter Pasture

Karun River

Malamir

Qal'ah Tul

Izah

Masjid Sulaiman

Bakhtiyari Road

KUHGILUYAH

Ram Hurmuz

49°

49°

33°

32°

Diz River

Dizful

Gutvand

Shushtar

Karkhah River

KHUZISTAN ('ARABISTAN)

Ahvaz

Generation

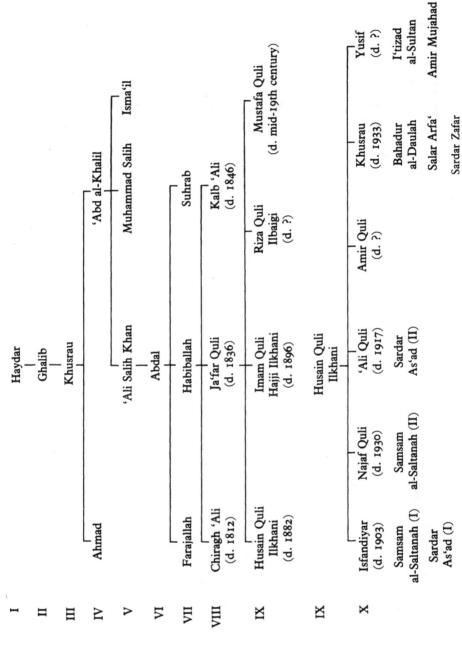

Genealogical table

IX — Imam Quli / Hajji Ilkhani

X —
- Muhammad Husain / Sardar Mufakham / Sipahdar
- Ghulam Husain / Shahab al-Saltanah / Sardar Muhtasham
- Lutf 'Ali / Shuja' al-Sultan / Amir Mufakham
- Nasir / Sardar Jang

X —
- 'Abbas Quli
- Sultan Muhammad / Mu'in Humayun / Salar Ashraf

X —
- 'Ali Akbar / Salar Ashraf
- Muhammad Riza / Sardar Fatih
- Mahmud / Hazhir al-Sultan

IX — Riza Quli / Ilbaigi

X —
- Ibrahim / Zargham al-Saltanah
- Imamallah / Sardar Hishmat
- Bahram

X —
- 'Azizallah
- Muhammad Murad
- Hadi

X —
- Darab
- Baqir
- Asadallah / Salar Mukarram
- Allah Karam
- Muhammad Karim
- Mirza Aqa

Genealogical table (based on Sardar Zafar's "Tarikh Bakhtiyari", pp. 91–6; on Government of India, Foreign Department, Secret E, Proceedings 3–33, December 1912, No. 29, Major Percy Cox to Secretary, Government of India, Bushihr, 25 October 1912; and on C. A. Gault, "The Bakhtiyari Tribe" (Isfahan, 1944), India Office Library, L/P&S/12/3546, pp. 42–50)

Introduction

Bakhtiyari. The name alone brings to mind many, and often conflicting, images, for which Victorian travelers are primarily responsible. Their accounts provided readers with the vicarious thrill of accompanying the dauntless but largely uncivilized and unprincipled herdsmen in their ceaseless and seemingly ageless quest of pastures for their flocks. Readers followed these tribes – often likened to those of the Old Testament – through heat, across flood-swollen rivers, up and over rugged mountains. Accounts were given of feuds, raids, and battles. The nomads, with their confusing and elaborate socio-political structure, were compared with the Highland clans. Observers often contrasted the nomads – free, courageous, simple, and open tribesmen – to their sedentary Persian contemporaries – servile, wily, suspicious, and decadent townsmen. (An ulterior – and often frustrated – motive of many of these writers, as they attempted to describe tribal organization and to locate the center of power, was to find the key to an understanding of this organization in order to further European political or economic ventures.[1])

Much of this romanticism, especially regarding the Bakhtiyari, lingers today in books, in films – even in that classic, "Grass" – and on television, where their struggle with nature and their supposed predatory habits have been graphically, but inaccurately, depicted. Today the name Bakhtiyari suggests to Westerners colorful carpets; the beautiful Soraya (Surayya), Muhammad Riza Shah's second wife; the shah's last prime minister, Dr Shahpour (Shapur) Bakhtiar; or perhaps even an All-American football player with the unlikely name of "Jimmy" (actually Jamshid) Bakhtiar. But to Iranians of an earlier era the name Bakhtiyari meant insecurity and fear, when powerful and arrogant khans, leading armed and mounted retainers, attacked or intimidated both settled populations and rival nomads. Conflicting images exist for Iranians, too. They praise Bakhtiyari participation in the deposition of Muhammad 'Ali Shah in 1909 and the restoration of the constitution; but they also view the subsequent Bakhtiyari role as both anticonstitutionalist and antinationalist.

Many contemporary urban Iranians no longer regard the Bakhtiyari and

I

the other nomadic confederations as a security threat; rather, they disdainfully see them as economic and social anachronisms out of touch with the goals and needs of a rapidly changing society. The descendants of the great khans of the past, moreover, are considered today as an eclipsed, fading element within the national elite. Contemporary urban Bakhtiyari who value their past have these same ambiguous attitudes, compounded by conflicting Bakhtiyari self-images and competing loyalties. They are proud of their past, though they have difficulty even in obtaining an accurate glimpse of their history and tend to emphasize only their powerful and independent khans; but at the same time they take pride in modern Iran, centralized at the expense of these khans and their tribal autonomy.

Perceptions and understanding of Bakhtiyari history have been greatly affected by the absence of sources both Bakhtiyari and Persian. (The Bakhtiyari dialect of Persian is not written; rather, literate Bakhtiyari write standard Persian.) Consequently, reconstruction of a narrative of pre-twentieth-century Bakhtiyari history may never be possible. Furthermore, the problem of interpreting Western sources raises serious issues for all observers. Especially critical for analysis is Bakhtiyari rationalization of all relationships in terms of kin. The seeming inexplicability of family ties and the welter of divisions, which often seem to lack functional significance, particularly puzzle Western observers, because of differing and even contradictory perceptions provided by sources and informants, whether they be the ruling khans of the late nineteenth and early twentieth centuries, lesser khans, individual Bakhtiyari, or outside Iranian and Western observers. The difficulty of consistent and meaningful historical analysis has been further compounded for all writers by their own initial assumptions, which have included the following: the basic social and political structure is confusing and cannot be explained except in terms of personalities; the Bakhtiyari have constituted a continuing, relatively changeless socio-political unit isolated for centuries; its leaders' roles date from antiquity; the link between the khan and his tribesmen, between power and the pastoral economy with its ties to the wider society, is self-evident, environmentally determined, and isolated. These assumptions are based on an almost inherent tendency toward romanticism and a misperception of the nature of so-called tribal society, especially with regard to the interaction between the Bakhtiyari and the larger Iranian political and cultural context – despite protestations to the contrary.

This study presents a sketch of Bakhtiyari history – which, in fact, is primarily the history of only one family, that of the ruling Duraki khans – and develops a thesis on the interaction of the Bakhtiyari with the state and greater Iranian society that has significant implications for

Bakhtiyari socio-political structures and their internal dynamics. In addition, this volume includes the texts, translations, and notes for official and personal documents relating to the Bakhtiyari in the period of 1144/1732 – 1299/1882.

The documents included here are either unique, such as Husain Quli Khan Ilkhani's "Kitabchah" (1290/1873 – 1299/1882), or little studied. All are inaccessible – possibly some have recently been destroyed in the revolution – and generally unknown to scholars. The official documents are from the chancellories of Nadir Shah, Azad Khan Afghan, Karim Khan Zand, Muhammad Sadiq, Fath 'Ali Shah's governors, Nasir al-Din Shah, Muzaffar al-Din Vali'ahd, and Mas'ud Mirza Zill al-Sultan; the personal documents were written by 'Ali Mardan Khan Bakhtiyari, Husain Quli Khan Ilkhani, Nasir al-Din Shah, and lesser Bakhtiyari leaders. These provide something of a textual foundation for Bakhtiyari history and provide some basis for analysis of Bakhtiyari society and politics and key Bakhtiyari and central government relations over a period of a century and a half. Thus the documents constitute an important corrective to later – especially Western and secondary – sources and assumptions, and their importance transcends this study.

Chapter 1

A historical and theoretical survey

Bakhtiyari history, stretching back to the fourteenth century, and the 200-year leadership role of the Duraki khans within it tantalize the social historian of Iran. There is great temptation to assume that the extraordinary continuity in the name Bakhtiyari can also be found in Bakhtiyari political, economic, and social organization. The historian is frustrated further because a narrative of Bakhtiyari political history cannot be reconstructed from primary sources until the late nineteenth century, and even then major parts of it remain fragmentary. The social scientist is likewise thwarted in attempting to obtain a detailed account of the Bakhtiyari social structure before contemporary times. Basic institutions, relationships, and values are obscured by the very nature of complex societies, by the gaps in and lack of sources, and by differences between internal and external perceptions of the Bakhtiyari.

Notwithstanding these difficulties, a hypothesis may be offered for heuristic purposes and tested against historical examples: the potential for tribal confederation is directly proportional to the strength of an external stimulus.[1] Pastoral tribes have made their most dramatic impact on history as confederations; their equally important economic contributions have been either ignored or assumed in historical sources. Historically, confederations have constituted impermanent and atypical groups.

The nature of pastoralism and of tribal socio-economic organization – as in the case of the Bakhtiyari – militates against the *sui generis* formation of tribal confederations. (Definitions of "tribe" and "confederation" emerge in subsequent discussion, as do the factors in the process of confederation formation.) Where no state structure exists or in tribal areas not under the control of an organized state, confederations tend to form only in response to conditions originating in adjacent areas – typically, a need for short-term common defense or an inducement for expansion or conquest. The confederations' strength tends to remain at a level approximate to the strength and duration of the external conditions: the confederation does not long outlast the existence of these conditions.

In tribal areas under the control of an organized state – the imposed control of a bureaucracy and army with a supporting ideology – the state itself can become the "external" stimulus. Tribes then form confederations to defend and expand their interests *vis-à-vis* the state, which itself may vary in the degree of its cohesion and authority. In these circumstances, the traditional, relatively decentralized state government may seek to utilize the power of tribal confederations for its own purposes of reinforcing internal cohesion by recognizing a confederation, or even by creating one. As such a government, however, becomes more centralized, it increasingly regards the existence of tribal confederations, even the ones it fostered, as antithetical to its interests. When the centralized bureaucracy becomes strong enough it attempts to limit the confederations' power; because the state controls greater resources and because of its superior organization, it usually succeeds in doing so.

Within an organized state the potential for tribal confederation thus tends to be proportional to the degree of bureaucratic organization. Periods when a Bakhtiyari confederation, or confederations – for example, the moieties of the Haft Lang and Chahar Lang of the eighteenth century – may have existed within the strong traditional state include the reigns of Shah 'Abbas I and Shah 'Abbas II; documentation supports the hypothesis in that circumstance for the periods of Nadir Shah, Karim Khan Zand, and Nasir al-Din Shah. Periods characterized by weak or nonexistent state structures – when smaller, competing segments characterized the Bakhtiyari and thus a competing Bakhtiyari unit could exist as an external factor – would possibly include pre- and late Safavid times, and this hypothesis can be supported by sources for the years preceding Karim Khan Zand's consolidation of his power, the reigns of the early Qajars, and the decade of World War I. ('Ali Mardan Khan's attempt to unite the Bakhtiyari in the mid-eighteenth century in order to rule Iran perhaps constitutes a variation of confederational formation for expansion.) An example of the Bakhtiyari under a centralized state – again, with the breakup into lesser units but in this instance state-initiated – is dramatically illustrated by Riza Shah's transformation of the Bakhtiyari confederational structure in the early 1930s and the elimination of administrative and military roles for the Duraki ruling khans.

"Bakhtiyari" appears for the first time in the fourteenth-century historical record as the name of a *tayafah* (tribe) that had entered Iran from Syria along with some 30 other such groups 100 years earlier in the thirteenth century.[2] Even so, the reference is not an unambiguous one: the text allows for a variant reading of that name. "Bakhtiyari" next appears on the historical record in Safavid sources,[3] where it refers to a geographic area and an administrative unit – an area of some 29,000 square miles (75,000 square kilometers) straddling the Zagros mountains between

5

Isfahan and Khuzistan – as well as to its inhabitants, a few of whom are designated by name. In the eighteenth century, Bakhtiyari leaders emerge as major contenders for power in the state, but their sons and grandsons become eclipsed in the early Qajar period of the first decades of the nineteenth century. Bakhtiyari leaders reappear on the provincial and national scene in the mid-nineteenth century and continue to play important roles – as tribal leaders – throughout the first third of the twentieth century.

Since the late nineteenth century, the term Bakhtiyari has acquired an ethnic, occupational – through association with pastoralism – and political emphasis as a great confederation of tribally organized pastoral nomads ruled and united by the *ilkhanis* and khans (the paramount and tribal chiefs). In addition, there has been a linguistic association of Bakhtiyari pastoralists with the Bakhtiyari dialect of Persian. In actuality, however, at least within the past century, the Bakhtiyari have counted in their number Turkic and Arabic groups, sedentary agriculturalists, and those Bakhtiyari resident in towns and places far from the the Bakhtiyari districts. The nomads themselves were no less dependent upon cereals they planted in both summer and winter pasture areas than on their flocks of sheep and goats. The confederation, although an administrative entity from the central government's perspective, was often politically fragmented, and seldom functioned as a unit except during the last decade of the rule of Husain Quli Khan (d. 1882), the first and most powerful ilkhani, and during the Constitutional Revolution. Nevertheless, Bakhtiyari legend supports notions of a common origin and unity, and group formation is rationalized in the Bakhtiyari patrilineal framework.

Between the fourteenth century, when the term Bakhtiyari first appears, and the mid-eighteenth century, the historical record provides only a narrow base for analysis. In summary, the term possesses two intersecting meanings from either an internal or an external political perspective, for it designates a tayafah of indeterminate size and organization and a geographic and administrative unit of Luristan. (Luristan is located in the central Zagros region between Kermanshah at the north and Ram Hurmuz and the Khuzistan plains to the south, and its population includes agriculturalists and pastoralists who are divided linguistically into two Luri dialects [of the southwest Iranian group], Lur Buzurg and Lur Kuchik.[4]) Safavid chronicles identify individuals who functioned as military leaders and civil administrators of the Bakhtiyari and adjacent regions, and who were, perhaps, Bakhtiyari themselves. If Chardin's seventeenth-century observations are assumed to include the Bakhtiyari as a Luri component, they may be further identified as pastoral nomads with an economy based on flocks traded in the nearby capital of Isfahan. Iskandar Baig Munshi, in addition, implies that Bakhtiyari were not peasants – he refers to *ra'iyats*, or peasants, *and* Bakhtiyari.[5] Chardin suggests a political structure when he mentions the autonomy of the Lurs, who were governed by subgovernors appointed from among themselves by the central government.[6]

Negatively, the few references to the Bakhtiyari in the Safavid period (1501–1722) suggests that they did not constitute a major political factor as a large Bakhtiyari unit until the seventeenth century. The Bakhtiyari occupied the midpoint of the Safavid power axis[7] in the Zagros, as it extended from Georgia to the Gulf; furthermore, it was strategically located in relation to the capital at Isfahan. Had there been a major Bakhtiyari confederation, this would have at least been noted in the chronicles. More probably the Bakhtiyari organized themselves into small groups and tribes – tayafahs or lesser units – which seldom, and then only under unusual circumstances, coalesced into larger ones. These small units were administered through local leaders, by Safavid governors who were not necessarily Bakhtiyari.

By the end of the seventeenth century – the era of accelerating Safavid decline – a shift in governmental–tribal relations presumably occurred, for the Bakhtiyari governorship emerged as an important administrative post. The *Tadhkirat al-Muluk* (1725), where it lists the ranks and honors given to Persian *amirs* (notables), notes that the governor of Bakhtiyari follows immediately after the four *valis* (viceroys) of 'Arabistan (or Khuzistan), Luristan Faili, Georgia, and Kurdistan.[8] In this same period both Persian and European sources[9] note the Bakhtiyari moieties of the Haft Lang and Chahar Lang for the first time and, in the mid-eighteenth century, the great antipathy between them. The Haft Lang and Chahar Lang may each have constituted a confederation, which may have been created by one of the more centralizing Safavids – Shah 'Abbas I (d. 1038/1629) or Shah 'Abbas II (d. 1077/1666). On the other hand, that division could have resulted from internal Bakhtiyari developments and have been used administratively, and hence reinforced, by the Safavids in the era of decline immediately following.

In the subsequent Afshar era, the Bakhtiyari were peripheral to Nadir's major concerns except as a threat to his southern flank; consequently, he sought to utilize Bakhtiyari military units in his eastern campaigns and to resettle large numbers of them in Khurasan. In both instances, it would appear on the basis of extant Haft Lang sources that he worked within the moiety framework of the Haft Lang and the Chahar Lang. During this period, with the continued decentralization of the state and the absence of Haft Lang leaders, the Bakhtiyari districts, too, would appear to have

7

been fragmented, and tayafahs challenged both Nadir Shah and the Haft Lang leadership.

Fragmentation persisted, and apparently increased, in the Bakhtiyari following Nadir's assassination in 1160/1747. Karim Khan Zand re-established central authority in south-central Iran and the Bakhtiyari when he asserted suzerainty over the Haft Lang through its own leaders, 'Ali Salih Khan and his son Abdal Khan, of the Duraki, one of the Haft Lang's major subdivisions, or *babs*. In addition, Karim had to establish his own power and destroy that of his Bakhtiyari co-ruler, 'Ali Mardan Chahar Lang. They had established rule in the name of a Safavid pretender, Isma'il III.

'Ali Mardan, about whom little is known other than his membership in the Kiyanursi bab of the Chahar Lang, may have emerged as a leader in the tumultuous Nadir Shah period. Possibly the Chahar Lang had constituted a confederation, but there was no single Bakhtiyari confedera-tion, for 'Ali Mardan, in a letter[10] to Haft Lang leaders appealing for unity, indicated contemporary Bakhtiyari fragmentation, and alluded to an earlier, presumably Safavid, harmony and unity. If the Bakhtiyari had been united, they might have prevailed over Karim Khan Zand.

Official Zand documents clearly reveal that the Haft Lang was treated as an administrative unit, and so corroborate traditional Bakhtiyari genealogies and history. In the *farmans* and *raqams*[11] (decrees) awarding *tuyuls* (land grants in return for service), governorships, exemptions, and admonitions to eighteenth-century Duraki notables, they are addressed with the titles of *sardar, baig, aqa, rish safid, zabit*, and *hakim*. These documents only suggest the relationship between these Haft Lang leaders and their tribes, and add little to our knowledge about Bakhtiyari commoners except their stratification within the organization into small groups headed by *kalantars* (deputies or bailiffs) and *kadkhudas* (head-men), with an interdependence between them and the Duraki khans, who were responsible for good administration. On an ideological basis, these same eighteenth-century documents indicate that the Bakhtiyari shared the prevailing Irano-Shi'i ethos. They often defied the rulers of the Afshar and Zand eras, but never challenged existing political and religious ideas and institutions.

Extant early Qajar documents relating to the Bakhtiyari are few until *c.* 1840. However, the far more numerous documents appearing between 1860 and 1880 reveal a significant number of khans competing within the tayafahs and at the level of what is to become the confederation of the whole of the Bakhtiyari.

A reassertion of central authority comes about in the mid-nineteenth-century Bakhtiyari and the adjacent areas to the south (notably the

northern edge of Fars and the borders with Kuhgiluyah and 'Arabistan)
through an alliance between the governors of Isfahan, the central government in Tehran, and Husain Quli Khan. Husain Quli had been one of the
contending Duraki khans and to outsiders appeared to be a rather unlikely
Bakhtiyari victor. His signal success was due to: his lineage, that of the
khans of the largest and certainly the most powerful Haft Lang bab;
primacy within it; political and military skills, which resulted in the defeat
of his most powerful Haft Lang and Chahar Lang rivals; collaboration
with and support of his three brothers; an increasingly broad network of
social, political, and economic ties, including those with ulema and great
merchants; and vast land holdings in Chahar Mahall to the east and in
'Arabistan to the southwest of the Bakhtiyari. Government support
increased and was demonstrated by additional land grants and exemptions, appointments, and titles – notably *nazim* (chief administrator) of the
Bakhtiyari in 1279/1862 and then ilkhani of the whole of the Bakhtiyari in
1284/1867.[12] The general result was good order, unification of the
Bakhtiyari, and an increase in Husain Quli's power to the extent that he
was feared both by elements within his own family and by the provincial
and central governments. Nasir al-Din Shah ordered his death, which was
carried out in 1882 by Zill al-Sultan, the shah's son and the governor of
Isfahan.[13]

Although an expected and feared general uprising of the Bakhtiyari did
not result, fragmentation characterized the tribes for the next twelve
years – exacerbated, too, by the Zill al-Sultan's fall from grace. Three
factions of the great khans (*khavanin buzurg*, a term which had been used
earlier but which generally specifies these later Duraki khans) then
emerged: Ilkhani, Husain Quli's sons; Hajji Ilkhani, Husain Quli's
brother's sons; and Ilbaigi, Husain Quli's half-brother's sons. These three
factions sought to form various political combinations in attempts to gain
pre-eminence, and there was no question that the office of ilkhani would
be filled by a candidate from one of these groups. During Husain Quli
Khan Ilkhani's rule of some twenty-five to thirty years, authority had
become even more firmly identified with his descent group; and their
wealth had so increased that none of the khans from other lineages could
hope to compete. In addition, Ilkhani, Hajji Ilkhani, and Ilbaigi ties
among the Bakhtiyari and with all factions of the Qajars were so
encompassing that all other Bakhtiyari leaders were removed from
contention, unless the government imprisoned the great khans and
confiscated their estates (which occurred in the 1930s under Riza Shah,
but from which Nasir al-Din Shah shrank out of fear of Bakhtiyari power
and because of his inadequate army). In 1894 an agreement was reached
by the Ilkhani and Hajji Ilkhani khans which excluded the Ilbaigi from

9

power and determined that the positions of ilkhani and *ilbaigi* (second to the ilkhani) would be limited to those two factions and would be based on primacy of age.[14] Within this general framework tribal, confederational, and family disputes – including those over the Bakhtiyari road (1897), oil agreements (pre-World War I), and the division of government positions following the Constitutional Revolution[15] – continued to be resolved.

The Qajar government's demands *vis-à-vis* tribal confederations and other autonomous groups were comparatively simple – recognition and submission characterized by payment of taxes, conscription of recruits, and observance of royal suzerainty. The Qajar government in nineteenth- and early-twentieth-century Iran maintained its position through its military superiority and through its greater prestige and authority, its access to Anglo-Russian support, and its ability to reward and divide by utilizing inter- and intra-tribal rivalries. In summary, the Qajars issued no order to the Bakhtiyari that could be ignored, thus insuring their exercise of absolute authority.

Increasingly, toward the end of the nineteenth century and the beginning of the twentieth, the British played a role in Iran analogous to that of the traditional decentralized Qajar state: British commercial and strategic interests required stability, but Britain lacked the resources to insure this directly and sought to obtain order by backing traditional leaders and institutions. The Tehran/Isfahan/Ilkhani and Hajji Ilkhani nexus was reinforced by the London/Government of India/'Arabistan/Ilkhani and Hajji Ilkhani connection.

Just as Husain Quli Khan Ilkhani had failed to expand Bakhtiyari power in the 1870s, so, too – although for different reasons – did his sons and nephews fail in the constitutional period, when the tayafah and Bakhtiyari leaders were only temporarily united. Both internal divisions and external opposition developed once Muhammad 'Ali Shah had been removed (1909) and replaced by Ahmad Shah; the decline of central authority stimulated internal rivalries and ambitions. Moreover, Bakhtiyari leaders – for example, Hajji 'Ali Quli Khan Sardar As'ad (II) – lost external urban support even as leaders of the government as they were identified with traditional values and came to be regarded as antinationalist and anticonstitutionalist; they had no alternative and acceptable ideology to offer to widen their Bakhtiyari power, and that base was suspect. The khans were also in danger of losing Bakhtiyari support, for as they moved away from problems of immediate tribal interest, they were also subject to the greater danger of loss of their power base and tribal support, diminishing their ability to play both Bakhtiyari and national roles.

The decade of World War I saw a resurgence of tribalism and fragmentation in the Bakhtiyari as the central government's authority and power collapsed. The British presence, too, was greatly undermined until the war's end. Furthermore, the senior Ilkhani and Hajji Ilkhani khans had moved to Tehran, leaving affairs in the hands of their sons and grandsons, who constituted a sizeable group that not only lacked authority but also competed for the same limited resources to maintain themselves and their *bastagan* (armed and mounted retainers). Order came only with the reassertion of power and authority at the center under Riza Khan Sardar Sipah (who later ascended the throne as Riza Shah).

Changes in the traditional Iranian system and the structure of the state began with Riza Shah and were continued by his son, Muhammad Riza Shah. These included the centralization of power and authority and the emergence of the nation–state, an expanded state role calling for economic and social progress. Even before Sardar Sipah was crowned as Riza Shah, the great khans – especially Khusrau Khan Sardar Zafar – perceived him and his policies as a threat to their autonomy and power. Nevertheless, their challenge to him failed because it followed essentially traditional lines while he utilized both the methods of the traditional Iranian system and those of the new nation–state. Tehran successfully identified the "feudal" Bakhtiyari leadership with the decadent past and with foreign domination. The new nation–state of Iran did not need to share authority and power; it had its own army and bureaucracy, as well as policies integrating Iranians into the national economy and promoting an "Iranian" identity through education and new national symbols.

Despite Pahlavi centralization, the form and function of the tayafahs have been more persistent than those of the great tribal confederations and less affected by external developments, because the former are derived from the exigencies of basic pastoral and agricultural production. Some 100,000 Bakhtiyari make the biannual migration, and still more follow traditional social and economic patterns.[16] Consequently, even today the earlier hierarchical structure headed by the ilkhani and the dual division of the families eligible for the position continue to provide the framework for traditional internal socio-political activities. Despite the state's assumption of their juridical and administrative functions, the tayafahs continue to align themselves into one of the great khan moieties of either the Ilkhani or the Hajji Ilkhani.[17] Pahlavi tribal policy of continuing to treat the Bakhtiyari as an administrative unit possibly resulted in a more precise delineation of internal and external social and physical boundaries, which may have strengthened both Bakhtiyari identity as a social unit with a given territory and the Ilkhani/Hajji Ilkhani framework for social, econo- mic, and political interaction.

The state's general economic and political policies, especially those of the past decade, have probably had an accelerating impact on change in the Bakhtiyari, particularly with the attraction of the oil fields and new industrial centers adjacent to that region, but the impact has probably been less far-reaching among them than among the Qashqa'i.[18] The reasons why the Qashqa'i were more affected by Pahlavi centralization are several. The location is one: Fars was more important and more affected by Pahlavi programs than the less heavily populated and more mountainous Bakhtiyari. Leadership is another: Qashqa'i khans have played important roles in Fars, but not on the national level, and their ability to maintain these roles and make the transition from Qajars to Riza Shah and then well into Muhammad Riza Shah's reign contrasts significantly with the case of the Bakhtiyari. In spite of Pahlavi centralization and modernization, then, those within the Bakhtiyari tayafah structure have continued to enjoy a degree of autonomy. Because of their location they have been largely peripheral to the nation–state and its new economy, whose opportunities have not been open to the Bakhtiyari unless they could leave the region; those who have moved from the Bakhtiyari, however, have become integrated into contemporary Iranian society. Even if the new Islamic Republic of Iran were to reverse Pahlavi centralization, there would be little likelihood of the re-emergence of a Bakhtiyari confederation.* The interaction of the Bakhtiyari and the government of Iran now enters yet another phase in its long history.

Change is the constant in Bakhtiyari–state relations and in Bakhtiyari structures as well. "Tribe", "confederation", and "state" are protean notions, encompassing a whole matrix of relationships, and as analytical categories they resist agreed-upon definitions. What makes the Bakhtiyari tribal are essential political relationships, but Bakhtiyari themselves would identify six characteristics, two of which may be shared by other tribal and nontribal populations in Iran. These two are: pastoral and agricultural production and a kin structure – either real or fictive – for socio-economic activity related to production. The other four political characteristics, which reinforce the first two and from a Bakhtiyari perspective make the first two "Bakhtiyari", are: a kin framework for integration into larger units (and, after 1867, into a confederation under the Duraki khans); an administrative unit within the state; identification with a specific territory; and symbols of a Bakhtiyari ideal of themselves as a socio-political unit relating to that territory, to their economy, and to the khans. Internal and external perceptions set the Bakhtiyari off from neighbors and settled society as a whole even though socio-political processes allow for the incorporation of outsiders into the Bakhtiyari.

* A single confederation in the future would be unlikely if there were a long period of political turmoil and uncertainty, for the tayafah leaders would compete among themselves – at least if this study's hypothesis is correct.

Tribe in the Bakhtiyari begins with the family, *khanivadah* or *vargah* (lit. tent), and ends with the tayafah* – the family's ultimate extension – which defines the limits of social and political activity.[19] (The units proceeding in order of size from the khanivadah include *tash* [*aulad*], *mal*, *tirah*, and, finally, tayafah. Tayafahs are grouped into nine babs, which in turn are grouped into the two moieties of the Haft Lang and Chahar Lang that constitute the confederation, *il*. There appears to be no written term, other than il, to designate the moiety level.) The family owns the flocks and adjusts to their needs within the ecological limits of their territory. This results in mobility and adaptability on an economic level and instability in group relations on a political one. The family unit takes on the key and enduring ideological role, forming the basis for everyday activity – and giving rise to most demands and conflicts – and providing the conceptual basis for the process of group formation ending in the tayafah and, ultimately, even the confederation. The further the socio-political level of organization moves from the family, the weaker the commitment to it and the identification with it, because the larger groupings have the potential for restricting adaptability and can serve important functions only in specific instances.

Despite the identification with the tayafah of a particular office – that of the kalantar – and the association of specific pastures and linked migration routes with the tayafah, this level of organization seldom serves as a corporate unit except in ideological terms, structuring subunits within itself and within the confederation. Most often the tirah, headed by kadkhudas, represents the largest unit defining effective corporate activity. The tayafah, a microcosm of the Bakhtiyari confederation, nevertheless constitutes the terminal unit of the "family's" functional limits, in which internal factors such as herding of flocks, pastures, water, and migration assume primary importance in the subunits' group formation.

The confederation of the Bakhtiyari (usually il, but also tayafah; *buluk*, or *bakhsh*, in colloquial and oral usage[20]) begins with the tayafah and terminates in either the moieties or the whole of the Bakhtiyari. The difference between the tayafah and the confederation is primarily one of function; size and organization, which may appear as additional variables, are derived from function. The confederation unifies the tayafahs for the resolution of internal disputes and for administrative purposes in the state system; it rallies the tayafahs for defense and expansion against the state and against neighboring tribes and communities; and, on an ideological level, it integrates the tayafahs into the greater cultural system.[21] The

---

* Note should be made that tayafah is used in sources to designate units ranging in size from the family to the confederation! The context in which tayafah is used identifies the referent. This characteristic is not restricted either to the Bakhtiyari or to Iran.

confederation is even less binding on its members – in terms of economic, social, and political activity, loyalty, and identity – than the tayafah; and it may even be perceived as exploitative, or as a structure whose goals are in basic conflict with those of the tayafah or the lesser units.

The confederational function is set off from the tribal one – this helps to account for the tribes' negative perceptions of the confederation – by the potential conflict of interest between the tayafah and the confederation, especially given the confederational leaders' dual power base and the exacerbation of internal competition for the limited resources of the confederational territory. Tayafah leaders depend primarily upon internal support as their power base, while confederational leaders possess an internal base but hold their positions of leadership in response to external stimuli and may draw support from the government, from land, and from leaders and groups external to the Bakhtiyari. During the late nineteenth century, leaders of the Bakhtiyari confederation – the Duraki khans, known collectively by that time as the khavanin buzurg, great khans – could only have been removed by a combination of the tribes and the state, thus limiting the tribes' independent action and power. The leaders of the confederation act as government surrogates in their role as administrators in the collection of taxes, conscription, and the maintenance of order. This results in one form of conflict of interest, but, in addition, the tribes could be exploited by confederational leaders who sought a broader, external role in the state. Those leaders who sought to form a state from the confederational base had to maintain its cohesion, but also had to appeal to those outside the confederation through an acceptable ideology reinforced by the expectation of meeting economic, social, and political needs. Finally, the confederational leaders' external support and internal domination gave them, at times, a monopoly of power, so they could reward and punish individuals or whole tayafahs and, despite internal opposition, award pastures, land, or exemptions to external groups in return for their support.

The great confederations commonly associated with Iran date only from the nineteenth century – scholars, of course, are aware of earlier ones, such as the Qara Quyunlu and Shahsavan – when the Qajars, who were possibly emulating a much earlier practice, invested leaders with the title and office of ilkhani, which gave its holders authority and power to act on behalf of the central government as official administrators of what were thus formally created and recognized as autonomous administrative units by Tehran. This occurred in 1234/1818 for the Qashqa'i[22] and in 1284/1867 for the Bakhtiyari.[23] The Khamsah confederation came into existence during Nasir al-Din Shah's reign; though its head never held the title of ilkhani, he functioned as such. The dates for the first appointment of an ilkhani for the Qajar confederation (possibly early nineteenth century and, given the confederation's relationship to the ruling dynasty, of special status) and for the Zafaranlu of Quchan are as yet unknown. None of the other Kurdish leaders possessed the title; nor did the Arab shaikhs who held like office as administrators for their respective areas.

The great confederations in Iran came about as the result of both designation and amalgamation. In designation, the central government possibly sought to centralize or to limit tribal autonomy when it selected a leader, not necessarily from within the group, as the one responsible for order, taxes, and conscripts. The Khamsah, formed by order of the Qajars and led by the Qavams, a Shiraz merchant–landlord family, are an example of this type.

Confederations also emerged through a process of amalgamation: a leader forged increasingly large and effective units, relying on a variety of leadership skills and symbols and manipulating the basic kin structures to achieve goals beyond those associated with the smaller groups. Over a period of time corporate interests would be identified with the confederation, but would be weaker than the corporate interests of the smaller units. The Qashqa'i provide but one successful illustration of this variation. They constitute a Turkic-speaking minority and their migration takes them through thickly settled agricultural regions in close proximity to urban areas – thus minority status is a factor for stimulus. Although this second model was commonly attempted in Iranian history, most tribal leaders failed (especially in times of a strong central government) because of internal and external opposition and the difficulty of obtaining outside support without threatening the central government. Even with the Qashqa'i, who pride themselves on greater autonomy, shahs elevated and deposed ilkhanis in ineffective attempts to control that confederation. Examples of failure to form such confederations are common in Bakhtiyari history up to the mid-nineteenth century. Husain Quli Khan Ilkhani, who succeeded, exemplified the third process, a combination of designation and amalgamation, in which the central government capitalized on a khan who was in the process of forming a confederation, and by assisting him with resources and thus retaining a degree of control over him, turned a potential threat to its own advantage.

The factor of state control constitutes a continuum, which may range from a fragmented polity to a centralized state maintained by a bureaucracy and a standing army, thus claiming a monopoly of the legitimate use of power – the modern state in the Weberian sense.[24] This analytical continuum accords roughly with Iranian historical reality. The eighteenth century – the first period for which a greater number of documents relating to the Bakhtiyari may be found – sees the final disintegration of the Safavid state, a resurgence of tribalism under short-lived confederations, the emergence of other local and provincial groups, and a breakdown of state functions. At the other end of this continuum are the Pahlavis, with a modern, centralized state; the Qajars of the nineteenth century are sandwiched in between. (The Zand decades, at least for the Bakhtiyari, approximate Qajar conditions.[25]) Pahlavi centralization contrasts with eighteenth-century fragmentation and Qajar decentralization. The Qajars tolerated and created confederations as autonomous, administrative entities rather than take on the expense and challenge of a standing army and centralized bureaucracy.[26] Furthermore, an Irano-Shi'i ideology – the Bakhtiyari are themselves Shi'a – persisted throughout these three centuries for these three states on the continuum. The Pahlavis, however, also attempted to stress Iran's pre-Islamic and future glory as justification for their centralizing policy and an insurance for dynastic loyalty.

The centralizing policies of the last decades have effectively destroyed only the power of the Bakhtiyari great khans, some of whose descendants have continued to play national roles until recently, though decreasingly as tribal leaders. The actual tribal role of the Duraki khans, except for its ideological function, has thus come to an end after some 200 years.

The Bakhtiyari and nomadism

The basis for our perceptions of the Bakhtiyari dates only from the late nineteenth century, when the confederation emerged under the leadership of Husain Quli Khan, the first ilkhani. Husain Quli Khan, or Ilkhani – and he is usually identified only by this title, awarded him in 1867 – became the archetypal ilkhani, or paramount chief, of the Bakhtiyari for subsequent holders of that office and for the Bakhtiyari as a group, as well as for observers and historians. Ilkhani was born into the khan's lineage (see Genealogical table) of the Zarasvand tayafah of the Duraki bab. Ilkhani first attained power within this family through the support of his three younger brothers, who helped him kill their uncle and then achieve authority over the Duraki. He assisted the Qajars in their subjugation of Muhammad Taqi Khan Chahar Lang, and they gave Husain Quli the support which enabled him to gain paramountcy over all the Bakhtiyari until his execution in 1882.

Ilkhani, like any successful tribal leader in this context, operated from a dual base – within the Bakhtiyari as its acknowledged leader and outside it as a major landlord and as the government official responsible for general order, taxes, and conscripts. This dual base could result in conflict of interest and required Ilkhani – or any who held that position – to balance internal authority and outside support. Formal recognition of this status came from the state in the form of offices and titles (nazim in 1862 and then ilkhani in 1867), incomes, and land. Ilkhani, unchallenged and unchallengeable so long as he retained Qajar support, increased his family's considerable wealth with additional land acquisition, through collection of dues and taxes, and through capital investment outside the Bakhtiyari. This wealth and power exacerbated Qajar concern about his ambitions, and Nasir al-Din Shah ordered Zill al-Sultan to assassinate him in 1882.

Ilkhani's Bakhtiyari domain not only included the nomads making up that confederation but also extended to include agriculturalists within Bakhtiyari and in immediately adjacent regions – the sphere of Bakhtiyari pre-eminence and influence. Significantly, Ilkhani, in his "Kitabchah",[1] did not distinguish between peasants and nomads; moreover, pastoral nomadism cannot be separated from agriculture in the Bakhtiyari economy except in terms of specialization and emphasis.

The Bakhtiyari pastoral–agricultural economy hardly distinguished them from their immediate neighbors, who consisted of a similar composite of nomads, transhumant agriculturalists–pastoralists, and sedentary agriculturalists. In Ilkhani's time, peoples adjacent to the Bakhtiyari – classified ethnically and regionally – consisted of the Lurs to the north, Arabs to the southwest in Khuzistan, and the Lurs of Kuhgiluyah and the Mamasani and the Buir Ahmadi to the south and southwest. Adjacent to the southeast corner of Bakhtiyari were the summer pastures of the Qashqa'i, perhaps the major threat, apart from the Qajars, to Bakhtiyari hegemony in the late nineteenth and early twentieth centuries. Further south and to the east – at least from the late nineteenth century – were the tribes of the Khamsah confederation. Chahar Mahall directly bordered Bakhtiyari summer pastures to the east and contained settlements of various sizes and a variety of Persian, Turkish, and Armenian agriculturalists and townspeople. No accurate census figures for any of these groups exist, but the Qashqa'i and the Bakhtiyari – certainly comparable social and political units during Ilkhani's lifetime – were the largest, and roughly equal in size. Sir Henry Rawlinson in 1836 estimated the Bakhtiyari to number 28,000 families.[2] In 1890, Isabella L. Bird Bishop estimated 29,000 and placed family size at eight.[3] In their more recent research, Fredrik Barth, William Irons, and Lois Beck have found family size of from five to six for nomadic groups.[4]

The bases of classification and identification from both within and outside the Bakhtiyari were economic and political; yet even Bakhtiyari utilized crosscutting linguistic, geographic, economic, social, and political classifications. Linguistically and traditionally the Lurs, who encompass the Bakhtiyari, have been divided into two Luri dialect groups – classified as a subsection of the southwest Iranian group that includes Persian and the dialect of Fars – coinciding with two geographic areas: Lur Buzurg (the Great Lur), composed of the Bakhtiyari, the tribes of Kuhgiluyah, and the Mamasani; and Lur Kuchik (the Lesser Lur), made up of the Faili Lurs to the north, between Bakhtiyari and Kurdistan.[5] Most Qashqa'i speak a western Ghuz Turkic dialect,[6] and the Khamsah is made up primarily of Turkic-speakers but includes Persian- and Arabic-speaking components. The Bakhtiyari under Ilkhani included members of all these linguistic groups.

What distinguishes the Bakhtiyari from comparable groups in the Zagros is the nature of the Bakhtiyari territory and its socio-political structure. Digard[7] notes that not only do the territorial size, range of resources, and relative completeness and compactness make the Bakhtiyari unique in the Zagros, but the social and political structures responding to ecological factors – and, it should be added, to historical factors – reinforce Bakhtiyari territorial integrity. To give but two brief contrasting examples, the tribes of Luristan to the north and Kuhgiluyah to the south are fragmented economically and socially. The Qashqa'i, more comparable to the Bakhtiyari in all respects, possess a more highly centralized political structure. Their summer and winter pasture areas are not contiguous and can only be reached by traversing a migration corridor that passes through a heavily populated agricultural and non-Qashqa'i region; consequently, more centralized control of migration is required.

The Bakhtiyari economy and society of Ilkhani's era were adapted to the Bakhtiyari territory. This was especially associated with the central Zagros mountains, through whose rugged terrain the nomads passed on their arduous and characteristic migration from winter to summer pastures and back again. The Bakhtiyari district – an administrative unit largely within the province of Isfahan under Zill al-Sultan, the Qajar governor contemporary with Ilkhani – totaled some 29,000 square miles, 60 percent of which is mountainous. This region encompassed an area west of Isfahan reaching to the plains of 'Arabistan and south from Gulpayigan to Ram Hurmuz (c. 31°N to c. 34°N and c. 49°E to c. 51°E), roughly between the Karun and Diz rivers and the central Iranian plateau. It comprised three major areas: winter pastures in the uplands of 'Arabistan, summer pastures on the plateau side of the Zagros, and the mountain-lined corridor linking the two somewhat hospitable areas. Certainly by 1864, if not earlier, the winter pastures were regarded as part of 'Arabistan, a jurisdiction where Ilkhani had specific responsibilities to its royal governor, but where taxes were paid to Isfahan. A small southeastern corner of the summer pasture area was treated as part of Fars. Given the inaccessibility of the region, the Bakhtiyari was usually beyond the direct control of the central government except in unusual circumstances and under the most determined ruler. Consequently local leaders could attain a degree of autonomy within the Zagros, and the government usually ruled indirectly through them.

The snow-capped Zagros tower to more than 14,000 feet above sea level in the Bakhtiyari and include such peaks as Zardah Kuh (14,920 ft), Kuh Rang (14,090 ft), and Shuturan Kuh (14,200 ft). Zardah Kuh is the highest point of the Bakhtiyari and successively lower and parallel ranges fall off both toward the Iranian plateau on the east and toward 'Arabistan on the west. The heavily faulted mountain ranges extend on a northwest–southeast axis and are separated by parallel narrow and deep valleys and by the streams and rivers that flow through them. The Bakhtiyari mountains give rise to three great rivers: the Zayandah, flowing east to Isfahan and the central deserts; the Karun, with many tributaries, zig-zagging tortuously south, west, north, and then south again as it cuts its way through the Bakhtiyari Zagros until it reaches the Mesopotamian lowland and finally the Persian Gulf; and the Diz, flowing in a general southwesterly direction on the northern and western reaches of the Bakhtiyari until it joins the Karun south of Shushtar. Lesser streams, considerably swollen during the spring melt, feed these three. Given the nature of the river beds and their seasonal flow, the three are navigable only by rudimentary craft, except for the lower reaches of the Karun, from Ahvaz to the Gulf, which lie outside Bakhtiyari proper. These rivers, including Ab Bazuft, a major tributary of the Karun, constitute a major obstacle for the nomads and their flocks during the spring migration.

The rivers are formed by the larger amounts of precipitation deposited by the westerlies in the form of snow in the winter and rain in the early spring months in the higher elevations of the Zagros, although sudden shifts in temperature will result in blizzards in April or even May. Thus the elevation of the Zagros provides the necessary moisture for vegetation and animals, but also contributes to the region's isolation.

The western boundary of the Bakhtiyari lies in northeastern Khuzistan, in the Mesopotamian uplands, which furnished the nomads with their *garmsir* (Persian for "hot country" [i.e., winter encampment grounds]) or *qishlaq* (the Turkish equivalent; both used interchangeably) that included settlements, fields, and pastures. These uplands were also the site for the fields and pastures of permanent sedentary agriculturalists. Moving eastward and higher from the garmsir, the Bakhtiyari passed through the connecting links of narrow valleys and passes to reach the intermontane valleys and meadows of the high Zagros that constituted the *sardsir* (Persian for "cold country" [i.e., summer encampment grounds]) or *yailaq* (its Turkish equivalent). Here the broad valleys extended to the eastern boundary of the Bakhtiyari at the edge of the central Iranian plateau, particularly the rich agricultural districts of Chahar Mahall (lit. the Four Districts, or Lar, Kiyar, Ganduman, and Mizdij). This region is broken by lower mountain ranges that provided both the summer pastures and fields for many of the nomads and the habitat of a permanent sedentary village population. Written sources often designated the garmsir as Pish Kuh, the sardsir as Pusht Kuh, and, occasionally, the area traversed between them as Miyan Kuh (lit. in front of, behind, and among the central massif), but Pusht Kuh usually sufficed for the last two. Except at the highest elevations, peasants lived in agricultural villages throughout the territory, and many practiced transhumant nomadism: that is, they accompanied their flocks of sheep and goats, or sent them with shepherds, to adjacent and higher elevations during the heat of summer and returned with them to their villages for winter, or even sent them to lower regions for that season.

The rains in the garmsir vary greatly but have averaged 12–15 inches per annum – the minimum for even marginal dry farming – in recent times, although in 1935, 26 inches[8] were recorded at one location. This amount of precipitation sufficed for pastures, which became increasingly dry and limited in the heat of summer, and for cereal agriculture, primarily wheat and barley. With irrigation the same region produced, as Ilkhani noted in his "Kitabchah", rice and garden and orchard produce.

Vegetation, affected by elevation and seasonal precipitation, was a key factor in Bakhtiyari pastoralism and especially in the biannual migration. The vernal migration began in late winter, by which time some of the flocks may already have been accompanied to pastures lower than the garmsir to take advantage of the earlier forage. In late March and early April, however, with temperatures climbing to over 100°F and the resulting desiccation of pastures in 'Arabistan, the Bakhtiyari as a whole – but in widely spread groups – began their characteristic six-week 80- to 100-mile journey to higher, cooler, and better-watered pastures in the sardsir. Some of the nomads remained in the garmsir to harvest wheat. In the sardsir a more plentiful supply of grass resulted from greater precipitation, up to 40 inches per annum, much of it in the form of snow that melted more gradually in the cooler mountain temperatures, thus providing needed moisture throughout the summer. Shortly after the nomads' arrival in the sardsir, winter wheat, planted before the previous autumn's departure for the garmsir, was harvested. Then, in early September, the return to the garmsir resumed, completing the cycle. This biannual movement between pastures and fields demonstrates Bakhtiyari sheep–goat specialization and, in addition, their dependence on agriculture. Furthermore, the migration allows for wider exploitation of the territory's resources. Finally, the migration is central to Bakhtiyari social and economic life, and serves to define what it means to be Bakhtiyari (even for those members who do not themselves participate in it); it is virtually a ritualistic act.[9]

Contrary to the popular and romantic image, the Bakhtiyari migrated with difficulty and great hardship and with the loss of animal, and occasionally human, life. Nevertheless, the Bakhtiyari welcomed the excitement of the migration and anticipated the delights of the cool alpine regions that they contrasted to the seared garmsir left behind. Migration constitutes an important aspect of Bakhtiyari self-image and ideology: an attempt to identify a specific territory as Bakhtiyari – one that encompas-

ses a range of ecologies – and to define themselves in opposition to
sedentary agriculturalists.

> O my Friend in the Hot Country, what do you wish me to bring you?
> The buds of the wild celery and snow-water are here at my side.
> Put melting snow in the water-skin of scented leather.
> And carry it to the Hot Country for the fever-stricken youth.
>
> ....
>
> The harvesters are set free [i.e., those who had remained in the garmsir to
> reap wheat and had finished] and have turned their faces toward the camp
> of the tribe (in the Yēlāq) [sic][10]

During the migration the nomads and their flocks had to cross cold,
swollen, and bridgeless rivers by swimming or by floating across on
inflated skin rafts, *kalaks*. (The rafts carried women, children, and young
animals – who thus avoided the dangers of drowning in the swift, icy
water – and goods and household items.) Some migration routes[11] crossed
the valleys and rivers and continued up and over the rugged mountains
through a very limited number of passes, some measuring over 11,000
feet! Unless the nomads pushed on through these bottlenecks the resulting
congestion exacerbated rivalries and invited raiding. Fodder was also
unavailable at the higher elevations, which, once reached, had to be
traversed without stopping. In addition to the steep mountain walls, rough
terrain, and rudimentary and dangerous trails, the nomads encountered
landslides, sudden storms, and dropping temperatures. The Bakhtiyari
frequently found snow in the passes through which they had to shovel
paths and over which they crossed in their cotton clothing and bare feet
(their *givah*, or traditional shoe, had a compressed cotton-rag sole that
would warp and disintegrate if it became wet). The length of the migration
varied, depending upon the location of a particular group's summer and
winter pastures.[12]

This migratory quest for pastures and water indicates the primary
economic role of sheep and goats, the largest and most important group of
animals owned by the Bakhtiyari. Curiously Ilkhani made few references
to them or to the migration in his "Kitabchah"; moreover, he provided no
evidence that he ever accompanied the migration or that he even owned
flocks. He referred, however, to one of his brothers or to sons who did
accompany the migration, presumably to supervise the movement of the
tribes and to settle disputes when they arose (which, perhaps from the
tribal viewpoint, constitutes the key aspect of chieftainship in the Zagros).
He often noted rainfall, or its absence, and its impact on the market price
of commodities such as wheat and livestock.

22

It has been suggested by Barth[13] in his study of the Basseri of Fars, and by Hole[14] in his work on the prehistory of Khuzistan, that the migration is necessary for the survival of these animals. Both argue that the nomads' flocks could not adapt to the extremes of cold and heat were they to remain year round in either of their pasture areas; snow in the sardsir and the desiccating heat of the garmsir would probably prevent flocks from grazing and fodder would have to be acquired for them.

Sheep and goats provided the nomads with food for their own subsistence and with products for economic exchange. The products the Bakhtiyari utilized from their flocks were milk and its derivatives: *rughan* (clarified butter or ghee), *kashk* (dried whey), *dugh* ("buttermilk" from churning), yogurt, and cheese – all to be consumed locally except for cheese and rughan, which were also traded or sold. The flocks at the same time yielded wool, hair, meat, hides, and dung. The meat of only a few animals was ever consumed by the Bakhtiyari, since animals herded to rural and urban markets possibly constituted the most important single source of Bakhtiyari income. Goat hair was spun and woven into strips of cloth to be used for the walls and roofs of tents, and twisted into rope. Sheep wool was carded and spun to be used locally for carpets and woven containers, but most of it was sold or traded in urban markets, and some of it was used in its raw form for felt.

Other Bakhtiyari domestic animals included horses, used for riding by the men and by the wives of the khans – only in the migration – and for exchange; donkeys, for transport; mules, for transport and exchange; dogs, for guarding the camp; chickens, for food; and cows and oxen, for food and transport and as draft animals. Of all these animals, Ilkhani was most interested in horses, and many pages of the "Kitabchah" refer to the various breeds he acquired, bred, or bestowed as gifts. In addition to animals the Bakhtiyari traded local produce consisting of charcoal, gallnuts, tobacco, cherry wood for pipestems, gum tragacanth, and wild animal skins – including fox, bear, and marten – for wheat and barley (unless they grew sufficient amounts for their own consumption), salt, tea, sugar, metal products, cloth, and tanned leather goods in urban or regional markets located on the periphery, or outside, of Bakhtiyari. Tea – earlier, probably water – milk, sugar, and wheat–barley bread were the staples of the Bakhtiyari diet. In times of shortage and famine they supplemented their grain flour with that ground from acorns (*balut*), which grew abundantly on scrub oak in the Bakhtiyari. Similarly, the Bakhtiyari utilized other seasonal plants – for example, the wild celery that grew in the Zagros – both for trade and for their own diet. This brief economic summary of Ilkhani's nineteenth-century Bakhtiyari – which is probably characteristic of earlier times as well – reveals not only the nomads' dependence on animal husbandry and agriculture, but the exploitation of all available resources.

In addition to nomadism, another response to the range of resources in a territory the size and complexity of the Bakhtiyari was agricultural specialization. Mid-nineteenth-century Europeans noted that permanent agricultural villages and settlements were found throughout the Bakhtiyari territory, except at the highest elevations, and especially in the border regions. Whole tayafahs, for example the Janiki Garmsir, were settled. Thus, paradoxically, the Bakhtiyari encompassed seemingly antithetical – certainly from a popular view – but complementary economies that resulted in greater utilization of a complex ecology. The agriculturalists focused on the development and protection of fixed resources of their land, crops, water, and dwellings and settlements. The nomads, on the other hand, centered their activities on movement and adaptability to their flocks' requirements for pasture and water, and given the limits and the nature of the Bakhtiyari territory, this necessitated a seasonal response. Apart from this fundamental difference – mobility versus settlement – the Bakhtiyari pastoral nomads differed from neighboring sedentary agriculturalists, and those in their midst, only in degree, for both shared the same pastoral and agricultural skills, complemented each other, competed for the same land, and experienced an overlap of ecologies. Moreover, both organized – or had the potential to organize – themselves on the same political basis, were dominated by the same types of leaders, had similar relationships with urban areas and the government, and shared many of the same values.

Jacques Berque has written: "Nomadism is an extreme case of a human society's adaptation to an unfriendly natural environment."[15] The classic Old World area of pastoral nomadism – except for Arctic nomadism – encompassed an arid zone that extended from the northern frontiers of China across Central Asia and the Iranian and Anatolian plateaus, through Mesopotamia and the Arabian peninsula, and across North Africa. This "unfriendly" environment had low rainfall, usually restricted to winter months, and hot, dry summers. Agriculture was often marginal and existed only in riverine areas, in oases, or where irrigation was possible, with the major exceptions to be found in Anatolia and the higher elevations of the western and eastern mountain fringes of the Iranian plateau, where dry farming was possible, and in the Mediterranean, Black Sea, and Caspian littorals. These better-watered areas were devoid of large numbers of pastoral nomads and the great confederations until the arrival of the Seljuqs in the tenth century and the subsequent Turkic–Mongol invasions. The seasonal nature of rain in the arid zone forced agriculturalists and pastoralists, were they to exploit this environment without altering it, into some type of cyclical movement in order to find grass for their flocks. In the Zagros this became vertical because of the increased precipitation at higher levels.

Two factors of pastoral nomadism prevailed in the Zagros in earlier times, as they have recently: a symbiotic relationship with the environment and sedentary society, and the exploitation of differing environmental niches necessitating movement between them. Nomadism *per se* has characterized history from the early beginnings; pastoral nomadism, however, could occur only after, or concomitantly with, the "food-producing revolution", during which animal and plant domestication took place, beginning before the tenth millennium BC. The recent archaeological investigations of Braidwood and Hole, Flannery, and Meldgaard, Mortensen, and Thrane[16] in the Zagros, a locus for the incipient domestication of sheep and goats and of wheat, barley, and legumes, give support to the hypothesis that pastoral nomadism – at least the vertical and transhumant types in West Asia – probably developed concurrently with agriculture.

Owen Lattimore analyzes and describes the process of the development of pastoral nomadism as it probably occurred in the area between the steppe and agricultural land in western China in the second half of the first millennium. Here again there were people practicing a mixed agricultural-herding economy. As these people were pushed further to the west and into the steppe by advancing agriculturalists, they emphasized pastoral production.

It was only when this diverging specialization had been carried to a certain point that the marginal steppe society ceased to be marginal and committed itself definitely to the steppe. Having reached that point it was ready to take advantage of a steppe technique of horse usage in order to increase the efficiency of life within the steppe environment.[17]

Lattimore, it should also be noted, allows for differing cultural and political relations between nomads and settled society depending on whether they are the "excluded" nomads of the steppes of Central Asia as described above or the "enclosed" nomads[18] more characteristic of the Zagros. The former are somewhat less dependent on settled society and are usually beyond its administrative and political reach, in contrast to the latter, who are integrated into the agricultural societies that encompass them.

The concept of the close relationship between nomadic and sedentary economies and societies in the Zagros is important because it shows the possibility for movement from one to the other under a variety of conditions, and the different ways in which man has responded to and exploited the same environment. In the Zagros there have been three major responses: the sedentary villager, who practiced dry or irrigated farming and who herded small flocks in pastures contiguous to his village; the transhumant agriculturalist–pastoralist with a permanent village base, who farmed and also maintained larger herds and moved them, often under the care of shepherds, to neighboring alpine pastures for the summer; and the long-range pastoral nomad, who may have had a permanent residence with sown fields in both the winter and the summer pastures, but who most often lived in a tent and was primarily dependent upon his relatively large flocks and moved in a seasonally cyclical and vertical sequence to maintain them. Bakhtiyari were to be found in all three categories, with the third group predominating. All three types relied essentially on cereals for food. The first two were more dependent on fixed sources of water, fields, and pasturage, whereas the third possessed greater freedom – but with limitations, specifically of general borders and traditional pasture rights – to move in search of them. The villager had to limit the herd size by the amount of available pasturage in the driest part of the year or provide for fodder storage, but the nomad could maintain larger flocks by moving them to pastures as they matured to optimum productivity.

Sedentary agriculturalists adapted to their environment, but pastoralists maintained a symbiotic relationship with it. The agriculturalists plowed and harrowed, fertilized and irrigated, or rotated planting of their fields. They seeded, weeded, harvested the crop, and stored seed for the next planting. Both the agriculturalist and the pastoral nomad were dependent upon rainfall, and both had little or no control over animal epidemics or over plant diseases and pests. But, unlike the agriculturalist, the nomad did little to change or improve his environment; if the pastures were poor he may have had the option to move on. He guided his flocks to pasture and water, protected them from predators and storms, and assisted in the birth and first suckling of the new-born. The nomad made little attempt to improve the blood lines of his flock, except perhaps in the case of horse and camel nomadism, and, other than isolation, he had no control over epizootic diseases. The unreliability of rainfall especially limited herd size and threatened the nomad with sudden economic disaster.

These paragraphs suggest a continuum, with the pastoral nomad at one end and the sedentary agriculturalist at the other, with a difference in degree and emphasis, as they practiced some of the same pastoral and agricultural skills, and competed for the same habitat or occupied complementary niches. The agricultural villages, like the nomads, shared corporate interests in community self-defense and sometimes in land usage and herding. The villagers did not have corporate interests organized around a migration, unless they were transhumant agriculturalist–pastoralist (in which case the migration was less complex), but they may have shared such interests in regard to water usage. Just as in migration, where coordination was necessary and a potential existed for hostile contact with outsiders as well as within the migrating unit itself, so did water usage require coordination and contain the germ of internal and external conflict.

Other similarities between the villagers and the nomads were that each group maintained territorial boundaries and identified itself with a name and through state political offices, activities, and administrative functions. Like the nomads, some villagers structured themselves in descent categories around which a variety of socio-political alignments may have been formed. Often identical outside groups – the ulema, tinkers, etc. – performed specialized tasks for both.[19] Nomads and agriculturalists, even when they might have shared the same values, were bound together as hostile units by mutual antagonisms that grew out of their competitive economic, and at times political, relationships. This antagonism may have served an ideological function as a possible mechanism reinforcing group loyalties.

The critical factor – in addition to an economic component of specialization – becomes one of relationships and the interaction between pastoral nomads and agriculturalists, which suggests political and historical factors. Dyson-Hudson has noted: "In short, to be a farmer or a herdsman is a matter of culturally conditioned choices, not merely a matter of ecologically conditioned responses; ecological niche and ethnic category can thus be seen as transformations of each other." He continues:

Perhaps we have here a most useful feature for grading pastoral systems, from which other features ought surely to follow: that is, the degree to which the pastoral occupation concerned is manipulated within a framework of natural conditions and processes – within and in response to which the pastoral occupation is conducted – and to what degree are they created by other populations in the same environment?[20]

Lattimore raises a similar question, but in a broader context of culture and politics, when he discusses the concept of excluded and enclosed nomads.

In the Iranian–Mesopotamian–Arab world the geographical and social pattern is much more confused than on either the west Roman or the Chinese frontier, a major phenomenon being that pastoral nomads were not only excluded on the north but enclosed in blocks of desert, semi-desert, and highland country within the general seep of civilization . . .

Leaving aside their differences, however, there are similar phenomena in all of these frontier histories. As in China, the range of military striking power exceeded the range of ability to conquer and incorporate; the range of uniform civil administration exceeded that of economic integration. The northern frontier at which an attempt was made to exclude the barbarians was also the limit beyond which uniform blocks of cultivated territory with a uniform complement of cities and administrative services could not be added to the state . . .[21]

In the case of the Zagros, unlike China and its steppe frontiers, nomads interacted in the framework of agriculture, cities and their central administration, and the great cultural tradition. Political autonomy and the means to extort dues are often said to characterize nomads, but agriculturalists also have demonstrated these abilities, but through the mechanism of urban society and the state.

Flock size, however, with the related factor of mobility with its mechanisms for expansion, defense, and the resulting experience that may be utilized for aggressive action, suggests at least a major economic difference, with significant political and cultural ramifications, between the agriculturalist and the nomad. There were economically marginal nomads who became sedentary or transhumant agriculturalists, but only some of the transhumant villagers, and only a very few of the sedentary villagers, had sufficiently large flocks to maintain themselves for long as pastoral nomads. Barth states that the average size flock needed to maintain a Basseri household consisted of approximately 100 sheep and goats, and that it was impossible for a Basseri household to subsist on less than 60.[22] The initial herd investment would prevent most peasants from engaging in nomadism, for, using Barth's figures, it would cost about $1,000 (1957–8) to obtain an adequate flock of approximately 100 sheep and goats. At that time the estimated annual median income for all peasant families in Iran – excluding casual agricultural labor and thus raising the figure – was only $112![23] Nor would it be possible – given agricultural specialization, pasture, water, and fodder constraints, and the need to utilize flock offspring to add to income rather than allow the flock to increase – for most peasants gradually to build a flock of sufficient size for nomadism. Dyson-Hudson's generalization should perhaps be modified to "a matter of culturally *and economically* conditioned choices. . .". (Poorer nomads, it should be emphasized, do maintain themselves with less than 60 animals by establishing animal and shepherding contracts, through seasonal agricultural or urban labor, or with a son in wage labor. Whole groups, such as tinkers and blacksmiths, of course, exist as nomads without directly relying on flocks.) Barth's relatively recent research thus corroborates Sir James Morier's observations of the early nineteenth century: "An I'liyát [nomad] of middling fortune possesses about a hundred sheep, three or four camels, three or four mares, ten asses, etc., which may yield him a revenue of forty to fifty túmáns. A man who possesses a thousand sheep, thirty camels, twenty mares, etc., is reckoned a rich man."[24]

In Hasanabad, a sedentary agricultural village in the Zagros near Kermanshah, the average number of animals per household was considerably less. "Most families in Hasanabad had no more than four or five of these animals [sheep/goats], but they are important because they belong solely to the villagers . . .". In this same village eight out of 42 households had 60 or more sheep/goats, and seven households had none. And in a village with a transhumant economy – also near Kermanshah – there were 33 households; ten of these had 60 or more sheep/goats, eight had between 40 and 59, and three had none.[25] In this latter village large flock owners hired shepherds and sent their sheep and goats with them to the Iran–Iraq border area for the winter; in mid-May most of these villagers moved in stages up to alpine pastures high on the mountain where their village was located and then returned, also in stages, beginning in late August, to their permanent stone houses. In contrast, Hasanabad families possessing large flocks occasionally moved to pastures at a higher elevation for a few weeks in summer when their local pastures became overgrazed. Except for these few families, it would appear that the sedentary and transhumant villagers did not have the minimum economic basis to maintain themselves if they were to leave their permanent residences; unless, of course, they were able, through the accumulation of capital or contracts, to acquire more animals, or unless they were able to establish client relationships with wealthier nomads. (It should be noted that the figures for Hasanabad were collected in 1959–60 and may reflect extreme cases or regional variations.)

The evidence cited here – except for Morier's – on comparative flock sizes is based on contemporary observations, and a question might well be raised as to the possibility that in earlier periods sedentary villagers possessed larger herds and that, in times of stress, they would have had the basic economic requirements to maintain a nomadic life style. Other important factors would be population density and availability of pasture and farm land; in both there could be considerable regional variation. The consequences of the drought of 1869–72 on human and animal population possibly allowed Ilkhani to give vacant pasture lands to dissident Qashqa'i. Although it is not certain that Barth's conclusions or Patty Jo Watson's figures for village flock size are wholly applicable to the past, one should be cautious before assuming any large-scale conversion of sedentary people into nomads. An increase in the relative number of nomads might more plausibly be explained by a combination of nomadic invasions and movements of such wholly new groups into a region, or a higher rate of population increase among nomads than among the settled population –

although Barth argues that in an attempt to balance resources with population, this surplus becomes sedentary, rather than the reverse.[26] Most likely, nomads in earlier periods encroached upon arable land, especially at times of weakened governmental centers or governments of nomad origin, but at the same time had a greater ability to absorb villagers.

The environment – topography, soil, fertility, water and drainage, animal life, plant cover, and constant modification due to climatic action, erosion, earthquakes, and other types of geological change – affected nomads and agriculturalists alike. These processes have only recently undergone detailed study; traditionally nomads and their flocks have often been cast as the villains responsible for such change in their "struggle" with agriculturalists. As an example: in southwest Iran the mountains have become deforested by the activity of charcoal burners and by overgrazing. Recent analysis of a similar geographic area has indicated that charcoal burners and overpopulation were among the major causes – not merely the grazing habits of goats,[27] which are also kept by agriculturalists. The resulting loss of plant cover increased erosion, and the streams and irrigation systems silted up and the contour of the land changed. Frequently, where there had been extensive irrigation, salinization occurred because of poor drainage, or the canal networks had not been maintained because of a weakened social and political fabric that had failed to provide the necessary security. Further deterioration followed as a result of a complex set of factors, until whole areas had been removed from cultivation.

Although nomads are frequently charged with disrupting irrigated agriculture, Ilkhani invested heavily in irrigation projects in his own villages and in the area under his control during the final decade of his life, a period when his power was relatively unchallenged. Moreover, farmans issued to Ilkhani note a number of villages, or their dependencies, which he had recently returned to cultivation. Najm al-Mulk, however, sent by Nasir al-Din Shah to gather incriminating evidence against Ilkhani, reported – and distorted – contrary evidence about the part of 'Arabistan bordering on the Bakhtiyari, which he charged had suffered from Bakhtiyari depredations.[28]

Historical problems of inter- and intra-national politics, population density, settlement patterns, and land use also affected the land and its inhabitants. Answers to many of these issues require further study. While past historians have placed great stress on the impact on certain societies of sudden, catastrophic, large-scale nomadic invasions, recent scholarship indicates that the slowly developing social, political, and ecological factors are probably more important to the history of man and his environment and society. At the conclusion of a careful and pioneering study of an area adjacent to western Iran, Robert McC. Adams writes:

With the collapse of Sassanian rule we have seen [in the Diyala plain] the onset of a slow, irregular, but decisive process of dissolution in the rural economy, which by Ottoman times may have reduced the area cultivated to a level comparable to that of the Middle Babylonian abandonment twenty-five centuries earlier. Both the deterioration of political control and ecological changes have been adduced as contributing explanations for this catastrophic decline, with the Mongol invasion having been an additional factor that probably in the long run was less important than either of the others.[29]

Historical processes such as the Mongol invasions, or the large-scale influx of whole societies of alien nomads, have affected the agriculturalists and their society and have had a significant impact on pastoral nomads as well. Many scholars[30] have noted that the arrival of Turkic–Mongol rule was followed by an increase of pastoral nomadism – consisting of the invaders themselves with their families and flocks – but sources also suggest the bedouinization of indigenous groups. Werner Caskel postulates that in third-century Arabia, "The transition of part of the population from settled life to nomadism is comprehensible by the decline of the southern Arabian [urban, mercantile] economy . . .".[31] A major problem in trying to uncover historical references to the process of nomadization is that it was often undramatic – the dramatic instances are noted in sources, especially when they provided dynastic leadership – continuous, and commonplace. Shifts from agriculture to nomadism may have occurred when the state adopted the administrative practice of the *iqta'* in Seljuq times (or its later manifestation, the tuyul, in the eighteenth and nineteenth centuries),[32] an important aspect of the pervasive Turkish military patronage system.[33] (The iqta'/tuyul practice perpetuated a military, usually tribal, elite, which received assignments of land, or its revenue, in return for service. Indirectly, this may have resulted in a reduction of peasant proprietorship and a decline in agriculture.) Similarly, the military and administrative practice of removing whole tribal groups to the marches and border areas, usually to ward off nomadic incursions – those of the Bakhtiyari and the Kurds under Nadir Shah, for example – may have extended areas of nomadism.

The historical problem of accounting for change, the nature of nomadism itself – especially the factors of mobility, flocks, and adaptability to ecological variation – and the nomads' political–military roles suggest a political difference between nomads and agriculturalists and invite comparison of the two in terms of their socio-political structures and responses to external political developments. Irons' work with the Yumut Turkman in the Gurgan plain demonstrates that an essential factor in their mobility was avoidance of government with its taxes and conscription, or resistance to imposition of dynastic control and its inherent interest in concentrating and centralizing power.[34] The Mongols under Chingiz Khan and his descendants exhibit the antithesis, an offensive rather than a defensive aspect of mobility, with the imposition of their hegemony over other nomads, over sedentary settlements, and even over states and empires – an attempt at concentrating power.

Herding and movement of flocks to pasture or assertion of power over neighboring agricultural hamlets may have involved only a family, or a small group, whereas the conquest of other tribes, a city, or a state required a larger and better-organized unit with leadership – a "tribe", in the case of nomads, or the state's army, which in the Iranian context would have had tribal components.

Despite corporate interests and needs, villagers did not usually have a political organization for potential conquest and expansion as did the pastoral nomads. They lacked the economic resources for arms and horses, and the experience gained from defense, which was usually provided for villages by their landlord, the government, or even pastoral nomads; nor was it likely that they would be willing to leave their capital investment and homes. Other major factors would have been the land system itself, which was characterized by internal competition for limited resources, and the relationship of the villages with the landlord, delineated by his arbitrary and autocratic power. The landlord was represented in the village by his headmen and, unlike the tribal khan, possessed no kin tie, either real or fictive, with his peasants. Generally – and historical and geographic factors impinge here – no peasant had "rights" to land unless he owned it, and in case of grievance against the landlord, he could have appealed to urban authorities or to the ulema, moved to vacant lands if such were available, or fled. This system worked to the peasant's advantage only when there were demands for peasant labor. Villagers appear to have lacked mechanisms to defend their own interests against the landlord, except as individual nuclear families; and these were powerless, since kin group membership was of little import to the landlord.

Among nomads lineage principles provided a framework for social and political organization and were more apt to operate in favor of the household or its functional extension in the aulad as herding camps (mals). The nuclear family formed the basis in fact and ideology for the larger segments in the pastoral nomadic structure. As Barth notes, "every Basseri obtains rights at birth in the pasture of his oulad [extended family]".[35] Utilization of specific pastures, in theory, may have been allocated or rotated by khans; indeed, nomads were expelled from them. In recent Bakhtiyari history, however, when a khan's power was primarily dependent upon the number of his supporters and when keen competition existed between an increasingly large number of eligible candidates for such positions, a khan emphasized his relationship to the nomads and feared their desertion to a rival. Bakhtiyari socio-political and lineage principles also functioned in favor of the family in migration, the defense of pastures and fields, and the raising of flocks, all of which also required economic resources, a degree of military skills, organizational ability, and experience and leadership – supplied largely by the khans. These qualities and abilities are commonly assumed when the term "tribe" is used in the Iranian context; popularly, the concept relates both economically to nomadism and politically to rule – in the case of the Bakhtiyari – by autonomous khans.

Chapter III

The khans and the tribal structure

The Duraki khans sought to unite the Bakhtiyari into an effective political force and from that base to influence affairs at the state level. Although ultimately unsuccessful – given the unstable socio-political tayafah structure of the Bakhtiyari – the khans sought to play a national role which has characterized much of Iran's history, and which has given rise to the truism that all the dynasties, except the Pahlavis, ruling Iran since the eleventh century have had an internal tribal base – the Seljuqs, the Mongols, the Timurids, the Aq Quyunlu and the Qara Quyunlu, the Safavids, the Afghans, the Afshars, the Zands, and the Qajars. However, once in power, these new leaders identified with state interests in order to maintain their positions and turned to curb their supporting tribes, whose political instability, conflicting interests, and potential for autonomy posed threats to the state's sovereignty and stability. The state prevailed – because of its greater economic, political, military, bureaucratic, and ideological resources – when it manipulated the tribal socio-political structure through divide and rule policies; conscription and warfare, especially utilization of tribal contingents in foreign wars; grants of land and incomes to tribal leaders; forced settlement and relocation; retention of hostages; confiscation; and extermination. The Pahlavis constitute the striking exception to this historical pattern, for their power was based on a standing army and not on tribal military contingents; Riza Khan, when his coup succeeded in 1921, was confronted with the same fragmenting forces and the problem of divided loyalties as he attempted to mold a unified nation–state. This threat persisted into the early 1930s, by which time the rapid changes in military technology and widespread urban support for the centralized state ended any major challenge the tribes could have posed.

The issue at stake for the Bakhtiyari khans, however, was not only the utilization of a pastoral base for an external role – the principal issue recorded in the sources – but, even more importantly, the manipulation of that pastoral base to maintain their own internal power. The khans' essential problem became one of identifying with exclusive, or particular,

34

tayafah goals, even though these may have conflicted with the confederation's inclusive, or general, goal of maintaining internal unity – and the khans required a united Bakhtiyari for their ambitions in the greater state. They had also to appeal for support to those outside the tribal framework without alienating internal support or threatening external rivals.

The uncertain position of the khans in the Bakhtiyari – including the Duraki great khans, and even the powerful Husain Quli Khan Ilkhani – *vis-à-vis* the tayafah structure was derived from the fact that they had little direct control over the Bakhtiyari economic base of pastoralism and agriculture, which was inherently unstable and regulated within the tayafah system. The great khans exercised indirect control of the Bakhtiyari pastoral–agricultural base through the juridical–political aspect of their intermediary role as arbitrators, judges, military leaders, landlords, and civil administrators. Ideologically, and in terms of the Bakhtiyari economy and its resulting socio-political framework, the great khans and their descent groups played a critical symbolic role, for they completed the Bakhtiyari hierarchical world and fitted it into the greater Iranian ethos.

From Ilkhani on – but possibly earlier as well – the Bakhtiyari structure came to consist of two major but interrelated components: first, the confederation of the whole of the Bakhtiyari, which emerged in the mid-nineteenth century and which the great khans administered until the 1930s; and second, tribes (tayafahs), which consisted of named, major units encompassing lesser ones in a segmentary pyramid, but which long predated the confederation and which were to outlast it. The confederation approximated pre-existing administrative, territorial, and ethnic divisions, but its formal structure came into being by imperial edict and by state support given to the ilkhani as the state's agent. The confederational framework, consisting of the political–administrative superstructure of progressively larger units, brought together the lesser units within it for defense, expansion, and administration. The confederation has been more subject to change because of the political competition among the great khans for dominance within it, the interjection of state politics and policies, and the somewhat ambivalent role of the great khans, who served as intermediaries between the state and the Bakhtiyari and who faced the dilemma of contradictory goals stemming from interests and ambitions peripheral to, or even beyond, the Bakhtiyari. The form of the tribes (at the tayafah level and below), on the other hand, has been more persistent and less affected by external developments than by basic pastoral and agricultural structures.[1]

The Bakhtiyari tayafah components begin with the family. (The classification and terminology in this book follow Digard's.[2]) The household – essentially, the nuclear family – owns the flocks and works together in the agricultural cycle, and, certainly in the case of the agriculturalists, constitutes the key economic unit. The yield of the flocks and of the land is largely utilized for family consumption; similarly, marketing is a family concern. The extended family comes together as an aulad, or tash, approximating to a descent group, which functions as a camp (mal) of from three to twelve tents and shares common herding, migrating, and defense interests. The camp – if not the family – constitutes the key economic unit for the pastoralists; a nuclear family could not long survive without the assistance afforded by the camp. At this level of integration decisions are reached by family heads. The tirah (roughly, subtribe) forms the next level; it comprises the maximum grouping of related camps and functions primarily around the corporate interests of migration and pasture "ownership". Tirahs come together to form tayafahs and are represented in them by kadkhudas. Tayafahs are headed by kalantars appointed from them by the khans. (The tayafah is a large entity; today, some tayafahs number 25,000 persons.[3]) If pasture rights are not derived from membership in the tirah, they are from membership in the tayafah.[4] Even though the tayafah may seldom have acted as a corporate group – its interests were usually defended at a lower level – it existed as a named entity with its own identity, as an endogamous unit, and as the khans' administrative unit. Thus the tayafah – indeed, the confederation – provided a conceptual framework for organizing people politically and administratively and attaching them to leaders. Eighteenth-century sources mention the offices of both kadkhuda and kalantar (the latter is not to be confused with the civil kalantar in urban areas),[5] but without delineating their functions; probably the kadkhudas represented the tribal units to the kalantars and khans, and the kalantars represented the khans to the tribes. The kalantars were wealthy, often owned land, married into the khan families as well as into important tirah families, functioned as petty khans, and have survived as leaders to the present. Theoretically, the kalantars were appointed, but it would appear that the office was often hereditary. The intermediary and uncertain position of the kalantar between particular interests of the tayafah and broader goals was similar to that of the khans.

Continuing with the confederational structure, each tayafah belongs to one of nine babs (here, lit. division); every bab has a dominant lineage, a subgroup in one of the tayafahs, from which khans are chosen. These babs are grouped into the two moieties of the Haft Lang and Chahar Lang; in recent history, five babs have been found in the Haft Lang – the Duraki, Babadi, Bakhtiyarvand (or Bahdarvand), Dinarani, and Janiki – and four in the Chahar Lang – Mamivand, Mamsalah, Mugu'i, and Kiyanursi.

The two moieties were finally unified in the confederation (il) of the Bakhtiyari after 1867 under an ilkhani. The pre-1867 confederational Bakhtiyari had the potential for crystallizing leadership at the highest, or confederational, level, but did not do so unless there was state intervention. For part of the eighteenth century the Haft Lang had a single leader, who may have had a counterpart in the Chahar Lang, though nineteenth-century sources provide no such evidence. It is possible that the Haft Lang leader was responsible to the central government for the Chahar Lang.

The primary role of the khans at the bab level was to mitigate competition between tribes for land and conflict with sedentary society, which probably constituted the major factors for strife; in addition, migration, with its potential for the exacerbation of intergroup rivalries, may have increased the likelihood of internal discord. All this, added to the pressures generated by disputes with other tribes, the defense of territory, the necessity for exchange with sedentary society, and the demands of the larger community (especially the Iranian government), seems to have necessitated the existence of khans or like leaders as mediators. These leaders and their people usually had "common" ancestors. Such leaders always possessed the characteristics of wisdom, courage, and generosity necessary for their chiefly function, which may have included coordination of the migration; assignment of pastures; appointment of headmen and agents; mediation of intertribal disputes; leadership for raids, defense, and battle; and issuance of levies, taxes, and fines.

The confederation, *Il Bakhtiyari* – the final, all-encompassing unit – is a further elaboration of Bakhtiyari political structure. Like the bab khans, the confederational khans could seldom count on the support of all the components of the confederation. The khans and their followers frequently had different interests and may actually have sought to weaken the power and ability of the ilkhani and the great khans to intervene and, especially, to collect taxes. Within the confederation, chains of command were established among the great khans through sons, brothers, uncles, and nephews. Although the great khans may have assisted the ilkhani and may have been obeyed because they were born into the chiefly lineage, they did not constitute a continuing administration; on the contrary, they could challenge the ilkhani and replace him. There was a line of communication from the ilkhani, great khans, and khans down through the kalantars to the lowest and smallest segment of the tribe; thus authority was delegated to those appointed by the khan to carry out his orders, but only for the duration of a specific task. The ilkhani maintained a rudimentary bureaucracy, with secretaries to keep records and to act as agents.

The power of the ilkhani and khavanin buzurg was both personal and vested in their chiefly office: it was based on the benefits they were able to dispense, the respect they may have commanded because of their lineage, their coercive capabilities within the tribe or confederation provided by a standing corps of loyal armed retainers, and the support given them by the central and provincial governments or outside sources of power, such as the British in the nineteenth and early twentieth centuries. These last associations were beneficial only to a few, other than the most important great khans and their supporters.

Khans generally had the greatest economic resources and widest ties within the Bakhtiyari and, outside it, with sedentary society and other nomads. This is illustrated by the large number of marriages among the great khans outside their tayafahs. In addition, inheritance practices in these families seem to have concentrated family wealth in the hands of favorite and more able sons.[6] The khans were the executives and retained the greatest coercive power within the tribe. Their power, though seemingly absolute, was limited by the power of the tribes' various segments to withhold their support or to transfer this support to a rival within the chiefly family, to another khan, or even to someone outside the group.

Accession to leadership of the bab was based on lineage; primacy of age; often mother's rank (if she were the daughter of a khan, she would be addressed by the title *bibi*, or honored lady); wealth; internal (including family and tirah) and external support; and perceived fitness for office, especially the virtues of courage, assertiveness, knowledge, sagacity, and generosity. Although one khan was regarded as paramount by his own bab or even other babs, several candidates competed for that position – brothers, cousins (father's brother's sons), and uncles (father's brothers). Occasionally a group went outside its own membership, or even outside the Bakhtiyari, to recognize a khan (e.g., the Duraki khans' earliest known ancestor, Haydar Kur, who, according to tradition, was a Papi Lur). Late in the nineteenth century, and possibly earlier as well, it would appear that eldest sons, usually the sons of bibis, were favored and were designated as successors by their fathers, although this was no guarantee of accession. The two dominant rivalries consisted of brother versus half-brother (same father) and nephew opposed to uncle (father's brother); given polygyny and the notion of the equality of all sons, these antagonisms should not be surprising. The Qashqa'i ruling khans constitute a striking contrast to the Bakhtiyari khans, as the former were monogamous and had fewer disputes over succession.[7]

The khans had to be able both to inspire and to provide maintenance for their immediate supporters. To act, lead, and live like a khan required a degree of wealth, especially in the form of regular incomes from tribal dues and land, and to maintain or to increase one's holdings required power – merely to retain one's leadership position often necessitated support from outside the tayafah and even outside the Bakhtiyari, where marriage alliances could play a key role. Khans sought wealth less for its own sake than for the power and prestige it helped to buy. Positions of power in the Bakhtiyari were insecure, for there were always rival claimants who acted as a check against the potential for despotism by allowing tayafahs and tirahs to transfer support and allegiance. In summary, power in the nineteenth-century Bakhtiyari was wielded by those born into ruling lineages who had the necessary ability to inspire family and tayafah support and the resources to maintain themselves as khans. Aspirations to greater power required outside assistance, and this usually meant the central government; however, the individual seeking greater power could be perceived as a potential threat by outside supporters. Political ties, reinforced by marriages, were first established within the Bakhtiyari tayafahs and then with neighboring confederations, but as the great khans began to play a national role, the quest was extended to the great national families. These ambitions and this pattern of marriage and political ties certainly distinguished the great khans from the lesser ones, from the kalantars and kadkhudas, and from Bakhtiyari commoners. Here, too, in addition to the political factor, both economic and symbolic factors may be found. Honor was accorded to, and great pride was felt by, those families who had married into the khan's family. On the level of the folk model, some idea of the status of the khans and the esteem in which they were held is illustrated by the healing power attributed to the uneaten food from a khan's plate and by the ceremony attached to his physical presence.

From the eighteenth century the dominant Haft Lang bab was the Duraki, which had its own lineage of khans, that of Haydar Kur, whose members belonged to one of the Duraki's component tayafahs, the Zarasvand. Nadir Shah bestowed the title sardar (commander) on 'Ali Salih,[8] an eighteenth-century Zarasvand of that lineage, and as the result of this formal award, family historians emphasize the distinction of that lineage. (The usual male honorific title of address at this time and until late in the nineteenth century was aqa [gentleman], pronounced "au", rather than khan, which was first used in written sources for 'Ali Salih. Even though members of major Haft Lang lineages may have lacked the formal award of the title khan by farman, by the end of the nineteenth century khan had become the customary male honorific.)

After 1867 the khavanin buzurg constituted the group from which the ilkhani was to be chosen by the shah. In the early eighteenth century the great khans possessed major land holdings in Chahar Mahall; functioned as government officials and military leaders there, in the Bakhtiyari, and on campaigns; and represented major Bakhtiyari components (after 1867 they represented the whole confederation). These great khans were part of a tribal/pastoral/nomadic world as well as the nontribal/agricultural/sedentary one.

The khavanin buzurg were set apart from the khans at the bab level by differences in degree of wealth, power, and function that were compounded by their involvement in state affairs as major landlords, government officials, and representatives of the confederation and the support given them by the state. To maintain their many positions they sought ties with Qajar factions, Qashqa'i khans, the Qavams of Shiraz, Arab shaikhs, the ulema, and the British. Such a range of ties is reflected not only in political alliances and rivalries but in marriage bonds as well. In the confederation, the khavanin buzurg held executive power, and retained the largest military units within it. Despite military superiority and government support, their power, like that of the khans, was limited by the competition within the Duraki lineage and by the ability of the Bakhtiyari components to withhold support or to transfer it to a rival. Similarly the state could recognize a rival and thus manipulate Bakhtiyari politics.[9]

The khavanin buzurg acquired income through their government ties, especially the revenues from ṭuyuls and from the collection of the confederation's taxes, dues, and assessments. An additional major source of income was derived from land outside the Bakhtiyari, especially in Chahar Mahall; between the Bakhtiyari and Isfahan, where the Duraki khans had been great landlords and officials at least from the late Safavid period; and in 'Arabistan. The great khans' surplus wealth was often considerable; it was reported that Husain Quli Khan Ilkhani entrusted 80,000 tumans on one occasion in *c.* 1882 to 'Arabistan merchants for investment.[10] The great khans' own flocks were possibly of minimal importance as a factor in their wealth, and with one exception the record fails to note the size of the khans' herds of sheep and goats; in any case, given the nature of pastoralism and its attendant problems,[11] no individual or group of leaders could successfully exploit this single factor of flocks for personal economic and political advantage. Husain Quli Khan Ilkhani's horses would constitute an exception.

An important issue – and one generally overlooked in sources – concerns the ruling khans' relationship to their Bakhtiyari followers, specifically as it dealt with economic and political structures. Although the Bakhtiyari were essentially nomadic pastoralists, they were also cultivators and grew agricultural produce. Flocks were owned by the nuclear family, but camping, herding, migrating, and defense required and resulted in increasingly large groupings which, from the perspective of the Bakhtiyari folk model, were formed on a kin basis. Such associations had access to the traditional pastures of their particular tirahs/tayafahs. Apparently the khans could assign or reassign pasture land as reward or punishment, but seldom did so.

The khans had little control over what might be called the economic base of the mode of production, which was controlled by family or extended family units. In terms, however, of the juridical–political aspect of the mode of production the role of the khans is more evident. After the mid-nineteenth century for the Bakhtiyari as a whole, but in earlier times for the two great divisions or even smaller units, the khans mediated within the Bakhtiyari, between them and outsiders, especially the central government, and integrated the Bakhtiyari into the larger social fabric. Their functions included the collection of tribal taxes and dues, maintenance of order, provision of cavalry forces, adjudication of disputes, and coordination of the migration.

Another aspect of the primary economic and political superstructure – an outgrowth of the mode of production and mainly ignored – is ideology, which incorporated political, social, and cultural values. Here the role of the ruling khans and descent groups is largely symbolic, yet crucial, as it completes the Bakhtiyari hierarchical world view and not only reinforces but justifies and legitimizes the lineage principles underlying internal Bakhtiyari relationships.

The Bakhtiyari folk model would appear to have shared in an Irano-Shiʻi hierarchical world view – God, the Imams and saints, the shah, the khans, and themselves. In addition power and authority were perceived concretely, not conceived abstractly, as wielded by individuals in specific situations. Thus power was seen when its holder, or his agent or writ, was present. His, or even at times her,[12] authority was acknowledged through submission, obedience, and deference. The khan was regarded as remote but accessible; powerful but one of the people; rich but hospitable, generous, magnanimous, and helpful; and omniscient and judicious but responsible. (Pasture rights were vested in the tayafah, but a powerful khan could dispossess dissident groups. Ideologically, the khan "represented" the unit.) Participation in the ruler's or khan's bounty of wealth and authority was by his grace, as all power and benefits were perceived as emanating from him in his position. In all manner of things the ilkhani, and most powerful khans, acted within the Bakhtiyari, as did the Qajar shahs in their realm, and was treated as pre-eminent. The khans also functioned within and held fast to the greater Irano-Shiʻi political ethos of their urban counterparts – the belief that legitimacy is vested in the Imams and is only held temporarily by secular leaders until the return of the

Twelfth (the last) Imam – so when they came to power they accepted the prevailing traditions and offered no alternative concept of power. Furthermore, if they achieved power – as Bakhtiyari leaders, as governors, or even as great landlords – they utilized power in the same way.

Significantly, the leading Bakhtiyari khans of the late nineteenth and early twentieth centuries – Ilkhani, his brothers, and their progeny – do not appear to have developed a distinctive Bakhtiyari ethos aside from identification with their own leadership. Nor were they above using "Lur" in its pejorative sense – in the manner of their sedentary counterparts – in reference to one of their own tribesmen, even though they took pride in their lineage, in pastoral life, especially horses and hunting, and in being Bakhtiyari. Although Bakhtiyari looked down upon members who settled in villages, the historical record does not reveal the intensity of the dichotomy between the Qashqa'i and the *tat* (the sedentary, non-Qashqa'i population).[13] The reasons are several: the Qashqa'i constitute a Turkic-speaking minority enclave surrounded primarily by Persian-speakers, Qashqa'i migration routes take them through a heavily populated agricultural region in proximity to urban areas, and they practice less agriculture than the Bakhtiyari. Furthermore, the Qashqa'i confederation was probably far more homogenous than that of the Bakhtiyari, which, in the late nineteenth century at least, included the Gunduzlu, a major Turkic-speaking dependency; smaller Arabic-speaking tirahs; and the Janiki Sardsir and the Janiki Garmsir, both of which were made up largely of sedentary agriculturalists – not to mention Qashqa'i elements.

In summary, within the Bakhtiyari, the family unit – the most exclusive group, but one which adopts members – takes on the key and enduring ideological role, forming the basis for everyday activity and giving rise to most demands and conflicts. In addition, the family provides the conceptual basis for the process of group formation ending in the tayafah and ultimately the confederation. The further a group moves from the family, the weaker the commitment to it and the identification with it. The tayafah, composed of autonomous segments – hence a microcosm of the Bakhtiyari itself – constitutes the terminal functional unit, in which internal factors such as herding of flocks, pastures, water, and migration assume primary importance in group formation. From the tayafah to the whole of the Bakhtiyari confederation, groups function within an essentially negative framework and align and define themselves through interaction with external factors – neighboring tribes, the state, or the broader ambitions of the khans. (Even though external threats, or negative factors, affected all units, the positive factors of pastoralism, with its internal focus, prevailed.) Consequently the basis for loyalty and identification depends less on kinship, even though it may provide the necessary terminology, than on economic, political, and moral expediency. Although groups were capable of significant expansion and contraction, specific group configurations were of short duration except as they reflected immediate self-interest. The confederation constitutes the most inclusive group and exerts the fewest actual demands on its members. Nevertheless, after the confederation's formation in the mid-nineteenth century, it provided the framework for the total world view, including integration into the Irano-Shi'i system. In earlier periods, that function may have been accomplished through the moieties of the Haft Lang and Chahar Lang, or possibly through the tayafah itself. (In the latter case, the general term Bakhtiyari may have been substituted for the specific name of a tayafah from that larger geographic or administrative area; this substitution may explain the relative absence of references to tayafahs in written sources.)

Even though the confederation – and earlier the Haft Lang and the Chahar Lang, or possibly individual tayafahs – provided for integration into the greater Irano-Shi'i system, it seldom furnished more than a vague, administrative identity. Moreover, the larger units did not unite the Bakhtiyari components in pursuit of common goals, and the khans made little appeal to their followers as Bakhtiyari. Possibly this identity was assumed or articulated only orally, but the absence of effective unity argues against such an identity. Even when the Bakhtiyari united, as they did in the Constitutional Revolution, a Bakhtiyari identity was peripheral to the factors underlying that unity. Appeal for action was based on personal ties and self-interest, as in the case of the khans' personal retainers and kinsmen, institutionalized in the bastagan system;[14] on the promise of reward of pastures or booty to whole tayafahs or their components; or on a call to defend traditional religious and political values.

There were several reasons for the khans' inability to rally the tribes on a Bakhtiyari basis. Possibly the family–tayafah nexus perceived the confederation, or the moieties, as a threat and as potentially exploitative: the confederation constituted the unit of taxation and conscription, and the focus of the great khans was often outside the Bakhtiyari, increasingly so after the Constitutional Revolution. The great khans had been land-lords and government officials, which reinforced their role as a link between the state with its culture and the Bakhtiyari. As a result, however, they could not articulate an alternative ideology without threatening their position either with the state or with the tribes. Possibly, too, they utilized the common Irano-Shi'i values as a means of broadening their bases outside the Bakhtiyari in order to consolidate their control of it or their relationship with the government. Finally, alternative values may have been seen as potentially disruptive by both khans and tribesmen – for example, Marxism attracted only a very limited Bakhtiyari following in the tumultuous period following World War I. When new ideas appeared, such as nationalism during the period of the Constitutional Revolution, the khans, notably Hajji 'Ali Quli Khan Sardar As'ad, responded as did their non-tribal counterparts – as Iranians, and not as Bakhtiyari.

The Bakhtiyari political system was divided into levels, with certain relationships, activities, and responsibilities associated with each level of organization; instability and change in these relationships; and diffusion of military power. This instability in relations and diffusion of military power was characteristic not only of the Bakhtiyari but of the Iranian political system as a whole. The Bakhtiyari used military force directly against other tribes or settled areas despite the basic idea that they were all subjects of the shah, and during the Constitutional Revolution the Bakhtiyari used force against the shah himself. The various tribes and subtribes within the Bakhtiyari used force against each other, against their khans, and against their ilkhani. Significantly, the highest authority at even the lowest level could, in effect, negotiate treaties, form alliances, and make peace independently of higher levels of authority. Thus, both intergroup and intragroup relations were based on a balance of power at each level – that of the tayafah, the il, or even the nation. Groups that opposed each other on one occasion could unite on another in opposition to some third group.

In the Bakhtiyari system the balance of power was among the various members of the chiefly hierarchy, who competed for the support of both their superiors and their subordinates, and at the same time formed alliances with members of other tribes to strengthen their position. Thus, the ilkhani of the Bakhtiyari competed with rival claimants – especially with half-brothers, nephews, and brothers; occasionally there was even competition between father and son – by seeking the support of bab khans, by concluding agreements with a Qashqa'i khan or an Arab shaikh, and by gaining the support of a superior authority, such as the shah's government or the British. The bab khans maintained themselves in the same manner. Bakhtiyari alliances were not based primarily on a theory of common descent, unless it suited the immediate purpose, but were extensively modified by negotiation and mutual agreement. Since these ties were derived from considerations of expediency rather than categorical loyalties, they tended to be brief. Exchange of daughters and sealed Qur'ans at the conclusion of these alliances, however, helped to strengthen them.

The Bakhtiyari system was thus characterized by continual internal shifts in the balance of power, frequently leading to a show of force and renegotiation of the positions of the khans, tayafahs, or confederacies involved. Groups at different levels were continually mobilizing for military purposes and redefining their position by violence or threats of violence, and political alignments rather than genealogy played the most important role. The Bakhtiyari system was not a political structure in which a central authority monopolized the use of military force and invariably imposed its will on subordinate local authorities. Only under the most effective khan, such as Ilkhani, or under the most extraordinary circumstances, such as the Constitutional Revolution, could unification of the polymorphic structure be brought about to form a confederation of all the Bakhtiyari. The Duraki khans, members of Ilkhani's own descent group, manipulated the tribal structure and utilized their incomes from land and government appointments to consolidate their position as Bakhtiyari leaders. Just as the Bakhtiyari economic base encompassed both pastoralism and agriculture, so the highest level of tribal politics and social structures incorporated tribalism and landlordism.

Unlike tribal khans, Iranian landlords – especially the great ones, who maintained armies and played significant provincial and national roles – exercised power autocratically and independently of their peasants. Their authority and power stemmed from the incomes of their land holdings, and ties to the government allowed them to maintain and arm retainers. By the last quarter of the eighteenth century – but possibly earlier as well – some of the Bakhtiyari khans (significantly, Ilkhani's ancestors) had become landlords and government administrators. Indeed, they may have been such even before they emerged as tribal leaders.

Comparatively speaking, the khans and landlords functioned similarly: both may have determined the use of the land, regulated disputes, mediated relations with the outside world, and integrated their tribes or peasants into the wider social and political fabric of Iran. Moreover, both were usually members of the local elite in provincial centers and often in Tehran as well. The central government used them to collect taxes, maintain order, and conscript. The khans, however, were regarded as kin by their tribesmen and were expected to be responsive to them. Incomes from land and appointments gave khans a degree of independence *vis-à-vis* the tribes' polymorphic system by allowing them to reinforce the kin tie with an economic tie, to utilize income to go outside the kin group for retainers, and to maintain and equip their retainers with better arms and for longer periods of time. Landlordism, however, held out the possibility of conflict with tribal interests. Following Ilkhani's death, tribal segments could once again limit the khans' independence that came from their dual roles, because of the increased competition among a large number of eligible khans for the office of ilkhani and its perquisites and because of the khans' unwillingness – even inability – to pursue national goals without a tribal base.

Chapter IV

The Bakhtiyari and the state through the eighteenth century

Historians, ancient, medieval, and modern, have been fascinated by nomads, whether it be Herodotus describing the Scyths – would that Xenophon's Carduchi could be directly linked with the Kurds of more recent history – or Ibn Khaldun attempting to understand history and culture and thus to explain the rise and fall of so many tribal dynasties in Islamic history; or Toynbee perceiving the repeated ebb and flow of history when he writes that the nomad, despite his superiority over agriculturalists,[1] is doomed:

Thus, in spite of these occasional incursions into the field of historical events, Nomadism is essentially a society without a history. Once launched on its annual orbit, the Nomadic horde revolves in it thereafter and might go on revolving for ever if an external force against which Nomadism is defenceless did not eventually bring the horde's movements to a standstill and its life to an end. This force is the pressure of the sedentary civilizations round about; for, though the Lord may have respect for Abel and his offering and not for Cain and his, no power can save Abel from being slain by Cain.[2]

The Bakhtiyari do not figure in classical accounts nor merit more than passing mention in medieval ones; they do, however, receive increasing notice from the eighteenth century on. In particular, nineteenth-century European historians and travelers project their own peculiar and romantic obsession with identity and origins onto the tribes they encountered in Iran. Kinneir, writing in 1813, strikes a recurring note that echoes in all subsequent accounts of the Bakhtiyari, including the Persian ones: "Those tribes in the southern provinces, indeed such as the *Bucktiari, Fielhi*, and *Mahmaseni*, trace their origin to the most remote antiquity, and are probably the descendants of the ferocious bands who inhabited the same country in the days of Alexander."[3]

The origins of the Bakhtiyari and their division into the moieties of the Haft Lang and Chahar Lang are puzzling, and some historians have sought etymological evidence for their roots, while others have scanned historical sources for clues to the solution of the difficult and probably insoluble problem of beginnings. Two contemporary Bakhtiyari historians[4] point out the similarities of spoken Bakhtiyari to Luri and Kurdi dialects and their relationship to Persian, and suggest that the Bakhtiyari have had a long residence in southwestern Iran. They also draw comparisons between Bakhtiyari costume and that depicted in Achaemenian and Sassanian reliefs and sculptures. One of these historians, the late poet, literary critic, and historian Husain Pazhman, writes that "Bakhtiyari" is synonymous with "Bactria".[5] Although both are derived from the same Indo-European root,[6] there is no evidence that the more recent pastoral nomads bearing that name came from that ancient state or region.

"Bakhtiyari" itself means bearer, or friend, of luck or good fortune, and it is probable that some leader was so known and his followers were identified with him and his name. This common enough process is illustrated by the Bakhtiyari tirah of the Ahmad Khusravi (i.e., the descendants of Ahmad the son of Khusrau), or by the late-nineteenth- and twentieth-century Ilkhani and Hajji Ilkhani moieties, which trace their descent to two brothers. Hajji Khusrau Khan Sardar Zafar, whose manuscript history "Tarikh Bakhtiyari" constitutes one of the most informative sources, posits that the conjunction of the name Bakhtiyari with the pastoral nomads subsequently known by it dates from some time in the Safavid period[7] (1501–1722).

The Bakhtiyari recall a number of legends about their roots, and, in so doing, perhaps correctly reveal a multiplicity of origins and no single one. A common myth notes Bakhtiyari arrival from Syria; interestingly, *Tarikh Guzidah*,[8] a fourteenth-century source that contains the first recorded reference to the Bakhtiyari, corroborates this tradition. Kinneir adds: "The tribes of *Louristan* trace their origin to the most remote antiquity; but say that their ancestors intermarried with several Turkish hordes, which they had invited from *Syria* to settle amongst them."[9] Another legend, less plausible, states that the Bakhtiyari were descendants of the men who were allowed to escape the fate of having their brains fed to the serpents sprouting from the shoulders of the legendary Zuhaq. Firdausi's *Shahnamah* – that great Persian epic of the eleventh century, which the Bakhtiyari regard as their epic – provides the obvious source for this myth. Similarly, myths exist regarding the division of the Bakhtiyari into Haft Lang and Chahar Lang (lit. seven legs and four legs). Khusrau Khan Sardar Zafar suggests that though the evolution of the names of these moieties are impossible to trace, they may have been based on a division of taxes between the two groups: the Haft Lang, the wealthier of the two, paid at a rate of one and three-quarters to the Chahar Lang's one.[10] Hajji 'Ali Quli Khan Sardar As'ad (II), like his brother Sardar Zafar, writes in his *Tarikh Bakhtiyari* that the two derived their names from tax assessments. All the tribes paid taxes in kind: the Bakhtiyari in mules, the Qashqa'i in sheep, and the Shahsavan in camels. The Bakhtiyari paid at the rate of three mules, with the Haft Lang contributing one and three-quarters (i.e., seven legs), the Chahar Lang one (i.e., four legs), and those tayafahs that had recently attached themselves to the two moieties one-quarter (i.e., one leg) – for a total Bakhtiyari contribution of "twelve legs" or three mules.[11] Yet another tradition relates that one of the early khans had seven sons from one wife and four from another, and the division resulted from the conflict between the two sets of sons over their patrimony – a frequent source of dispute among the Bakhtiyari.

The earliest known written reference to the Bakhtiyari dates from approximately 1330 AD and is found in the previously mentioned *Tarikh Guzidah* (*Select History*) by Hamdallah Mustaufi Qazvini.[12] (The earliest mention of the Haft Lang and Chahar Lang appears as late as *c.* 1740 AD in Muhammad Kazim's *Namah 'Alam Ara Nadiri*.[13]) The *Tarikh Guzidah* names the Bakhtiyari (the quality of the manuscript allows for the variant reading of "m kht ri" as well as "Bakhtiyari") and the Ustiraki, which appears in nineteenth-century lists as a Haft Lang component, as two of some thirty tayafahs that came from Syria to join the thirteenth-century Atabaig Hazaraf. Amir Sharaf Khan Bidlisi's *Sharafnamah Tarikh Mufassil Kurdistan*, written *c.* 1596 and probably based on the earlier *Tarikh Guzidah*, repeats the account of the *Tarikh Guzidah*. The *Sharafnamah* adds that Shah Tahmasp I (930/1524–984/1576) entrusted the leadership of Lur Buzurg, which was known – according to the source – as Bakhtiyari, to Taj Amir Khan of the Ustiraki, the major *'asha'ir* (tribe) of that *quam* (people), in return for an annual payment of a large sum. Taj Amir was unable to make the payment and was subsequently killed by Shah Tahmasp I. In his place the shah appointed Mir Jahangir Bakhtiyari, who was regarded as the leader of that *alus* (people) and who promised to make an annual payment of the equivalent of 10,000 mules to his treasury; this payment was to be guaranteed by Shah Rustam, governor of Luristan. Significantly, in return, Jahangir Khan was given the right to collect the taxes of certain districts of Khuzistan, Dizful, and Shushtar; these districts had formerly been entrusted to Arab leaders in those areas.[14]

Iskandar Baig Munshi's *Tarikh 'Alam Ara 'Abbasi*, postdating the *Sharafnamah* by about fifty years, refers to a rebellion that included the *qaba'il* (tribe) of Bakhtiyari Lurs* and the *ru'aya* (pl. of *ra'iyat*, peasant) of the Jaki and Javanaki (possibly Janiki – an important agricultural region

---

* Lur, or its Arabic plural, *alvar*, is used to identify both "Lurs" as an ethnic group and pastoral nomads as an occupational entity.

and dependency subject to the Bakhtiyari ilkhani in the late nineteenth century), and the indemnity that the insurgents were forced to pay.[15] This same source also notes the bravery of Jahangir Khan Bakhtiyari and 200 of his men in fighting the Qizilbash of Rum,[16] eastern Anatolian Turks who had earlier been Safavid supporters. *Tarikh 'Alam Ara 'Abbasi* then notes the appointment of a Jahangir Khan, together with several others, to be in charge of the Karun river diversion into the Zayandah river (the connecting link between the two rivers being in the Bakhtiyari yailaq).[17] Sardar Zafar adds that Jahangir was related to the Safavids through his mother.[18] Finally, Iskandar Baig Munshi, in a list of the leaders of Kurdistan and Luristan, makes passing reference to Khalil Khan, son of Jahangir, as governor of Bakhtiyari Luristan.[19]

Possibly there are few references to Bakhtiyari because they were subsumed as Lurs. Chardin, that perceptive and reliable observer of late-seventeenth-century Safavid Isfahan, makes no reference to the Bakhtiyari directly but notes the pastoral nomads of Luristan when he writes:

To the East of *Ispahan*, and near adjoining to his territory lyes the Province of Lour-Estom, which is held to be a part of ancient *Parthia*, extending on Arabia's side toward Basra. The peoples that Inhabit it, never mind the building of Cities, nor have any settl'd Abodes, but live in Tents, for the most part feeding their Flocks and their Heards, of which they have an infinite number. They are Govern'd by a *Kaan* who is set over them by the King of *Persia* but chosen from among themselves: and for the most part all of the same Race, the Father Succeeding the Son. So that there still remains among them some shadow of Liberty; however they pay both Tribute and Tenths. This Province furnished *Ispahan* and the Neighbouring parts with Cattel; which is the reason that the Governor of these People is greatly respected in those parts. *Soleiman* the third therefore at his coming to the Crown, commanded the General of the Musquetteers to send Royal Habit and Commission into all the Grandees. But the General of the Musquetteers having had some quarrel with this Governor who is call'd *Lour-Manoushar Kaan*, neglected to do him that Honour, putting off his sending the King's Present to him till six Months after. The *Grandee* impatiently brook'd the contempt; and being sufficiently convinc'd who was the occasion of it, for madness he tore in pieces the Habit which was presented him, saying withal. I value not the Habits, nor the commissions which the King of Persia's General of the Musquetteers sends me.[20]

In summary, the term Bakhtiyari first designates a tayafah, but it is also used to identify a region of Luristan. Safavid chronicles mention individual leaders who, perhaps, were Bakhtiyari themselves – Jahangir is specifically identified as a Bakhtiyari chief (amir). Furthermore, the name is associated with the important commodity of mules, which, of course, presupposes mares and asses. If Chardin's description is assumed to include the Bakhtiyari as a Luri component, they may be further identified as pastoral nomads with a prosperity based on flocks traded in nearby urban centers. Iskandar Baig Munshi, in addition, implies that the Bakhtiyari were not peasants – he refers to ra'iyats (or peasants) *and* Bakhtiyari. Chardin suggests a hierarchical political structure when he mentions the autonomy of the Lurs and the fact that they were governed by appointees, who functioned as subgovernors, chosen from among themselves by the central government. Moreover, that position passed from father to son.

Had the Bakhtiyari constituted a major confederation during the Safavid era this would have at least been noted in the chronicles, as were the Turkic confederations. This suggests that the Bakhtiyari were at best secondary in the major political network of the Safavids, which was dominated by the rivalry between the Turkic tribes and the Persian administration. Possibly Bakhtiyari importance increased after the seventeenth century, when Shah 'Abbas I shifted the capital from Qazvin to Isfahan. In addition to having a strategic position in relation to the capital, the Bakhtiyari region occupied the midpoint of the Safavid power axis that extended in the Zagros from Georgia to the Gulf.[21] The Safavid record fails to refer even in passing to Haydar Kur, the earliest known ancestor of the Duraki khans, who, if family tradition is correct, probably lived in the reign of Shah 'Abbas I (996/1588–1038/1629).

Nevertheless, the importance of the Bakhtiyari governorship as an administrative post at the end of the Safavid era is revealed in *Tadhkirat al-Muluk* (1725), where, in a listing of the ranks and honors given to Persian amirs, the governor of Bakhtiyari follows immediately after the four valis of 'Arabistan, Luristan Faili, Georgia, and Kurdistan. "After him [i.e., the vali of Kurdistan] comes the ruler of the Bakhtiyari tribe [il], who in former days enjoyed great esteem and respect."[22] In addition this source notes that the Bakhtiyari is to provide 3,370 tumans and 3,320 dinars as emolument for the governor and that 361 Bakhtiyari are on campaign in Iraq.[23] (*Tadhkirat al-Muluk* does not mention whether these governors of Bakhtiyari were themselves Bakhtiyari.)

Significantly, *Tadhkirat al-Muluk* makes no reference to the Bakhtiyari as a tribal confederation, and, seemingly, the late Safavids administered the Bakhtiyari as another province. In this same era – roughly the middle of the eighteenth century – references are found in both European and Persian sources to the moieties of the Haft Lang and the Chahar Lang. Jonas Hanway notes, in *The Revolutions of Persia* (1754), the division of the Bakhtiyari into the two major components of the "Cahar Ling" and the "Efh Ling" and the rivalry between them. No evidence is to be found that could account for this division.

Hypothetical history is generally of little value, but it may be useful to chart the degree of centralization of the state and its possible effect on the Bakhtiyari from the time of first reference in the fourteenth century to 1722 and the capture of Isfahan by the Afghans.

Hamdallah Mustaufi's fourteenth-century *Tarikh Guzidah* adds little to our knowledge of the Bakhtiyari other than first mention and this silence persists down to the very end of the sixteenth century. We can assume that they practiced a mixture of agriculture and pastoralism, were organized socially and politically around those tasks, and were affected in terms of external relations by contemporary developments, institutions, and practices. These would include the decentralization of power during the thirteenth century under the Ilkhanids and then its fragmentation in the fourteenth and fifteenth centuries under the Timurids and Aq Quyunlu. Furthermore, the Bakhtiyari were affected by the movements of whole peoples, especially the Turkic tribes, in adjacent regions. The arrival of Turkic elements in the Bakhtiyari may date from this time; de Planhol certainly goes too far in ascribing the formation of the Bakhtiyari confederation to the arrival of Mongol–Turkic nomads in this period.[24] The Turkish military patronage state system[25] – dating back to the tenth-century Seljuqs, and based on the practice (first identified as iqta' and then as tuyul) of granting land or its income in return for military and administrative service – was the dominant institution and presumably affected the Bakhtiyari as it did all other groups. It allowed for diffusion of power and regional autonomy, which was checked by the appointment of provincial and regional governors responsible for military levies, taxes, and good order, and by control of the state's agents with appointments, tuyuls, exemptions, divide and rule policies, and retention of family members as hostages at court. In this pre- and early Safavid period, which was characterized by decentralization or fragmentation – though even in times of fragmentation, a tribe's proximity to the center of power could affect it in much the same way as if it were part of a centralized state – the Bakhtiyari could have consisted of autonomous competing groups indirectly administered through their own or state-appointed leaders.

The systems that followed in the eighteenth century were affected not only by Safavid political practice – essentially that earlier decentralized, even autonomous, Turkish military patronage system modified toward a more centralized, bureaucratic system during the reigns of the two 'Abbases – but also by Safavid political theory and ideology. This ideology helps to explain the importance and number of Safavid puppets and pretenders. (There were some eighteen between 1722 and 1729; the last,

Isma'il III, died in 1187/1773.[26]) Tahmasp Quli (Nadir or Nadir Quli) manipulated the Safavid ethos when he ruled first through Tahmasp II (1135/1722–1145/1732), whom he deposed, and then through Tahmasp's infant son, 'Abbas III (1145/1732–1148/1736). Tahmasp Quli, however, consciously broke with the Safavid tradition with his election and his coronation as Nadir Shah in 1148/1736, as well as with his attempt to found a new dynasty and his efforts to unite Shi'i and Sunni Islam.

The persistence of Safavid values throughout most of the eighteenth century is striking, despite the decline in Safavid power that began with the reign of 'Abbas II (1052/1642–1077/1666) and culminated in the loss of effective power with the capture of the capital of Isfahan by the Afghans in 1135/1722. The authority of Safavid shahs rested on three bases: as earthly representatives of the Twelfth Imam, including claimed descent from Musa al-Kasim, the Seventh Imam; as spiritual leaders of the Safaviyyah order; and as successors to Iran's pre-Islamic monarchical tradition of divine rule. As Savory notes, "Ithna 'Ashari [Twelver] Shi'ism was therefore the most important element in Safavid religious propaganda and political ideology."[27]

The power of the Safavids was derived initially from the followers of their Sufi order, the Safaviyyah, and especially from the Qizilbash (Turkic tribes of Azerbaijan and eastern Anatolia), but this charismatic tie was greatly weakened by Shah Isma'il I's defeat at Chaldiran in 920/1514,[28] and by continued rivalry between the Turkic military leaders and an essentially Persian bureaucratic class. The increasingly disruptive role of the Turkic tribes continued until Shah 'Abbas I broke their power and replaced these unreliable and unruly tribal contingents with an imperial army composed of slaves and freedmen, based somewhat on the Ottoman model. Shah 'Abbas I thus brought to full development the practice of relying on an army loyal to him and on the Iranian bureaucratic tradition at the expense of the tribal element, whose interests were often in conflict with those of the state.

Nadir Shah – indeed, his own line of successors, the Afshars, as well as 'Ali Mardan Khan, Karim Khan Zand, subsequent Zand claimants, and the Qajars – was in no position to assert the authoritative link to the Imams except through Safavid puppets or collateral ties (e.g., Shahrukh, Nadir's grandson, whose mother was a Safavid). The inscription on the seal of 'Abbas III – Nadir's second puppet – unduly emphasizes 'Abbas III's relationship to the Imams and his descent from Shah Safi (the Safavids' eponymous ancestor, who founded their order), 'Abbas I, and Tahmasp.[29] By the time 'Abbas III died (1148/1736), Nadir had so consolidated his power that no Safavid and his supporters could success-fully challenge him. He engineered his own election to the throne by assembling notables, and based his authority as Zillallah (Shadow of God [on earth]) on his *de facto* power as victor. Possibly as the result of the weakness of his claim to rule and the continuing challenge to his legitimacy by the Shi'i ulema and Safavid pretenders, and in order to disassociate himself further from the Safavids, Nadir sought to replace Shi'ism with Sunnism.

> . . . if the people of Persia desire that we (Nadir) [*sic*] should reign they must abandon this doctrine which is opposed to the faith of the noble predecessors and the great family of the Prophet, and (they must) [*sic*] follow the religion of the Sunnis. Since the Imam Ja'faru's-Sadiq was descended from the Prophet . . . the faith . . . of the people of Persia is clearly this religion. They should make him the head of their sect.[30]

With this forced, but futile, abandonment of Shi'ism, Nadir perhaps hoped to unite all Muslims under his eventual rule; but more immediately and importantly, he sought to please his army, the base of his power, which was composed chiefly of Sunni Afghan and Turkman tribal contingents. Despite this break with two centuries of Shi'i rule, further symbolized by the shift of the capital from Isfahan to Mashhad – Khurasan being Nadir's home province and close to his political and military base – the Afshars emphasized continuity through administrative and military procedures and practices such as land usage and grants, titles, and military recruitment of tribal contingents.

All subsequent rulers in the eighteenth century claimed to rule as Zillallah with the backing of their own tribal cores – Bakhtiyari, Zand, Afghan, or Qajar. Even as late as 1194/1780, by which time their last Safavid puppet had died, the Zands appealed to Safavid sentiments. Whereas Nadir sought to establish his independence from Safavid authority, by means of the inscription on his seal he sought to link himself to the Prophet: "The Seal of State and Religion [i.e., Muhammad] having been displaced, God has given order to Iran in the Name of Nadir."[31] Except for Azad Khan, subsequent rulers, even though Sunni, appealed to the populace on a Shi'i basis. Shahrukh, for example, who continued Afshar rule in Khurasan albeit with the support of Ahmad Shah Durrani – from 1161/1748 to 1210/1795 – associated his name with 'Ali's on his seal: "Through Shahrukh the Safavid religion and fortune found order in the world, through the benevolence of His Excellence, Murtaza ['Ali]."[32] Both 'Ali Mardan and Karim Khan Zand were Shi'a. None of 'Ali Mardan's seals survives,[33] but on the coins struck during his regency for Isma'il III, he refers to himself as "bandah Isma'il", or the slave of Isma'il,[34] the puppet supported by 'Ali Mardan and Karim. 'Ali Mardan used the title "Vakil Isma'il", regent of Isma'il; while Karim, after he defeated and killed 'Ali Mardan, styled himself as "Vakil al-Ra'aya", regent for the people. (Customarily, the title has been "Vakil al-Daulat", regent of the state.[35]) Karim formally deposed Isma'il III in 1172/1759 but bothered neither to replace him nor to take the title of shah for himself. The underlying assumption of Karim's long rule (1163/1750–1193/1779) was that he was directly appointed by God as Zillallah; the succeeding Qajars (1208/1794–1342/1924) emphasized the same legitimizing principle, though it was weakened by their acquiescence to Anglo-Russian imperial aims and by the consequent attacks on them by the ulema.

Shi'i ideology and the pattern of the great king persisted from the Safavids on without serious challenge. None but Nadir Shah in the case of religion and Karim Khan Zand in the case of formal title departed from the Safavid precedent established by Shah Isma'il I. This would suggest widespread support of and identification with an abstract, distant, but attractive ideal; Kasravi some years ago noted the charismatic appeal of the Safavids in eighteenth-century Luristan.[36] No model other than kingship was likely; rule patterned after that of a tribal khan was a possibility, but a khan's government was too personal and decentralized for dynastic continuity in the state. Furthermore, the role of a tribal khan, such as a Bakhtiyari great khan, was but a weak one within the tribal confederation, unless the khan had significant external support or opposition; outside support was necessary to overcome internal resistance to concentration of power, and opposition reinforced a sense of cohesion. (This was a factor at the state level as well, where external threats such as the Ottomans, Uzbegs, Russians, or British allowed the shah to manipulate Shi'i identity and to hold out the promise of reward for success in battle.)

The Safavid model represented a modification of the Turkish military patronage state system, and a linking of the Iranian monarchical tradition, including its implicit if not explicit centralization, with a diffusion of power and regional autonomy. Political identity was linked with the center on the one hand and the smaller tribal units, the tayafahs, on the other. Even confederational identity, in the case of the Bakhtiyari, was shaped by state activity with the recognition of an ilkhani or its equivalent. Moreover, the state had ready access to reserve military units without having to bear their direct cost, and the degree of mobilization was determined by the perceived nature of the threat; and the same principle and system were used at the tribal level.

Throughout the Safavid, Afshar, and Zand eras this interplay of tribal power, religion, authority, and symbol existed, as did the attempt to accommodate these to the Iranian urban populace and the bureaucratic tradition. All of these matters touched on the Bakhtiyari, who emerged in this century as important military and civil leaders, as dissidents on both the national and the local scene, and as tuyul holders and landlords outside the Bakhtiyari region in Khurasan and Qum. From the Safavids on, an increasing number of sources are to be found that relate the Bakhtiyari to key institutions, individuals, and developments and that provide more of a basis for describing and analyzing their social, economic, and political roles. Moreover, it must be remembered that groups such as the Bakhtiyari define and redefine themselves, but within the parameters of basic and persisting structures.

Military, tribal, and civil appointments (including governorships of major provinces), awards of titles and land, and recognition of Bakhtiyari power characterized the emerging roles, responsibilities, and rewards of the Duraki khans during the Afshar and Zand periods. This historical process stretched back through the Safavid era; the eighteenth century marked an expansion of the Bakhtiyari role not only in central and southwestern Iran but in the whole of the empire. Official eighteenth-century documents clearly indicate that the Haft Lang was treated as an administrative unit but do not delineate the relationship between these Bakhtiyari and their khans.

The earliest extant document relating to the Duraki khans is possibly a forgery. This farman,[37] issued in the name of 'Abbas III in 1144/1732, describes Khalil – presumably this would have been 'Abd al-Khalil, great-grandson of Haydar Kur, of Sardar Zafar's genealogy (see Genealogical table) – as hakim and farmanfarma (governor) of 'Arabistan Bakhtiyari, Chahar Mahall (or 'Arba'ah), and Faridan. This would establish a genealogical link with the name of someone who was known to be in the khans' family tree but who held a high position in a region associated with them. (Does this represent a need on the part of 'Ali Salih, who was to seek a comparable appointment from Karim Khan some thirty years later?) This document would also link the Duraki khans to Mizdij, where by 1173/1759 they were major landowners, and to the sayyids at the shrine of Baba Haydar there. Possibly Khalil was granted such an important post because he had consolidated Bakhtiyari tayafahs, produced a sizeable armed force, and played a key role in Nadir's cause in central and southwestern Iran. Subsequent official documents issued to 'Ali Salih and Abdal, 'Abd al-Khalil's son and grandson, refer to them usually as leaders of the Haft Lang or as less important appointees with local responsibilities (i.e., zabits [revenue collectors] or tuyul holders); consequently Khalil may have united only the Haft Lang.

Father Krusinski, an eighteenth-century Carmelite, notes the antipathy between the Haft Lang and Chahar Lang factions ten years before the issuance of this farman:

Some leagues from that City [Isfahan] there were two very great Nations, who lived under Tents, after the Manner of the *Tartars, viz.* the *Lorians* and *Bachtilarians*. Each of them was able to raise an Army of 20,000 Men, one of which was sufficient to force the Rebels [the Afghans] to raise the Siege [in 1722]. But because each Army was divided into two Factions, like the rest of the Kingdom, and because each of those Factions was for depriving the other of the Honour that might accrue to it of having delivered the Capital, they could never agree to Make War together; so that this Army, which, if they had been united and acted in Concert, would have infallibly defeated the Rebels, and saved the King and the Capital, was defeated itself, and put to flight because they were divided into two Bodies . . .[38]

Muhammad Kazim adds, however, that the two factions were united against Nadir in 1732, and this unification may have been the work of 'Abd al-Khalil and 'Ali Salih. Consequently, Nadir, before he could deal with the Ottoman threat in the north, had to put down the Bakhtiyari rebellion, and, in so doing, he imprisoned thirty khans and kadkhudas. 'Ali Salih (*not* to be identified with his contemporary 'Ali Salih Baig of the Duraki), one of those imprisoned, said that the tribes would continue in revolt because there were no leaders left to guide them, but that if he were released he would quiet the tribes and produce the 10,000 to 12,000 troops that Nadir had previously requested. Fifteen khans were released, the rest were kept as hostages, order was restored, and the troops were con-scripted. This contingent then went on to subdue the Lurs.[39] (According to another, but unavailable, chronicle by Muhammad Kazim[40] dating from the same period, Nadir himself, after a siege of twenty-one days, had defeated the Bakhityari.[41]) As punishment, and in an attempt to diminish the Bakhtiyari threat and to fortify the northeastern marches, Nadir sent 3,000 Haft Lang families to Khurasan; in 1743, however, 2,000 "returned to their own country, where they retired in the mountains resolving to shake off the Persian yoke. Nadir being apprehensive that others would follow their example, sent a great body of Ousbegs [Turkic tribes from Khurasan] to keep them in awe."[42]

Bakhtiyari elements, however, continued to challenge Nadir. 'Ali Murad (of the Mamivand, a Chahar Lang bab) had distinguished himself by helping 'Ali Salih subdue the Bakhtiyari rebels, and although 'Ali Murad was not a major Bakhtiyari leader he had achieved fame in Nadir's campaign and victory against 'Abdallah Pasha in Azerbaijan. The *Namah 'Alam Ara Nadiri* reveals that 'Ali Murad was charged with inciting the Bakhtiyari in Nadir's army to return home, and with raising a force of in-surgents to take Isfahan and to restore Tahmasp II, the Safavid whom Nadir had deposed, to the throne. 'Ali Murad was able to seize an Ottoman mule laden with gold; he then returned to Bakhtiyari and raised an army purporting to number 20,000, which grew along with his success. It is stated that he gathered together the leaders of the Haft Lang, Chahar Lang, and the Lurs of Khurramabad, and exclaimed:

If I decide to become king, I shall cast coins in my name and have the *khutbah* [the Friday prayer testifying to the legitimacy of the ruler] said in my name. All of the leaders of the army from Iraq ['Ajam], Fars, and Hamadan are loyal to the Safavids. They will follow me, and after I end Nadir's rule, I shall go to Khurasan, and I shall free Tahmasp, who is now in prison there. The Royal Name is a great name, and if God is with me the people will follow me. Shah Tahmasp will be satisfied with only Iraq ['Ajam] and Khurasan, and I shall be content with Hamadan, Fars, and Kerman.[43] (free translation)

The speech apparently had its effect, and 'Ali Murad ordered coins to be struck[44] – yet another sign of legitimacy – with the following inscription: "I am enraged, and I shall create a tumult and mint gold coins until their rightful master be found."[45] Nadir Shah began a pincer movement to put down 'Ali Murad's rebellion, but a shipment of 10,000 tumans on their way to Nadir for transport was intercepted by the rebel, who had something of a Robin Hood reputation. When 'Ali Murad was finally encircled, his troops fled, and he disappeared into the fastness of the mountains, where he was finally captured and executed. This time Nadir had 10,000 Bakhtiyari families transported to Khurasan.[46]

Some Bakhtiyari (or at least Duraki) support for Nadir Shah, and the presence and role of the Bakhtiyari in Khurasan, is attested to by a raqam[47] issued by Nadir to 'Ali Salih and dated 10 Muharram 1158/12 February 1745. This document identifies 'Ali Salih (of the Duraki) with the military title of baig, and as the holder of the tuyuls of Jam and Bakharz (whose assessments were to maintain his troops or to provide for the expenses of administering the Bakhtiyari in that area?). The injunction in this raqam is to bring the tuyuls into production – implying that they had been out of production – for it had been reported that 124 *zauj* (1 zauj = an area that could be plowed by a yoke of oxen) in Jam and 202 zauj in Bakharz had lapsed into uncultivable status, and then there could be sufficient income for both the holder's function and the owners'. 'Ali Salih went on to distinguish himself in Nadir Shah's attack and conquest of Qandahar. Nadir granted 'Ali Salih three raqams in Jumadi I 1159/ May–June 1746[48] (the latter two were issued on the same day), and in these he is identified with a variety of military titles, including *minbashi*, commander of 1,000 (the number of Haft Lang, or Bakhtiyari, cavalry?), and sardar, roughly colonel, the highest rank awarded him. In addition, other titles in these three documents relate both to military and to tribal roles: baig (chief) and rish safid (elder, or highest ranking – lit. white beard). In one of these raqams 'Ali Salih is styled as rish safid of the Bakhtiyari, but in the next, issued only two days later, as rish safid of the Bakhtiyari Haft Lang. (This ambiguity persists in the documents issued in the eighteenth century.) Presumably, with this title, he functioned as a type of military governor. Furthermore, Nadir granted 'Ali Salih the considerable sum of 5,600 rupees.

These Afshar documents assert military and administrative roles for 'Ali Salih, who commanded a Bakhtiyari contingent of cavalry, held tuyuls both in the Bakhtiyari Kuh Mali (Pusht Kuh?) and in Khurasan, was awarded additional incomes (a mill and exemptions), and was responsible for the administration of Kuh Mali in Bakhtiyari. He is established as a historical figure. In addition, and importantly, these documents allude to an internal Bakhtiyari hierarchical structure headed by khans with kadkhudas and kalantars subordinate to them.

After Nadir's assassination in 1160/1747, the Bakhtiyari displaced to Khurasan returned to their home territory. In the prevailing anarchy 'Ali Mardan, a member of the chiefly lineage of the Kiyanursi bab of the Chahar Lang, attempted to establish, and in 1164/1751 succeeded in establishing, a joint suzerainty with Karim Khan over much of southern and central Iran in the name of Isma'il III. (Another Bakhtiyari, Abu al-Fath, played a key role as governor of Isfahan, and he may have been used by Karim Khan to counter 'Ali Mardan, who killed him in 1750.[49])

It remains unclear whether the Haft Lang supported the Chahar Lang's 'Ali Mardan. The only extant document produced by 'Ali Mardan consists of his letter[50] written in reply to one by Abdal, son of 'Ali Salih, and Aqa Muhammad Salih, 'Ali Salih's brother. 'Ali Mardan's letter of 1162–4/1748–50 – a critical period in his rivalry with Karim Khan – raises more questions than it answers, but it establishes Haft Lang and Chahar Lang disunity. Had Abdal and Muhammad Salih originally proposed a meeting to discuss joint Haft Lang and Chahar Lang support for Shahrukh, who was upholding the Afshar banner? (Shahrukh issued 'Ali Salih a raqam[51] in 1163/1750, and 'Ali Salih must have died shortly after this, for there are no further documents awarded to him.) Or were they covering family interests, in offering support to 'Ali Mardan in his cause in return for concessions? Or had Abdal and Muhammad Salih broken with 'Ali Salih, who enjoyed Shahrukh's support? (The tie between uncle [father's brother] and nephew [brother's son] in the Bakhtiyari is one of either great tension or close support.) Or had 'Ali Mardan learned of Abdal's support for his co-ruler but rival, Karim Khan Zand? (In the year 1164/1751, Karim Khan appointed Abdal as the governor of Iraq 'Ajam, that important area to the west of Isfahan.[52])

Karim Khan succeeded in ridding himself of his co-ruler in 1754, when his forces finally isolated and killed 'Ali Mardan Khan near Kermanshah. Karim next had to face Azad Khan Afghan, one of Nadir's generals in Azerbaijan, who continued to challenge Karim until 1757. Meanwhile, Abdal had transferred his support to Azad Khan, who issued him two *hukms*, or decrees[53] (both bear identical dates in 1167/1754): in the first, Abdal was given his father's governorship of Pusht Kuh in the Bakhtiyari, and in the second, Abdal was appointed zabit of Chahar Mahall. Only six months later, Karim in a farman[54] exhorted Abdal to acknowledge his suzerainty once again.

These documents suggest, and others confirm, that Abdal Khan was an important landlord in Chahar Mahall. These sources also link justice and good administration with the peasants' prosperity and contentment. As is evidenced by a petition – and by the farman[55] granting it, issued by Karim Khan in Rabi' I 1173/October–November 1759 – Abdal Khan sought title, or recognition of ownership, of some sixteen villages and their dependencies that had come into his family's control through inheritance, through purchase, or possibly as tuyuls that he was hoping to appropriate as private property.

Abdal and his son Habiballah dominated the Haft Lang, if not the Bakhtiyari, throughout the Zand era, but the Zand transfer and resettle- ment of Bakhtiyari – Chahar Lang? – near Qum,[56] far to the north of Bakhtiyari, suggest not only Zand apprehension but the Haft Lang leaders' inability to maintain order and control over the Bakhtiyari. Abdal never fully regained the confidence that he had enjoyed early in Karim's rule. Significantly, though, the principle of administrative responsibility for Bakhtiyari no longer resident in the Bakhtiyari region seems to have been established,[57] and not just for those settled in Qum but for those in adjoining provinces as well. Such responsibility would also have served to reinforce political and perhaps even ethnic ties between the khans and the Bakhtiyari.

The Haft Lang may have been formed into a confederation by 'Abd al-Khalil Khan and his son and grandson, 'Ali Salih and Abdal; and in the decade following the Safavid loss of power and the loss of Isfahan to the Afghans, Khalil may have forged a confederation of the whole of the Bakhtiyari, or at least the Haft Lang, with the assistance of Safavid pretenders or Nadir. If so, the latter did not tolerate it for long. Khalil may have drawn the Bakhtiyari together from a base of Bakhtiyari, or tribal, leadership, Safavid–Afshar civil and military appointments and support, and land holdings in Chahar Mahall. He may not, however, have been a Bakhtiyari, but may have consolidated the tayafahs through his other roles.

Late-nineteenth-century family traditions assert that 'Abd al-Khalil was the great-grandson of Haydar, who was a Papi Lur and not a Bakhtiyari. Haydar, the son of a khan, was forced to flee Luristan as a young man, becoming a shepherd for a Bakhtiyari of the Duraki. When Haydar was discovered to be, in fact, a khan, he married his benefactor's daughter, and assumed leadership of the Duraki.[58] This tradition probably represents an attempt on the part of the "Haydari" lineage in the eighteenth or even the nineteenth century to assert a Bakhtiyari link, in order to appeal to the tribal ethos as the means of reinforcing existing political, administrative, or economic relationships.

The official documents add little to our knowledge about Bakhtiyari commoners and the lesser khans except their organization into small groups and units headed by rish safids, kadkhudas, and kalantars, with an interdependence between these leaders, the khans, and the great khans, and with the great khans, at least in the Haft Lang, ultimately responsible to the government for the good administration of the whole. The Bakhtiyari economic contribution and military roles are noted, as is the fact that they fought not only for their leaders but against them as well. Consequently the government sought to control them through governors and by resettlement in Khurasan and Qum. The Bakhtiyari tribes and their khans, Haft Lang as well as Chahar Lang, seemed to have shared the prevailing eighteenth-century Iranian ethos, especially as it related to authority. Throughout the eighteenth century, the Bakhtiyari supported various Safavid pretenders or those who upheld Safavid legitimacy. Bakhtiyari support for the Safavid and Shi'i cause sprang, no doubt, from both religious fervor – an appeal to religious values was used to settle a major dispute between the Babadi and the Duraki – and political opportunism; hence the willingness of some Bakhtiyari to support Nadir and Azad Khan. The Bakhtiyari often defied the rulers of the Afshar and Zand eras, but they never challenged existing political and religious ideas and institutions by offering new ones. Moreover, whoever sought to rule central and southwestern Iran had now to contend with that strategic region and the newly expanded role of its Bakhtiyari inhabitants.

Chapter V

The Bakhtiyari and the nineteenth century

The role of the Bakhtiyari in nineteenth-century Iran, and especially Husain Quli Khan Ilkhani's consolidation of Bakhtiyari rule, are either taken for granted or largely ignored in contemporary sources. To complicate the historian's task further, only five documents awarded to Ilkhani's immediate Duraki predecessors are extant – in contrast to the significantly larger number for a comparable period in the eighteenth century – and four of these are dated 1815 and one 1825.[1] Perhaps other documents have simply been lost or destroyed. Their absence also holds out the possibility that the Duraki khans' power had been eclipsed by rival Bakhtiyari factions as a result of their opposition to the Qajars, who by 1795 had wrested power from all rivals and attained the throne. Fath 'Ali Shah's marriage to Zainab Khanum, sister to 'Ali Khan, the important Chahar Lang leader, could even suggest Chahar Lang ascendancy. It is also possible that the Bakhtiyari were peripheral to major Qajar concerns, which were focused in the north or in Fars. In addition, for the first half of the nineteenth century, contemporary Persian and Western sources provide only the most general information on the Bakhtiyari, except for some travel–military reports; this also gives support to the supposition that the early Qajars paid minimal attention to the Bakhtiyari, who were relatively unimportant to them.

Travel–military reports suggest, however, that the potential strategic and commercial importance of Bakhtiyari – astride the shortest route between Isfahan and the Persian Gulf – was not lost on European powers. Increasingly, such sources provide more detailed information for analysis. The most important of these accounts is Sir Henry Layard's *Early Adventures in Persia, Susiana, and Babylonia;*[2] even Bakhtiyari chronicles and histories rely heavily on Layard. Layard spent the months from October 1840 through August 1841 among the Bakhtiyari as the guest of Muhammad Taqi Khan, the most powerful Chahar Lang leader. Layard's Muhammad Taqi Khan had the potential of consolidating his position to challenge the Qajars. This was not to be realized by him but by his Haft Lang rival, Husain Quli Khan. Husain Quli, on the basis of his Duraki position, family support and wealth, Qajar patronage, and possibly charisma, emerged as the pre-eminent Bakhtiyari and then as the first ilkhani of the whole of the Bakhtiyari. Although Husain Quli Khan Ilkhani, like Muhammad Taqi Khan, was brought down and executed by the Qajars, unlike his predecessor he made a permanent impact on Bakhtiyari and Iranian history.

Qajar chronicles, except for that of Zill al-Sultan,[3] Ilkhani's royal patron and then rival, give Ilkhani little mention, and when they do it is an admixture of awe and fear. Zill al-Sultan, governor of Isfahan and 'Arabistan, reported that Ilkhani's name and not his was feared there.[4] Similarly, I'timad al-Saltanah, Nasir al-Din Shah's secretary, in recording his surprise at Ilkhani's execution, referred to him as one of the powerful notables in Iran and only added that he had been poisoned – actually strangled – by Zill al-Sultan.[5] Likewise, Ilkhani's own documents, including his "Kitabchah", are frustratingly undetailed. Although a narrative of nineteenth-century Bakhtiyari history cannot yet be written, the sources together allow, at least, for a sketch that approximates to historical reality.

Eighteenth-century documents assign the Duraki khans the pre-eminent role in the Haft Lang, link them to the Pusht Kuh tuyul, and allude to their possible domination of the Bakhtiyari. Both Haft Lang power and the Pusht Kuh tuyul passed from father to son – from 'Ali Salih to Abdal to Habiballah. The four 1230/1815 documents, however, assign Pusht Kuh to the same family of Duraki khans but through a collateral line, to Abdal's second son, Farajallah, and then to his son, Ilyas Khan. In the absence of corroborating evidence, this transfer can best be explained by family division over state and Bakhtiyari allegiances. The Farajallah–Ilyas faction may have supported the successful Qajars Aqa Muhammad Shah, Fath 'Ali Shah, and then Muhammad Shah, and may have been rewarded for this support by central government backing in the Bakhtiyari. At the same time, Habiballah, who may have died in this period, and his three sons Chiragh 'Ali, Ja'far Quli (the father of Husain Quli Khan Ilkhani), and Kalb 'Ali aligned themselves with Qajar rivals and, after their defeat, were bypassed in the government's designation of its representative in the Haft Lang or in the Bakhtiyari.

(This split may have been healed in the 1840s with Husain Quli Khan's marriage to Ilyas Khan's daughter Mihrijan. This marriage, too, may inadvertently have resulted in the preservation of the five Ilyas Khan documents. In the 1840s Husain Quli was emerging as the dominant Duraki khan; furthermore, marriage both as an alliance mechanism and as a means of healing political divisions was a common feature of late-nineteenth- and twentieth-century Bakhtiyari history. Mihrijan was Husain Quli Khan's most important wife, and mother of 'Ali Quli Khan

Sardar As'ad [II] and Khusrau Khan Sardar Zafar. The preservation of these Ilyas Khan documents by Sardar As'ad in his collection is accounted for by this marriage, but further suggests that had Sardar As'ad's paternal grandfather occupied a position comparable to his maternal grandfather's he, too, would have been awarded similar documents that would have been preserved by Sardar As'ad as well.)

One of the 1230/1815 documents further identifies Ilyas Khan as landlord of Chaqakhur, a strategic and well-watered plain in the Bakhtiyari yailaq, the center of the Duraki summer pastures, and a traditional locus of Duraki power. This would confirm Ilyas Khan's Duraki, and possibly Haft Lang, dominance.

The last of these early Qajar documents, the 1241/1825 farman, recognizes Ilyas Khan's authority but makes reference to Husain Khan and Aqa Muhammad Hasan as his subordinates and as petitioners. (The contents of their petition remain unknown.) Husain Khan is identified as ilbaigi of the Duraki and the Babadi; he cannot be identified as a Duraki khan and may have been a Babadi khan. Ilbaigi, as the title of a Bakhtiyari office, first appears in this document and then only later in the nineteenth century as a subordinate to the ilkhani and finally as second in command to the ilkhani. The Duraki and the Babadi were linked in eighteenth-century documents with the Duraki dominating. Was Husain Khan appointed from the Babadi because of Duraki divisions? Later in the 1840s a Babadi insurrection was put down by the Duraki khans. Aqa Muhammad Hasan was Suhrab Khan's son (Suhrab was Abdal Khan's third son), and possibly Aqa Muhammad Hasan represented Duraki interests, with Husain Khan representing Babadi, in the petition. They are commanded to obey Ilyas Khan.

Other pre-1840 sources, although clearer, are seldom specific in identifying individual Bakhtiyari, but they do add general information. Watson reported that Aqa Muhammad Qajar's attempts to defeat and subdue the Bakhtiyari were unsuccessful.[6] Some control over them was imposed by 1813 by Muhammad 'Ali Mirza when he defeated As'ad Khan,[7] a Bakhtiyarvand khan and a notorious brigand who had dared raid as far north as Tehran.

The sources agree that Bakhtiyari cavalry played an important role in the shah's army – contributing in one instance 200 cavalrymen to Tehran and 200 to the royal governor of Shiraz[8] – and in provincial levies. They disagree on the precise amount paid to cavalrymen: Malcolm states that it was 5 to 6 tumans a year – officers received *c*. 15 to 20 tumans[9] – and Morier would give them the slightly larger sum of 8 tumans per annum.[10] In addition both men and officers received allowances of fodder for their mounts. Note is made of the tuyul base, or the continuation of the traditional land-based Turkish patronage system, but in certain instances soldiers were paid by the government through their khans.

Two sources provide conflicting population estimates. Morier, 1814–15, estimates Bakhtiyari population at 100,000 families, or *c.* 500,000 individuals;[11] and Rawlinson, 1836 – and the intervening 21 years cannot account for the difference – in a more detailed and probably more accurate report based on his own direct Bakhtiyari contact, places their population at 28,000 families.[12] He also provides the first record of Bakhtiyari tax assessments: a total of 14,000 tumans – an amount that remains constant throughout the nineteenth century. The Haft Lang with a population of 7,000 families paid 4,000 tumans; the Chahar Lang, 8,000 families, 4,000 tumans; the Dinarani, 5,500 families, 2,000 tumans; and the Bakhtiyari dependencies, 7,500 families, 4,900 tumans.[13] Morier notes the favored position of pastoral nomads over peasants in regard to taxes:

The existence of these migratory tribes being advantageous to the government, they are little oppressed. They are taxed at certain established rates upon each head of cattle, and are called upon to serve in the king's armies. They pay at the rate of five piastres for each camel, one piastre for each cow, the same for mares, one 'abbasi or quarter-piastre for a sheep. When they cultivate the ground, they are fined according to the rates exacted from the other Rayahs. Should they not be cultivators, each ten Khaneh or houses provided one horseman mounted and armed; and each five, one footman, or Tufenkshi. . .

The I'liyáts are not compelled to bestow their labour upon public works, like the other Rayahs – they keep exclusively to their tents and tend their cattle. The Taxes they pay are levied by their chiefs who account with the government. Those who are inclined to elude taxation frequently do so by secreting their cattle in the mountains.[14]

(Such favored treatment may have sprung from the governor's recognition of the pastoralists' flocks as a necessary privilege for their economic and military roles, but also from the difficulties in collecting taxes from them.) Nine years after Rawlinson's estimate Baron De Bode notes that the "Chehar-langs are taxed at 15,000 tomans, but it is rare that this tax can be regularly levied, for it is only by main force that they can be compelled to pay it".[15]

Despite the general nature of the pre-1840 sources, the Bakhtiyari that emerges in them is a familiar one. The Bakhtiyari tribes were divided into the Haft Lang and Chahar Lang, the subdivisions of the former included the Duraki, Babadi – who were certainly rivals on the basis of the oath of 1230/1815[16] – and Bakhtiyarvand, and there were tayafahs independent of the moieties. The Bakhtiyari, in addition to their economic contribution of animals and animal products to the general economy, paid taxes and furnished troops for the central and provincial governments. In return

65

they were paid and maintained. The Bakhtiyari khans on occasion served as state officials, most often as military leaders. The khans were sometimes confirmed in their position as military leaders and administrators, but this depended on their ability to maintain order, pay the tax, and produce conscripts. For this they were given gifts of land or tax-collecting rights. To lessen any threat posed by powerful leaders the central government kept members of the leading khans' families, or in some cases the khans themselves, near the court. These hostages also helped to insure the payment of the tax. The central government resorted to wholesale movement of tribal groups, particularly to the marches, where their threat was greatly diminished and where their presence would aid in maintaining the borders against invaders. The last such movement of Bakhtiyari occurred during the reign of Fath 'Ali Shah, who moved groups of them to the Tehran vicinity.[17]

Muhammad Taqi Khan's life – as presented by Layard[18] – furnishes a pattern that anticipates Husain Quli Khan Ilkhani's to a startling degree. This suggests no mere accident, especially since it follows from what little remains of eighteenth-century fragments that leadership in the Bakhtiyari adhered to a pattern of economic, social, and political relationships. Muhammad Taqi Khan, a member of the ruling family in the Kiyanursi bab of the Chahar Lang, had first to establish himself there, but to do so had to eliminate his chief rival, his uncle. This characteristic rivalry, not only over political leadership but over disputed inheritance of family estates, suggests that land with its assured incomes was the *sine qua non* for power. Muhammad Taqi Khan next demonstrated leadership, military, and diplomatic skills that went beyond the Kiyanursi to embrace others in the Bakhtiyari and outside it to Arab, Kuhgiluyah, and even urban factions. As the crisis built between Muhammad Taqi Khan and the governor of Isfahan, Britain – a new but increasingly important nineteenth- and twentieth-century element – entered as a potential ally. The central government, too, was able to manipulate the same Bakhtiyari structures and their processes, and given its determination in this instance and its greater resources – economic, political, and symbolic – brought him down.

Briefly, during the second quarter of the nineteenth century most of the Bakhtiyari was under the governorship of the Georgian eunuch, Manuchihr Khan, Mu'tamid al-Daulah, and the provinces under his authority included Isfahan, 'Arabistan, and most of Luristan. Mu'tamid al-Daulah's jurisdiction thus encompassed the Bakhtiyari region, which, in this period, was characterized by internecine fighting: in the Haft Lang, the Duraki Ja'far Quli Khan and his brother Kalb 'Ali Khan opposed the Bakhtiyarvand As'ad Khan and his son Ja'far Quli Khan; and in the

Chahar Lang, the Kiyanursi descendants of the eighteenth-century 'Ali Mardan Khan faced each other, 'Ali Khan opposing his brothers Hasan Khan and Fath 'Ali Khan. 'Ali Khan was emerging as the most powerful, but aroused the suspicions of the Qajars, who instigated Hasan Khan and Fath 'Ali Khan to turn him over to Fath 'Ali Shah, who had him blinded. Hasan Khan, supported by the central government, then dominated the Chahar Lang. 'Ali Khan's sons were hidden away and raised in the security of one of their father's villages in Faridan, near the Chahar Lang summer pastures. At the age of eighteen one of these sons, Muhammad Taqi Khan, killed his uncle Hasan Khan, regained the disputed patrimony, and won Kiyanursi support as its leading khan. He then married his uncle's daughter "in order to bring the blood feud to an end; she was from her rank considered among the tribes as his principal wife".[19]

Muhammad Taqi became known as a forceful and just leader, and though he was a tribal khan and the owner of large herds he demonstrated equal or greater interest in agricultural matters: crops, irrigation systems, acquisition and expansion of agricultural land on the borders of Bakhtiyari in Faridan to the east and Ram Hurmuz to the southwest, breeding of horses, and marketing of agricultural produce. His interests in establishing order and stability were germane to his concern for agricultural production and marketing, and may have been a factor in winning the support of Bakhtiyari groups – such as the Janiki Garmsir – that were almost wholly settled and essentially agricultural.

Muhammad Taqi Khan, like Husain Quli Khan after him, used this dual base to expand his power, first in Bakhtiyari and then outside it. The Janiki Garmsir alliance was one example of the former; furthermore, Muhammad Taqi's mother came from this group, thereby giving him maternal ties within it. The Sahuni, another Chahar Lang *tayafah*, threw its support behind him, in return for which he assigned it new pastures, using its leader, Shafi' Khan, as his chief agent. (Layard refers to him as Muhammad Taqi Khan's vizier.[20] Interestingly, Shafi' himself was not from the Sahuni but was an Afshar, and possibly allied with Muhammad Taqi Khan as a means of strengthening his Sahuni position.) Outside the Bakhtiyari Muhammad Taqi Khan established ties with Shaikh Thamir of the Ka'b Arabs, who were then given grazing rights in the Bakhtiyari garmsir, and more tenuous ones with the Buir Ahmadi; Muhammad Taqi's sister had married Khalil Khan of the Buir Ahmadi. However, in expanding his own and his supporters' interest and in building alliances, Muhammad Taqi Khan alienated key groups that were to be utilized by Mu'tamid al-Daulah to bring him down. Opponents included family members, Haft Lang and Chahar Lang khans, and leaders of neighboring tribes.

The scenario of Muhammad Taqi's downfall began when Mu'tamid al-Daulah proposed to accompany troops through Bakhtiyari to collect the tax arrears of Shushtar, Dizful, and Havizah. Muhammad Shah – according to Layard – offered Muhammad Taqi Khan the governorship of Bakhtiyari and 'Arabistan if he would cooperate with Mu'tamid al-Daulah and allow his own brother 'Ali Naqi Khan, who had been a hostage at court, to guide Mu'tamid al-Daulah through Bakhtiyari to 'Arabistan. It would have been possible but difficult to move the Isfahan troop and its three guns through the Bakhtiyari mountains without the assistance of 'Ali Naqi Khan. Muhammad Taqi faced a predicament for he, too, was being pressed to pay arrears in his taxes to the amount of 10,000 tumans. He could not quickly collect that amount without weakening his own relationship with his tayafah, because the collection could only have been made forcibly. The tayafah knew this; in addition, other khans supported Mu'tamid al-Daulah because they hoped to replace Muhammad Taqi Khan. Finally, Muhammad Taqi Khan was charged with corresponding with 'Ali Riza Mirza, Zill al-Sultan, Muhammad Shah's exiled uncle in Iraq, who had reigned briefly in 1834 as 'Adil Shah. Not only was Muhammad Taqi Khan's political position in danger, but as a rebel his life was at stake and – an added threat – his property would be confiscated.

Layard's visit was fortuitous for it held out a glimmer of hope for Muhammad Taqi that assistance might be forthcoming from the British. He was aware of the strained relations between Iran and Great Britain over Afghanistan and the suspension of diplomatic relations between them. With the British occupation of Kharg Island (1838) near the head of the Persian Gulf there had been rumors in 'Arabistan and Luristan of an impending British invasion. Layard reported:

He probably hoped that if war were to break out between England and Persia he might avail himself of the opportunity to proclaim his independence. He had at his command many thousands of the finest and most daring horsemen and most skillful matchlockmen in Persia, and he had reason to believe that the force already at his disposal might be greatly increased should he bring about a general rising against the Shah, to be supported by English money, bayonets, and artillery. He was desirous, therefore, of communicating with the British authorities at Karak, and learning whether, in the event of war, they would be prepared to accept his assistance, and to enter into an agreement with him to protect him against the vengeance of the Shah, and to recognize him as the supreme chief in Khuzistan on the conclusion of peace. He accordingly begged me to proceed to that island in order to ascertain if possible, the intentions of the British Government, and to submit his proposals to the command of the British forces there.[21]

Layard had discussed the importance of trade with Muhammad Taqi Khan (along with "English money, bayonets, and artillery") and had raised the possibility of opening a road through Bakhtiyari that would join central Iran with the Persian Gulf and international trade; therefore, Muhammad Taqi Khan had also authorized Layard to inform the British that, if they would begin to trade with the Bakhtiyari, he was prepared to build roads and provide security for their goods on them. Layard so informed Captain Hennell, the British resident in the Persian Gulf at Kharg Island, who in turn communicated the following information to India:

[Muhammad Taqi Khan] . . . had been grievously offended by the present Government of Persia, and was not disposed to submit any longer to the tyranny and extortion to which he had been subjected, but whether to raise the standard of revolt in his own behalf, as a lineal descendant of Alee Mardan Khan, the Bakhtiyaree Monarch of Persia, or whether to support the claims of Ally ['Adil] Shah (the uncle of the present king) to the throne, were points on which he had not yet determined.[22]

Neither military nor economic support from the British materialized for Muhammad Taqi Khan; most importantly Iran and Britain were not to enter into war over Kharg, and the speed of developments in 'Arabistan precluded any assistance that might have been given even if Britain had had such a policy of support for autonomous leaders in southwest Iran. (Such a policy emerged only late in the nineteenth century and early in the twentieth in response to increased Russian political and economic competition.[23] Layard's and Hennell's perception of the khans as autonomous, just, and legitimate rulers, with full support of their tribal confederations and anxious to be freed from the Tehran yoke with British assistance, characterizes the attitude subsequent British officials in southern Iran held toward the tribes there.)

Shortly before Layard's departure for Kharg Island, Muhammad Taqi Khan had not yet decided how he should receive Mu'tamid al-Daulah. The governor's troops had passed through the most rugged section of Bakhtiyari, and as they moved into the lower, broader, and more agricultural valleys the troops plundered and exacted provisions from the countryside, adding to the instability of the area. Muhammad Taqi Khan's brothers and the other khans – especially Shafi' Khan – advised him to allow the Iranian regiment to proceed through Bakhtiyari to 'Arabistan to collect the tax there. They also urged him to collect as much of the Bakhtiyari tax as possible, but not to call up his forces and give the governor a pretext to attack.

Mu'tamid al-Daulah and his two regiments advanced to the plain of Malamir – the site of the medieval capital of the Atabags of Luristan – where negotiations continued for forty days. The governor renewed the shah's original promise, offered a *khal'at* (royal robe of honor), and swore on a Qur'an that no harm would befall Muhammad Taqi Khan and his family. Muhammad Taqi Khan, suspecting a trap, vacillated between attacking the governor's camp and temporizing in the hope that it would leave.

'Ali Naqi Khan, Muhammad Taqi's brother, who had been kept as hostage in Tehran by the shah and who had recommended a policy of acquiescence, was fearful that if the Bakhtiyari attack were successful the shah would only seek retribution with a larger force. During the period of Muhammad Taqi Khan's indecision Mu'tamid al-Daulah suddenly struck camp and left for Shushtar, and before his departure Muhammad Taqi presented him with traditional gifts of five Arab horses, twelve mules, a shawl, and 200 tumans. In addition, he had provisioned the governor's troops while they had been in the Bakhtiyari district.

'Ali Naqi Khan accompanied Mu'tamid al-Daulah to Shushtar, and as they proceeded other khans were invited to join the governor's party. Failure to do so would have been taken as a sign of disrespect or even of disloyalty. These khans were, however, imprisoned in Shushtar, and Muhammad Taqi Khan himself was ordered to appear. He refused unless given further assurances. This was rejected and he was declared *yaghi* (a rebel); Mu'tamid al-Daulah prepared to attack. The khan then offered additional hostages from his family as a sign of his fidelity to Muhammad Shah; Mu'tamid al-Daulah asked for his eldest son, Husain Quli Khan (not to be confused with Husain Quli Khan Ilkhani), and at the same time swore on a Qur'an that if this demonstration of loyalty were given he would return to Isfahan.

At approximately the same time the governor of Shiraz marched to Bihbahan and thus prevented any support from there or from Kuhgiluyah from reaching the Bakhtiyari. Muhammad Taqi Khan was consequently cut off from any hope of aid except from the Ka'b Arabs, since Mu'tamid al-Daulah had the active support of sections of the Lurs and Arabs and the assistance of Ja'far Quli Khan of the Haft Lang and 'Ali Riza Khan of the Chahar Lang. The governor had by now obtained the neutrality and even support of tribal leaders who formerly had recognized Muhammad Taqi Khan's suzerainty, but who now saw his rapidly weakening position. And those sections that had remained loyal were afraid, in the absence of many of their own men, to send the remainder as support, fearing reprisal from the Iranian government or attacks by bandits or the governor's forces.

Mu'tamid al-Daulah failed to keep his promise after Husain Quli Khan had been surrendered to him, and he next ordered Muhammad Taqi Khan to present himself or his son would be killed and the Bakhtiyari garmsir, the winter pasture in 'Arabistan, would be devastated. (This was in late spring 1841 at the time of migration and just before the wheat crop harvest.) The khan then decided to seek haven with Shaikh Thamir of the Ka'b Arabs in Fallahiyah (present-day Shadagan), whose swamps afforded a natural refuge. With Muhammad Taqi Khan's departure, the imprisonment of leading khans and personages of 'Arabistan, and the presence of unpaid and poorly disciplined provincial troops, the area from Dizful south to Bihbahan became insecure and unsafe. People from the towns fled into the mountains to escape exactions and threats. Some of the Arab shaikhs fled across the border into Ottoman territory.

Shaikh Thamir gave order to the Ka'b to leave their villages, burn their wheat, open the dykes and flood the land, and flee into the swamps surrounding Fallahiyah. Mu'tamid al-Daulah advanced slowly into this area supported by the leaders of Havizah and the shaikh of the Bavi tribe, having first won their support by promising them authority over the Ka'b tribes. The governor sent one of the Bakhtiyari hostages as his emissary to Shaikh Thamir and Muhammad Taqi Khan, and renewed the earlier promises if he would surrender.

Muhammad Taqi Khan, isolated and supported only by Shaikh Thamir, submitted, but upon arrival in the governor's camp was imprisoned. Mu'tamid al-Daulah then demanded an indemnity of 12,000 tumans from Shaikh Thamir, who, after a meeting of Arab shaikhs and the few remaining Bakhtiyari, decided to attack the governor's camp to free Muhammad Taqi Khan. The attack was unsuccessful although other khans were freed, and the governor, rather than counterattack across the swampy terrain and bridgeless canals, decided to return to Shushtar.

Meanwhile, Muhammad Taqi's family fled toward the mountains, hoping for refuge with the Buir Ahmadi and then the Qashqa'i. Their hopes were dashed when Khalil Khan Buir Ahmadi turned them over to Muhammad Taqi Khan's chief rival and cousin, 'Ali Riza Khan – son of Hasan Khan, whom Muhammad Taqi had killed – who had just been appointed by Mu'tamid al-Daulah as head of the Kiyanursi. Those leaders who had supported Muhammad Taqi Khan were either captured or killed; their positions were filled by partisans of the major khans who had the support of Mu'tamid al-Daulah. Muhammad Taqi's relatives were finally delivered over to the governor, and they accompanied Muhammad Taqi Khan to Tehran, where they were all imprisoned. In 1851, a decade after his capture, Muhammad Taqi Khan died.[24]

The struggle for supremacy in the Bakhtiyari now began. 'Ali Riza Khan was recognized as khan of the Kiyanursi in Muhammad Taqi's place, and after his death in 1295/1879 this position passed to his son Mirza Aqa Jan, who was murdered by his brothers in 1889. From 1841 on, however, these Chahar Lang khans were to play only a supporting role and never again a dominant one (Mirza Aqa Jan Khan married the daughter of Husain Quli Khan Ilkhani); Bakhtiyari paramountcy was to become the monopoly of the Duraki khans.

Layard probably overestimated and overemphasized Muhammad Taqi Khan's power; although Rawlinson in 1836 and De Bode, who was travelling with Mu'tamid al-Daulah when he was in pursuit of Muhammad Taqi, corroborated Layard's assessment. All three, given their wishful thinking and assumption that a Bakhtiyari khan was an autocrat, misunderstood the nature of Bakhtiyari society and politics. Rawlinson[25] estimated that Muhammad Taqi Khan could field 10,000–12,000 troops; Layard guessed at 15,000.[26] Even had the whole of the Bakhtiyari been under Muhammad Taqi Khan, it is unlikely that 25,000 families – using their Bakhtiyari census estimates – could have furnished that number of troops (roughly two families providing one fighting man), even for the briefest of campaigns. (During the Constitutional Revolution at the end of the first decade of the twentieth century, when the Bakhtiyari were relatively united, the khans fielded a total of *c.* 2,000 troops!) At issue for the Bakhtiyari would have been not only expenses and a socio-politically decentralized structure, but defense of families, fields, pastures, and flocks in the absence of their men.

Furthermore, Muhammad Taqi Khan, contrary to the impression left with Layard in 1841, was far from being the all-powerful khan of the Chahar Lang, let alone of the Bakhtiyari: he was opposed by close family members, especially his cousins, the sons of his uncle, Hasan Khan, whom he had killed; he had virtually no Haft Lang support; major Chahar Lang tayafahs were independent of him; and where he had external support, those leaders had lost the support of the central government. As he was without internal dominance, helpless before the government's greater resources and ability to manipulate the Bakhtiyari system – especially by rewarding those khans and tribesmen who collaborated with it – and denied the state's legitimacy, with its symbols, and the power that its support meant, his ambitions were doomed to failure.

Muhammad Taqi Khan, however, is an important Bakhtiyari historical figure. He was the last of the Chahar Lang to hold significant power, and his defeat relegated them to a subordinate position under the Haft Lang and perhaps accelerated their sedentarization – largely achieved by the 1920s. Muhammad Taqi Khan loomed large and noble in defeat (from Layard's account and subsequent Persian translations) in Bakhtiyari leadership myth and affected subsequent leaders. And his pattern of leadership was to be repeated, but with greater success – or in effect reversed – by Husain Quli Khan.

Extant primary sources pertaining to Husain Quli Khan – including his own "Kitabchah",[27] or journal of some ten years – do not allow reconstruction of a narrative of his life. These sources do, however, provide an approximate framework for this extraordinary Bakhtiyari leader's life. The first period spanned the time of Muhammad Taqi Khan's fall in 1841 to 1862, when Nasir al-Din Shah awarded Husain Quli the title and office of nazim of the Bakhtiyari.[28] During these two decades Husain Quli began the internal process of gaining power in his family, and, from that base, acceded to leadership of the Duraki, the Haft Lang, and finally the Bakhtiyari. The second phase – consolidation and reinforcement of this internal power through continued but expanded external alignments with the Qajars – continued from 1862, culminated with the award of the title and office of ilkhani in 1867,[29] and ended in 1878. During the last eight years especially, Nasir al-Din Shah issued Husain Quli a variety of decrees regarding his Chahar Mahall estates and his role as administrator and military leader. Some of these same documents extend his ties to a number of Qajar princes and, in effect, recognize his eldest son, Isfandiyar, as his successor. In this period, too, Ilkhani began making entries in his "Kitabchah", whose pages reveal him as tribal leader, landlord, and notable who increasingly had an impact outside the Bakhtiyari. The third and final period of Ilkhani's career extended from 1878 to 1882: his perceived challenge by the Qajars, his execution by them in 1882, and the immediate aftermath of his death. The Qajars saw him as a threat, undermined him through his family, but resolved the question of Bakhtiyari leadership within his family framework.

Throughout Ilkhani's life, and within the totality of the Bakhtiyari and the state – and the Bakhtiyari cannot be considered apart from the state – the very basis of his success rested primarily upon his juridical–political functions. Economic and symbolic factors were entwined with those primary functions, but were subordinate to them. Family and state backing led to Ilkhani's success, and their absence resulted in Muhammad Taqi Khan's failure. Historical examples of accession to power, with its attendant components of rivalry and the marshaling of resources and support, emphasize the importance of kinship and marriage – not simply for the Bakhtiyari and other tribal groups.

Not surprisingly, one commonplace aspect of family rivalry in the nineteenth century was that between nephew and uncle (brother's son and father's brother). The case that probably first comes to mind is the competition between Muhammad the son of 'Abbas Mirza and the latter's brother for the throne at the death of Fath 'Ali Shah in 1834. Similarly, there are the three striking instances in the Bakhtiyari: *c.* 1836, Muhammad Taqi Khan Chahar Lang vs. Hasan Khan; *c.* 1846, Husain Quli Khan (later, of course, Ilkhani) vs. Kalb 'Ali Khan; and 1881–2, Muhammad Husain Khan vs. Husain Quli Khan Ilkhani. At the end of the century, too, the lines of rivalry are between the sons of Ilkhani and their father's two brothers, Hajji Ilkhani and Ilbaigi. In these Bakhtiyari cases leadership of the tayafahs and potentially much or all of the Bakhtiyari was at stake, but in the first example cited there was the additional factor of revenge for the father's death – 'Ali Khan had been murdered by his brother Hasan Khan.

'Ali Khan's son, Muhammad Taqi, killed his uncle, Hasan, to avenge his father's death and emerged as the paramount khan of the most important Chahar Lang bab, the Kiyanursi; he was eighteen. He also married his father's brother's daughter, and his only other wife was from the Bahmah'i, one of the Kuhgiluyah tribes south of the Bakhtiyari. Significantly, Muhammad Taqi Khan came to the height of his power at a very young age; as a result he had only two wives, and one of these was estranged and the other lacked Bakhtiyari links. Furthermore, his sons were too young to be married, as were his brothers, who could not yet provide marriage ties to other segments of the tribes. In addition, his sister had been married outside the Bakhtiyari to Khalil Khan of the Buir Ahmadi, another Kuhgiluyah tribe. Once he had demonstrated his leadership abilities, could he expand or even retain his power? To compensate for the lack of affinal relatives and ties, Muhammad Taqi Khan's "staff" was drawn from a variety of Bakhtiyari tayafahs with which he had alliances; these included the Janiki Garmsir, his mother's tayafah; the Sahuni; and the Gunduzlu, a Turkic-speaking remnant of the Afshars allied to the Bakhtiyari.

If Muhammad Taqi Khan aspired to suzerainty over the entire Bakhtiyari he failed, and the reasons include a lack of sufficient support in the Bakhtiyari and probably even in the Chahar Lang; the absence of intratribal ties; the alienation of Chahar Lang sections as the result of brother–brother and then uncle–nephew rivalry; and the absence of government backing. Possibly, too, there was the problem of liquidity, for his capital was in flocks and newly acquired land[30] and he could not, or possibly he was unwilling to, provide maintenance for more than key supporters; and he lacked affines within the Bakhtiyari who might have given support on the basis of a patronage relationship, and those outside the Bakhtiyari were minor in political terms.

Husain Quli Khan succeeded in all areas in which Muhammad Taqi Khan had failed. Husain Quli was the eldest son of Ja'far Quli Khan Duraki and Bibi Shahpasand of the Bakhtiyarvand. Ja'far Quli was killed in battle, *c.* 1836, by Ja'far Quli Khan of the Bakhtiyarvand;[31] and leadership of the Duraki was assumed by Kalb 'Ali Khan, his brother, who had been designated guardian of his nephews, Ja'far Quli's four minor sons. These were Husain Quli and Imam Quli, born to Bibi

Shahpasand, and Riza Quli and Mustafa Quli, sons of Mihr Banu of the Dinarani. After the death of his father Husain Quli entered the service of Mu'tamid al-Daulah and assisted him in the capture of Muhammad Taqi Khan in 1841. According to family tradition the young Husain, in his early twenties, so won the confidence of Mu'tamid al-Daulah that he was appointed a Bakhtiyari governor.[32]

Meanwhile, Husain Quli and his brothers had broken with Kalb 'Ali Khan in a dispute over what they considered to be their rightful inheritance, especially the ownership of certain villages. Most of the other Haft Lang khans gave Husain Quli their support, but a dissident group rallied around Kalb 'Ali Khan, who was finally defeated and killed by his nephew's forces in 1846.[33] Husain Quli's only Duraki rival was thus removed. Layard reported earlier that Kalb 'Ali was regarded as the "legitimate" head of the Haft Lang, and that he was noted for his peacefulness, generosity, and religious devotion. Almost in contradiction, Layard noted that Kalb 'Ali was neither obeyed by Haft Lang tribesmen nor considered a threat by the government.[34] There is no record of the disputed patrimony between Kalb 'Ali and his four nephews; if the wills of Sardar As'ad[35] can be used as an example and if they indicate customary practice, then presumably Ja'far Quli and Kalb 'Ali had inherited, or held, estates in common, no final division of them had been made before Ja'far Quli's death, and his sons challenged their uncle's division.

(Note should be made that Husain Quli Khan had a number of advantages over others in the past who had attempted to assume the dominant position in the Bakhtiyari. He had the collaboration and support of his three brothers [although in this period Mustafa died]; Riza Quli Khan forced the submission of the Chahar Lang and, in turn, continued to recognize his brother's authority. Husain Quli also won the support and recognition of Mu'tamid al-Daulah and the sanction of the central government in Tehran – Amir Kabir, Mirza Taqi Khan, who attempted to introduce internal reforms as prime minister at the beginning of Nasir al-Din Shah's reign, entrusted Husain Quli Khan with the suppression of revolts by the Babadi.[36] The Babadi territory was in the southern portion of Bakhtiyari, and part of it was contiguous to the Qashqa'i. Kalb 'Ali's son, Abdal Khan, had married one of his daughters to a Babadi khan in an attempt to establish alliances with this important and rival group, and similarly Mustafa Quli Khan, Husain Quli's youngest brother, had married a Babadi woman. The strategic location of this pasture in relation to the Qashqa'i was to be a continuous problem for Husain Quli Khan.)

Husain Quli Khan – in the first phase of his career from the fall of Muhammad Taqi Khan until he was awarded the title of nazim in 1862 – married judiciously and produced six sons who lived to play adult

75

roles.[37] During his lifetime he had a total of eight wives, who bore him
twelve daughters in addition to his six sons; marriages were arranged for
his children that strengthened his position in the Bakhtiyari. His first
wife, Bibi Khanum, was from the Khadir Surkh, a Zarasvand tirah, and
she bore him three sons – notably Isfandiyar, the eldest, who was
appointed *sarhang* (colonel) and first entitled Samsam al-Saltanah and then
Sardar As'ad (I) – and three daughters. His second wife, Bibi Mihrijan,
was regarded as his paramount wife since she was his only spouse who was
the daughter of a khan from a ruling descent group, in fact Ilkhani's
own – she was the daughter of Ilyas Khan, the son of Farajallah Khan,
younger brother of Habiballah Khan, Ilkhani's paternal grandfather, and
hence a parallel cousin. Bibi Mihrijan gave birth to two sons, 'Ali Quli (the
famous Hajji 'Ali Quli Khan Sardar As'ad II), who along with Isfandiyar
was his father's favorite, and Khusrau (later entitled Sardar Zafar), and
three daughters. His other marriages were less notable except for that with
the daughter of 'Ali Riza Quli Khan, brother of Muhammad Taqi Khan,
who had acceded to dominance of the Kiyanursi and of the Chahar Lang
following his brother's capture. This marriage produced the illustrious
Bibi Maryam, Ilkhani's favorite daughter, who was independent and
strong-willed, and who played a major role in Bakhtiyari politics, especially during World War I. She was married first into the Chahar Lang and
then to a parallel cousin; significantly, then, she was first married back
into her mother's family – an exception, as will be seen, from the usual
preferred pattern of marriage to father's brother's son. Ilkhani's other
wives were one whose origin is unknown (a *sighah* [temporary wife]?), one
from the Zarasvand, another an Isfahani, and two from the Raki Bab, a
Babadi tirah. (To settle that dispute? In return for support against the
remaining Babadi?)

Ilkhani's twelve daughters made a total of fifteen marriages, which –
together with their brothers' marriages – were potentially significant in
Ilkhani's political career. One daughter never married and four remarried,
and two of the latter married their deceased husbands' brothers. Three
marriages were with Ahmad Khusravi men (the beginnings of reinforcement of the bastagan system?), seven may be classified as parallel-cousin
marriages (three of these were second marriages), two were with Chahar
Lang, one with Babadi, and two with unidentified husbands (one of whom
was possibly a Bakhtiyari with Arab antecedents). The predominant
marriage pattern for this group of daughters was parallel-cousin, which
was utilized as a means of obtaining continued family–tayafah support, of
retaining some control over the wealth that accompanied these brides, and
of keeping their sons in the family. Possibly it was also a means of
lessening uncle–nephew tension over inequities in inheritance. The other

1. Husain Quli Khan Ilkhani *c.* 1879

2. Husain Quli Khan Ilkhani and retainers *c.* 1879

3. Husain Quli Khan Ilkhani *c.* 1879

حسب الفرمایش مقرب الخاقان حسین قلی خان
ایلخانی بختیاری کار حوض اتمام پذیرفت ۱۲۹۲

4. The Dasht Gul pools and canals

"By order of the Great Khaqan, Husain Quli Khan, Ilkhani of the Bakhtiyari, the work of the reservoir and waterway was completed, 1292 [/1875]."

5. The second and third generation Ilkhani, Hajji Ilkhani, and Ilbaigi khans c. 1911 (seated: Sardar Zafar, 3rd from left; Sardar As'ad, center; Samsam al-Saltanah, 3rd from right)

6. Isfandiyar Khan (left of the far tent pole) and Imam Quli Khan Hajji Ilkhani (to its right) c. 1893

7. Hajji 'Ali Quli Khan (later Sardar As'ad II) at the center of a Bakhtiyari reception tent *c.* 1893

8. Bakhtiyari tents at Chaqakhur *c.* 1893 (the khans' tents are of Indian manufacture and the others are of black goat hair)

9. Hajjiyah Bibi Nilufar (d. 1913), daughter of Husain Quli Khan Ilkhani and full sister to Hajji 'Ali Quli Khan Sardar As'ad and Khusrau Khan Sardar Zafar

marriages were possibly arranged as part of a settlement of a dispute or as a means of establishing an alliance. In the case of daughters, since their names have not always been recorded, it is difficult to discern whether their mothers' status was a factor in the selection of husbands – e.g., were daughters of higher-ranking mothers married to men of the same rank as their mothers?

The desire to broaden alliances within the Bakhtiyari would seem to characterize Ilkhani's sons' marriages, and it is striking how few cousin marriages were made. (The apparent lack of parallel marriages may be explained by the fact that the khans usually took two or more wives, only one of whom would necessarily be a parallel cousin. Furthermore, the khans continued to take wives throughout their lives.) Ilkhani's six sons made a total of twenty-three marriages, which produced thirty-five sons and twenty-eight daughters. Of all these marriages only four were parallel-cousin. In addition there were two Duraki–Zarasvand marriages, which, of course, were in the khans' own tayafah. All the other marriages cut across Bakhtiyari tayafah lines. Outside the Bakhtiyari there were two urban marriages – one with the daughter of Qavam al-Mulk of Shiraz and the other with an unidentified Tehrani, presumably non-elite. There was also a marriage with an unidentified Arab woman.

Ilkhani's only full brother, Imam Quli Khan, known after 1882 as Hajji Ilkhani, was regarded as second only to his older brother. Hajji Ilkhani's first wife was the daughter of a leading Chahar Lang khan, Abu al-Fath of the Kiyanursi, and she bore Muhammad Husain Khan, his most important son and the one who ultimately challenged Ilkhani. This marriage, like Hajji Ilkhani's second, was probably arranged as part of a settlement between two factions – Haft Lang and Chahar Lang in the case of the former, and nephew and uncle in the case of the latter. Even though Hajji Ilkhani's most important son, at least in the nineteenth century, was a product of the first marriage, his second wife, Hajjiyah Bibi Zainab, a parallel cousin who was the daughter of Abdal Khan, son of Kalb 'Ali Khan, was regarded as his most important one. Three of his other marriages were with Bakhtiyari women who represented three different tayafahs, and one was with a village woman.

Hajji Ilkhani thus had a total of six wives, who bore him nine sons and seven/eight daughters who lived to adulthood. His daughters' known marriages totaled seven – three were parallel-cousin, one Chahar Lang, one Bakhtiyarvand, one unknown, and one to a Chahar Mahalli. (The khans had extensive land holdings in this rich agricultural region between the eastern boundary of Bakhtiyari and Isfahan, and they borrowed cash from the wealthy landowners in that region: possibly the marriage was arranged with one of the sons of such persons.) Hajji Ilkhani's nine sons made twenty-five marriages and in turn produced forty-five sons and twenty-three (?) daughters. Of these marriages eight were parallel-cousin, and three were made with Zarasvand women. The others again covered a cross-section of Bakhtiyari tayafahs. These sons also married two elite women from Tehran and two other Tehranis whose fathers cannot be identified.

Less is known about Riza Quli Khan Ilbaigi, the half-brother to the other two, who functioned in a role akin to finance minister for Ilkhani. After Ilkhani's death Riza Quli held office both as ilkhani and as ilbaigi until the two major factions of the Ilkhani and Hajji Ilkhani excluded him and his sons from power and office in the 1890s. Ilbaigi had eight wives, and only one of these marriages was parallel-cousin – with Hajji (*sic*) Bibi, daughter of his uncle, the aforementioned Kalb 'Ali Khan. One of his wives was a Bahmah'i, another a villager, and the rest were drawn from different Bakhtiyari tayafahs. Ilbaigi fathered fourteen sons but only six daughters, according to available sources. For these six only four marriages are noted, all parallel-cousin. (If, indeed, he only had six daughters, this was possibly a factor in his inability to match the alliances established by the other two factions.) The fourteen sons had at least seventeen wives, and of these six were parallel cousins, one was a Usivand woman, and the others remain unknown. These marriages produced fifty-five sons.

From the limited information on the marriages of the three brothers and their children one could generalize that daughter marriages were arranged to reaffirm family ties and to lessen family tension. The sons often included a parallel cousin among their wives but then chose brides from a range of tayafahs as a means of broadening their base of outside alliances and support. (In subsequent generations more and more marriages were made with the national families – to use Bill's classification[38] – as these khans began to play an increasing national role after the Constitutional Revolution. This process, however, had negative repercussions on their support within the Bakhtiyari.)

The mystique of rulership and its importance on both the actual and symbolic levels are revealed by the fact that the khans were not always bound by the same rules that applied to other tribesmen. In the marriages described above, for example, the khans took brides outside their own tayafahs but did not usually reciprocate with their own sisters or daughters. Marriage, from the khans' viewpoint, exacerbated rivalry at the same time as it aided alliance formation; both were affected by the problem of inheritance. One's mother's status would appear to have been a factor in determining one's share in an estate, but, more importantly, the absence of clearly defined and accepted rules governing inheritance – Qur'anic division notwithstanding – contributed greatly to family tension.[39] Patrilateral parallel-cousin marriage constituted a family's attempt to retain a daughter's offspring and any wealth that accompanied her at marriage within its purview.

Another important aspect of rulership and marriage was the tension between Bakhtiyari and Islamic egalitarian values, on the one hand, and a family's dynastic interest in perpetuating its economic and political dominance, on the other. Ilkhani's favored treatment of his eldest son, Isfandiyar, and of his highest-born son, 'Ali Quli – which included frequent appointments as his representatives and as military leaders for Bakhtiyari militia in the various Qajar courts, and frequent mention in his "Kitabchah" – would suggest dynastic concern on his part. 'Ali Quli's wills clearly demonstrate this when the major portion of his estate is awarded to his favorite son. Uncle–nephew rivalry was another facet of egalitarian–dynastic tension, and either egalitarian ideas or dynastic ones could be used as propaganda in the struggle for power.

Parallel-cousin marriage, also, served a dynastic function, and perhaps served as a mechanism to propitiate egalitarian pressures. Possibly the tension that arose between nephew and uncle resulted when a marriage did not occur with the latter's daughter, or in the event of its failure and an accompanying quarrel over its settlement, or even from disputes involving promised gifts in lieu of a share in inheritance. This conflict may have been masked by uncle–nephew rivalry. (A similar tension may have arisen over the question of a woman's share of her father's estate, placing her and her son in competition with her son's father's father's brother, yet another uncle.)

An additional and complicating factor for marriage and inheritance questions was the institution of the office of ilkhani with its attached revenues and incomes. As a result, for those eligible a prebendal system intruded on the existing patrimonial system, and competition increased with the hope of the ilkhani's perquisites as a prize. For example, the large village of Gutvand in 'Arabistan was attached to the office of ilkhani.[40]

Marriage and family relationships were as critical for Ilkhani's administration of the Bakhtiyari as for his dynastic concerns. Even a cursory examination of historical data relating his political–juridical, economic, ideological, and symbolic roles reveals the extent to which he resembled a non-tribal magnate. The proto-elements, or the bases for forming the state in the Weberian sense[41] – army, bureaucracy, and legitimacy – emerge in Ilkhani's rule of the Bakhtiyari of 1862–82. Ilkhani possessed an undifferentiated and personal bureaucracy larger than, but similar to, Aqa Muhammad's when he established Qajar rule at the end of the eighteenth century. Ilkhani employed five munshis, or secretarial agents; in addition, one of his brothers, Imam Quli Khan Hajji Ilkhani, served as his executive, and his half-brother, Riza Quli Khan Ilbaigi, functioned as his finance minister. Ilkhani's sons – especially his favorites Isfandiyar Khan and 'Ali Quli Khan – served him in a variety of military, diplomatic, and administrative roles. Ilkhani's sons and nephews performed military, police, and administrative functions under their fathers and uncles in the Bakhtiyari and adjacent regions. The younger khans served as officers from six months to two years in either the shah's bodyguard or one of the Qajar princes' militias; they would then return to the Bakhtiyari to be replaced by another brother or cousin. Most obtained their first titles in this manner; but, more importantly, they established contacts with members of the Qajar family and their ministers. Muhammad Husain Khan, Imam Quli Khan's eldest son, served for eight years with the Vali'ahd in Tabriz before being recalled to enter the service of the Zill al-Sultan. Isfandiyar Khan, Ilkhani's eldest son, was a sarhang of the Bakhtiyari *savars*, or cavalrymen, in the shah's and the Zill al-Sultan's militia. To maintain these savars the Bakhtiyari khans had been given Mizdij, a section of Chahar Mahall, as tuyul savar; Hajji 'Ali Quli Khan, another of Ilkhani's sons, was placed in charge of it.[42]

The favored sons were placed advantageously in terms of future roles and preferments. Qajar documents recognize Isfandiyar especially and imply recognition of him as heir. The younger brothers recognized and accepted their subordinate position, possibly out of consideration for continuity of family domination, and in this particular generation family tension was expressed between cousins and between uncles and nephews – especially between Muhammad Husain and his uncle, Ilkhani – rather than between brothers.

Ilkhani was attended by his *yatims* (lit. orphans, essentially non-Bakhtiyari clients), who served as his household and were responsible for his tents, flocks, horses, weapons, and entertainment. On the military side he was attended by his bastagan, primarily drawn from the Ahmad Khusravi, who formed the core of his cavalry; his army and cavalry could expand to *c.* 2,000, building upon the Bakhtiyari segmentary structure.

The political relationship, including its military component, established by marriage is revealed in the bastagan system. These same khans, their full and half-brothers, and their parallel cousins (and there is no evidence for examples earlier than the late nineteenth century) utilized what they called their bastagan (sing. *bastah*, lit. tied) as retainers. Informants invariably link their fingers or tie an imaginary knot around a finger to show the nature of this relationship between a bastah and his khan. Although the bastagan of more recent times all appear to have been recruited from the Ahmad Khusravi, a tirah of the Duraki and one claiming a common lineage with the khans (Ahmad and 'Abd al-Khalil were the two sons of Khusrau, and the major lineage traced its descent from the latter and the bastagan from the former), it is possible that they were also drawn from other tayafahs/tirahs. It is also possible that a similar relationship was established through marriage and the bride's agnates were expected to function as bastagan, and in the case of daughter marriage her affines were regarded as bastagan.

The Ilkhani–Hajji Ilkhani tie with their Ahmad Khusravi bastagan provides the model for the relationship. Emphasis in it always fell on patrilineal descent and marriage. Secondary marriages occurred between the khans, or their sons, and Ahmad Khusravi women, and marriages were also arranged between the daughters of the khans and their less important wives and Ahmad Khusravi men. A bastah was obliged to provide service to the khan, military and political, and the khan helped in his maintenance, directly with gifts of cash or kind and indirectly through his participation in booty and dues collections. This economic factor is downplayed by informants who have been, or are, bastagan. Such links as established through the bastagan system or similar ones through marriage acquired great significance for a khan aspiring to compete for offices and positions.

Accession to and continuation in the office of ilkhani required family, tribal, and imperial support; family division and withdrawal of royal favor resulted in Ilkhani's death in 1882. Potential family disputes and rivalries were manipulated by Nasir al-Din Shah and his governors. The basis for the essential disagreement between the three brothers and their twenty-nine sons–although in 1882 perhaps only six counted politically–was probably over the question of anticipatory inheritance and the division of villages and incomes acquired during Ilkhani's tenure in office, and over the division of power in the event of his death. (It should be remembered that there existed only a vague principle of succession to power favoring the eldest male best suited to serve, and that inheritance did not need to follow an assumed Islamic division.) Presumably each of the three khans had separate estates but also shared properties in common, and specific ones were allotted to the office of ilkhani; this is noted by Sardar Zafar[43] and, in addition, this practice and the accompanying problems of division are suggested by Sardar As'ad's two wills.[44] Given the relationship of land and wealth to power – especially for the maintenance of bastagan – and the greatly increasing number of khans in subsequent generations eligible for important tribal roles, this division and its ramifications took on great importance, as it would directly affect Ilkhani's six sons and the other two brothers and their sons.

The very first document – a farman of Rabi' II 1279/September–October 1862[45] – issued to Husain Quli Khan recognizes him as responsible for establishing order in the Bakhtiyari. This farman awards him the title of "nazim of the Bakhtiyari" and appoints him to that office with an annual stipend of 500 tumans. This unusual title and office (lit. regulator or orderer) implied that Husain Quli had brought order to the Bakhtiyari; he did so on the basis of family and Qajar support. The next two extant documents – a farman (?) dated Zi al-Qa'dah 1279/April 1863[46] and another farman of Rabi' II 1280/September 1863[47] – hold him responsible for good order and security. The first of these charges that Bakhtiyari attached to him – presumably Duraki – have assaulted and killed twelve peasants in Junaqan after Husain Quli Khan's departure (on the autumnal migration?), and he is held responsible and is to obtain restitution. Thus, he was accountable for specific Bakhtiyari outside of tribal territory. (Junaqan happened to be one of his properties in Chahar Mahall.) The other farman commends him for his service and maintenance of order, but it also sets down his Bakhtiyari responsibilities as follows: collection and remission of taxes, maintenance of order among the tribes and security on roads and highways, and capture of thieves and rebels. From the state's perspective, he was a local leader appointed as administrator, tax collector, and policeman. Presumably other Bakhtiyari held similar posts, but not necessarily with the same title.

The next phase of Husain Quli's career, the 1862–78 period of consolidation and expansion of his power, culminated in the farman of Sha'ban 1284/December 1867[48] – issued again by Nasir al-Din Shah – that recognizes him as "ilkhani of the tribes of the Bakhtiyari". Although this farman explicitly grants him the military rank of *sartip* (brigadier), the emphasis in this important document expands his role to that of a confederational leader – not only in terms of the title, which has medieval roots and associations with tribal confederations, but practically in the admonition to the Bakhtiyari: "the khans and leaders of [tribal] military contingents, and kadkhudas and rish safids of the tribes and sections of the Bakhtiyari, are to consider him to be endowed with this rank and status [of ilkhani] and recognize respect toward him, to be in keeping with this rank and appropriate to this status, to be incumbent on them". His Bakhtiyari position, reinforced by the state, went beyond that of nazim and became in effect, that of leader of the Bakhtiyari confederation. (When Bakhtiyari secondary sources mention Husain Quli Khan as ilkhani of the Bakhtiyari, they almost always include "*kul*", or "the whole", before Bakhtiyari , which is implied in this and subsequent documents to mark this singular achievement.)

These earliest documents emphasize Ilkhani's juridical–political role within the Bakhtiyari and within the state. Increasingly, Ilkhani's full brother, Imam Quli, was to serve internally as judge and mediator and as coordinator of the migrations, and his half-brother, Riza Quli, as fiscal manager, although Ilkhani seems to have delivered the taxes personally to Isfahan each year. Ilkhani functioned as general executive and commander in chief, integrating the Bakhtiyari into the state economically and politically and, ideologically, into the larger Irano-Shi'i ethos. As his "Kitabchah" and letter to Nasir al-Din Shah in 1878 note, he personally led the Bakhtiyari cavalry in the regions contiguous to the Bakhtiyari which were sensitive to the potential of Bakhtiyari hegemony. His sons and nephews led contingents assigned to the shah and the Qajar princes. These, and later documents, also deal with the ideological and symbolic aspect of this juridical–political role, internally and with the state. Ilkhani is styled as "khaqan", or great khan, a title used for the shah as well as earlier illustrious Bakhtiyari mentioned in eighteenth-century documents. And he is specifically identified with, and was commended to, a range of powerful Qajar princes: Farhad Mirza, Mu'tamid al-Daulah; Hamza Mirza, Hashmat al-Daulah; Muzaffar al-Din Mirza, Vali'ahd (crown prince); Kamran Mirza, Nayib al-Saltanah; Ziya' al-Mulk; and especially Mas'ud Mirza, Zill al-Sultan. Muhammad Taqi Khan's only known tie to a Qajar prince was to one in rebellion and living in exile! Ilkhani's links to Qajar princes were strengthened by gifts and by the younger khans' military service in their various provincial militia. Furthermore, support for succession in his family was implied when Isfandiyar, Ilkhani's eldest son, was appointed "sarhang"[49] of the Bakhtiyari cavalry in the shah's service, and again when other sons were given responsibilities and titles. The significance of titles and Qajar ties was not lost on the tribesmen, and Ilkhani's power, exercised in the name of the shah, would be less subject to internal fragmenting factors.

Perhaps surprisingly, even Husain Quli Khan Ilkhani had little direct control over the pastoral base of the Bakhtiyari, which was controlled by family units or their extension. Flocks were owned by the nuclear family, but camping, herding, migration, and defense required and resulted in increasingly larger groupings that were formed on a kin basis. Such associations had access to the traditional pastures of their particular tayafahs and controlled pasture usage through *bunchaqs* (agreements or contracts).[50] Apparently the khans could assign or reassign pasture land as reward or punishment but seldom did so. In the nineteenth century demographic factors were probably of greater significance in terms of pastures than khan–tayafah relationships; the famine of 1869–72 reduced both human and animal populations, and pastures and agricultural land may have been opened up. In the nineteenth century as a whole there may even have been surplus pastures,[51] for Ilkhani found pastures for various Qashqa'i rebelling against their ilkhani, without, presumably, displacing Bakhtiyari.

The Bakhtiyari economic base, an aspect of the larger and essentially pastoral–agricultural economy of the state, was controlled indirectly by Ilkhani through his collection of surpluses in the form of taxes for the state. His letter to Nasir al-Din Shah[52] emphasizes that he collected the tax thirty-one times. There are no references to Bakhtiyari revolts against Ilkhani, and his reputation for just administration is possibly derived from his fairness on tax issues. Riza Quli Khan, responsible for the actual collection, did not have such a reputation. Although some of the khans' income must have been derived from tax collecting, no references to personal use of taxes or even the total amount collected are made by Ilkhani. Ilkhani usually refers to tax assessment merely as *maliyat*, but there were two main types of taxes collected in the Bakhtiyari: the *gallahdari* or *maliyat shakhi* (flock or horn tax) and the *khish* (plow tax). The first of these was collected in the spring, and after 1898 for those tribes using the Bakhtiyari road it was levied at the bridges. In 1910 it was levied at the rate of 15 qirans for every mare, for every 4 donkeys or cows, and for every 20 sheep.[53] Both Sardar As'ad and Sardar Zafar in their histories state that the maliyat was based on mares. This would reflect the development of these taxes from Safavid, or even earlier, times and reveals the relationship between the assignment of land to pastoral leaders and the reciprocal obligation of furnishing cavalry forces. Both these khans would disagree with the fixed rate of 15 qirans per mare as recorded in the above British source. Sardar Zafar writes: "I have heard that one mare is worth four tumans [for tax purposes] and for others ten, two, or one. This discrepancy is dependent upon the wealth of the tayafah. For the richest the value of a mare is less, and for the very wealthy a mare is worth only five qirans."[54] Sardar As'ad agrees with this.[55] The tax rate varied, and the wealthier paid at a lower rate. This indicates the greater influence of those who were affluent, and who may have contributed cavalry forces in an earlier period; however, in this late Qajar period the khans were also awarded specific grants in cash and kind by the government for the use of their cavalrymen. A variation of this practice was in operation in the Bakhtiyari at this time: those tayafahs that supported the ilkhani were assessed at a lower rate. Indeed the Ahmad Khusravi paid no taxes because of the military support they gave Ilkhani as bastagan. Also, it was perceived that if a wealthy pastoralist like Ilkhani or Muhammad Taqi Khan (the latter was supposed to have owned over 10,000 sheep alone) paid at the same rate, he would jeopardize his flocks. A standard tax rate, combined with the expense of hiring shepherds or herdsmen, the poorer standard of care such clients would provide, and the greater potential for the loss of whole herds through disease, would perhaps have discouraged the accumulation of wealth in the form of herds and flocks – especially of horses, which were needed for cavalry. This variable tax was an important political device and allowed the khans, especially the ilkhanis, to reward and punish with the authority of the central government. It was from these taxes that the annual assessment for the Bakhtiyari tribesmen of *c.* 15,000 tumans during Ilkhani's tenure in that office – he never mentioned the amount in either his letter or his "Kitabchah" – was paid to the central government through Isfahan. Walter Baring, who visited Ilkhani shortly before his death, reported the Bakhtiyari tax to be 14,000 tumans,[56] and J.R. Preece noted in 1895 that the Bakhtiyari tax was 15,000 tumans and 20,000 tumans for Chahar Mahall.[57] Presumably, the last amount was for the agricultural villages there – some of which were the khans' property – and not the small fields that the tribes tilled in their summer pastures.

The plow tax for sown land was levied at the rate of 1 qiran per khish or plow (the amount of land farmed by a plow) and 20–25 *manns* (1 mann = 6½ pounds) of grain per khish.[58] According to Sardar As'ad this was levied only on cultivated land in the garmsir;[59] but he did specify whether this tax was on the tribal lands or on the khans' personal estates there. (Sardar As'ad excluded their Chahar Mahall properties, probably because they were not a part of the Bakhtiyari assessment but a part of that of Chahar Mahall or Isfahan.)

What was the burden of taxation for pastoralists? Agriculturalists complained about tax exaction to Qajar officials and to British travelers. Walter Baring noted in 1881 that a Bakhtiyari village of 200 families paid Ilkhani 5,000 manns of grain and 300 qirans annually (he did not specify whether this was the tax or the landlord's share): "I suspect, however, this statement is exaggerated, as the peasants are clearly inclined to overstate what they have to pay in order to excite commiseration, but on the other hand their authorities greatly understate the amount they exact."[60] Agriculturalists paid from a third to two-thirds of their yield to the landowner, and, in comparison, their tax was relatively small, but taxes and the landlord's share – not easily evaded – were a far greater burden for agriculturalists than for pastoralists. In the mid-nineteenth century, Baron De Bode observed the disparity that sedentary Haft Lang in 195 villages in Burburud were required to pay 7,873 tumans in cash and 530 kharvars of grain as their tax, but "the Iliyat migratory Bakhtiyari who are more numerous, only pay 3,600 tumans".[61]

Baring, in 1881, reported a Bakhtiyari tax rate of 25 qirans per 100 sheep – a very low rate by contemporary standards.[62] Continuing to use Baring's data: the Bakhtiyari numbered 30,000 families, and assuming that each family owned 100 sheep/goats and that each sheep was valued at 10 qirans (Baring quoted a price of 10–15 qirans), the total value of

Bakhtiyari herds was 3,000,000 tumans (1 tuman = 10 qirans; *c.* 27 qirans = £1 in 1882). By this very approximate calculation, the Bakhtiyari should have paid a total tax of 12,000 tumans, which is close to the 14,000 tumans actually paid. (The constancy of the Bakhtiyari tax over two decades paralleled that of state expenditures.)

Other taxes, however, were collected from the tribes. These included the *sursat*, or purveyance tax, provisions in kind for the khan or his agents, which amounted to 1 mann of bread, 1 load of wood, 1 mann of barley, 1 load of straw, 2 fowl, ¼ mann of oil, and 10 eggs; the *dar qishlaq* (lit. gate of the winter pasture), which was 5 qirans per flock of sheep but which was not regularly levied (no Bakhtiyari source makes reference to it); and a tax in cash and kind on salt springs.[63] Most Bakhtiyari tribesmen did not pay a grazing tax, unless the seldom-levied dar qishlaq is counted. If non-Bakhtiyari tribes grazed on Bakhtiyari land they were charged a small tax, '*alafchah*,[64] for this privilege.

Ilkhani's internal juridical–political role was strengthened not only by his designation as administrator–tax collector but also by the incomes from his Chahar Mahall and 'Arabistan estates, which allowed him – and the other khans with land holdings – to maintain a more or less permanent body of armed retainers, essentially their bastagan, beyond those provided for by tuyuls and specific grants. Significantly, when Husain Quli Khan was entitled Ilkhani, the tax assessments of his Mizdij estates were specified in farmans,[65] and, in effect, his ownership of them was acknowledged. Significantly, perhaps twelve of these villages had been recognized as belonging to his great-grandfathers. Had they been confiscated by the early Qajars, and then restored to him? Some of his estates in Mizdij, and others in 'Arabistan, had been brought into production by him and were regarded as his property. This was the result of the political stability he maintained, his capital expenditures for irrigation systems, and his effort to extend fields and to develop production.

It is not yet possible to arrive at any estimate of Ilkhani's estates or actual wealth. His office carried with it the annual stipend of 1,000 tumans,[66] but official documents provide only elusive clues to the extent of his incomes and holdings; he makes no direct mention of them. Najm al-Mulk calculated that Ilkhani obtained 20,000 tumans from his 'Arabistan military role.[67] An added problem is posed by real estate, as there was always the problem of ambiguity of ownership, not only from the viewpoint of the government but from that of his brothers, nephews, and sons. (No doubt this was a factor in his sons' decision to hold property jointly until their sons compelled them to divide it.) Ilkhani indicates indirectly that he is a man of great wealth when he mentions expenses of 15,000 tumans for his stay at court in Tehran, or that Zill al-Sultan's visit with him has cost 5,000 tumans. Similarly, he notes the expenditure of 6,000 tumans for mirror work on the Karbala shrines and the expenses of his family on their various pilgrimages to Mecca. In addition, Ilkhani cannot disguise his wealth when he makes numerous entries in his "Kitabchah"[68] of the mares or stallions he has obtained for 400–600 tumans.

Horses, wealth, and power came together in 'Arabistan. His horses seem to have been pastured and bred there, or on that side of Bakhtiyari. First, he had access to the important bloodlines from Arabia west of that region. Second, he played important military and political roles there and had established patron relationships with a number of 'Arabistan leaders. (This would have included merchants, for Najm al-Mulk estimated – though he may have exaggerated – that Ilkhani had given 80,000 tumans to 'Arabistan merchants for investment.[69] The patron–client relationship both actual and symbolic is indicated, in the "Kitabchah", by the numerous "gifts" of horses made by Arab shaikhs, which in turn allowed Ilkhani to bestow these prized animals on Qajar princes. Third, 'Arabistan – given the factor of distance from the capital and poor communications – was an area where Ilkhani could expand his influence and power; this may have been a factor in Qajar perceptions of Ilkhani as a threat.

Bakhtiyari interest in 'Arabistan dates at least from the Safavid period, when Jahangir Khan was given the right to collect taxes from certain of its districts. Also, we have seen that Muhammad Taqi Khan's and Ilkhani's interest in 'Arabistan expressed itself in economic and political terms (i.e., acquisition of estates and political alignments with governors and tribal leaders against, or in support of, the central government). The khans, both as tribal leaders and as landlords, found the movement in a southwesterly direction into 'Arabistan a natural one. Rivals occupied Bakhtiyari borders and prevented significant movement except towards the southwest. Furthermore, the terrain resembles the Bakhtiyari garmsir and could be exploited by both pastoralists and agriculturalists. There was some expansion in an easterly direction toward Isfahan; the nineteenth-century khans significantly increased their holdings in Faridan and Chahar Mahall by purchase, gifts, or harassment. This last tactic involved raiding a village periodically at harvest time until the peasants and landlords were willing to meet their terms. But further movement here was hindered by the existing land-owning pattern and by the watershed of the Zayandah river near Isfahan. Some of the richest farming land on the Iranian plateau, however, is located in this area along the terraces of the Zayandah as it flows to Isfahan and beyond. This land commanded a premium price, and its proximity to Isfahan, a major administrative center, precluded harassment and subsequent sale or expropriation. The khans preferred territory that was adjacent to the Bakhtiyari and hence under their own authority rather than that of the central government. This left only 'Arabistan.

'Arabistan fulfilled all their requirements. The rugged Zagros mountains effectively cut this province off from the remainder of Iran; it was contiguous to the Bakhtiyari; and land and water were available. Water existed in the form of numerous rivers flowing from the Zagros to the Gulf; and land existed in the forms of *khalisah* (crown property), which could be purchased or leased; dead lands, where cultivation would give the cultivator certain rights; and villages, available through regular purchase. Oppressive taxation and levies and governmental neglect contributed to a depressed state of agriculture in 'Arabistan under the Qajars.[70] After the opening of the Karun to international commerce in 1888, however, Isabella L. Bird Bishop, a perceptive late-nineteenth-century traveler, reported increased agricultural activity along its banks and in the province:

A great change for the better has taken place in the circumstances of the population, and villages, attracted by trade, are springing up. . . The landtax is very light, and the cultivators are receiving every encouragement. Much wheat was exported last year, and there is a brisk demand for river lands on leases of sixty years for the cultivation of cotton, cereals, sugar-cane, and date palms. . .

One interesting feature connected with these works is the rapidly increased well-being of the Arabs. In less than a year labour at 1 *kran* a day has put quite a number of them in possession of a pair of donkeys and a plough, and seed-corn wherewith to cultivate Government lands on their own account, besides leaving a small balance in hand on which to live without having to borrow on the coming crop at frightfully usurious rates.

Until now the shaikhs have been able to command labour for little more than the poorest food; and now many of the very poor who depended on them have started as small farmers, and things are rapidly changing.[71]

The Bakhtiyari khans' land was concentrated in three parts of post-Ilkhani 'Arabistan: the immediate areas adjoining Shushtar, Ram Hurmuz, and Bihbahan. (In the early twentieth century the khans were acquiring land even farther to the south in Liravi.) Much of the 'Aqili land, near Shushtar, was to become the property of Sardar Muhtasham, one of Imam Quli's important sons. Ram Hurmuz, after Ilkhani's death, became the winter seat of the Bakhtiyari khans, and one of them was usually its deputy governor under the governor of 'Arabistan, whose capital was usually Shushtar. According to John Gordon Lorimer's *Gazetteer of the Persian Gulf, 'Oman, and Central Arabia*, the Bakhtiyari khans owned all the villages (*c.* 27) in the Ram Hurmuz district.[72] During the first decade of the twentieth century, the Ilkhani and Hajji Ilkhani khans owned 3,600 khish[73] in this area, and as landlords their share of the

1906–7 crop amounted to 22,650 *Ramuz manns*[74] (a Ramuz [Ram Hur-muz] mann was equivalent to 106 English pounds). They paid 15,000 tumans per annum tax to the governor of 'Arabistan.

The agricultural taxes are generally collected in kind at the rate of one-fourth of the gross produce in the case of wheat, barley, linseed, cotton, beans, and tobacco, and at the rate of one-third in the case of rice and sesame. Unirrigated crops ordinarily pay revenue in cash at the rate of 33 Qrans [qirans] per Faddan [khish]. (One good authority, however, states that the annual payment to the Persian Government is only 10,000 Tumans, and that the tax on agriculture is 1/5 of produce in all cases.) In 1904 the revenue collections in kind consisted of 2,000 Ramuz Manns of wheat, 12,000 of barley, 100 of beans, 1,500 linseed, 70 of tobacco, 12,000 of rice, and 1,000 of sesame, and their total value was estimated at 55,000 Tumans: in the same year the area cultivated by rainfall was 2,000 Faddans and yielded 6,500 Tumans in cash.[75]

In his "Kitabchah", Ilkhani gives no hint either of his wealth or of his impending troubles with the Qajars, but in a letter written by him to Nasir al-Din Shah, who scrawls his reply and the date ([12]95[/1878]) in the margins,[76] he expresses his particular frustration in dealing with Farhad Mirza, Mu'tamid al-Daulah, the governor of Fars. Ilkhani begins this letter with the customary formula recognizing the shah's authority and majesty. Next he acknowledges receipt of the shah's letter, no longer extant, in regard to the Qashqa'i. From other sources, primarily Ilkhani's own "Kitabchah", we find allusions to differences between the Bakhtiyari and the Qashqa'i. One reference alludes to a *tafriqah* of Muhammad Shah in regard to the 'Ali Shaikh (a Bakhtiyari tribal section?). This was possibly an order that allowed a Bakhtiyari section to move into Qashqa'i territory, but their tax was assessed with the Bakhtiyari tax. Another source of Qashqa'i conflict mentioned in the "Kitabchah", which might have been the occasion for the shah's concern, involved the flight of the Darashuri, a major Qashqa'i section, from their own territory to the Bakhtiyari, where they were given pastures by Ilkhani. Their continued presence in the Bakhtiyari would have exacerbated relations with Mu'ta-mid al-Daulah, who was emerging as Ilkhani's bitterest enemy, and Saulat al-Daulah, the Qashqa'i ilkhani. Finally, the third possible source of conflict to which this mention of the Qashqa'i might refer involved a jurisdictional dispute over the town of Falard, which is situated in northern Fars at the point where Qashqa'i and Bakhtiyari summer pastures meet. Its taxes were collected by Ilkhani but paid to Fars; it is possible that they were sometimes paid to 'Arabistan. Later in his letter, but also in his "Kitabchah", Ilkhani mentions the Qashqa'i attack on Falard. Possibly this was the result of continued support for Qashqa'i dissidents.

Ilkhani then directly implores the shah to heed his side of the conflict with the Qashqa'i. He goes on to recount that he has served thirty years and as head of the Bakhtiyari has transformed them "into the likes of the peasants of Linjan". He relates that he has also collected and submitted thirty-one Bakhtiyari taxes (covering thirty-one years?) and that his account is in order and cleared. In addition he has served the government by spending six months on the Isfahan side of the Bakhtiyari and six on the 'Arabistan side with Bakhtiyari cavalry keeping order in these adjacent regions. He adds that two of his sons, Isfandiyar and 'Ali Quli, are both serving in the shah's guard.

Ilkhani laments that despite this record of service he is being attacked by Mu'tamid al-Daulah. One of the charges against him is that he was responsible for instigating the conflict with Khuda Karam Khan Buir Ahmadi and his son Muhammad Husain Khan. Ilkhani counters that Mu'tamid al-Daulah was responsible for 10,000 tumans' damage to the peasants of Falard. References are made to Zill al-Sultan, and to the fact that without his support Ilkhani would be at a complete loss. (Several years later Ilkhani, of course, was to lose this support and be strangled in Zill al-Sultan's prison by order of Nasir al-Din Shah.)

Ilkhani concludes by noting his age, service, and fatigue and asks to be relieved of his responsibilities. If this request is granted he will journey to Najaf (one of the Shi'i shrine cities) to pray for the shah. He also argues that he is not indispensable, since his brothers and sons are fit to carry on his duties. Sipahsalar had already turned down this request, doing so because he wanted to use Ilkhani as a means of checking the power of the two powerful governors, Zill al-Sultan and Mu'tamid al-Daulah. Ilkhani, if he were seriously desirous of stepping down, had no recourse but to write to the shah. This communication with Nasir al-Din also allowed him to present his case directly and might have been conceived as a means of gaining imperial support at the expense of the prince–governors.

Nasir al-Din Shah, with his customary curtness, replies in the margins that he is satisfied with the good order of the Bakhtiyari and Ilkhani's services. "It is as you have written . . . you have served excellently . . . you must continue to do so." Thus, he rejects Ilkhani's resignation and refuses to grant him permission to go to Najaf. He is to follow Sipahsalar's orders, and Nasir al-Din Shah concludes by writing: "Be assured of my favor to you and your sons, and never think of resigning from service."

The "Kitabchah" provides no hint of internal family rivalry. Imam Quli had always respected Ilkhani's seniority, and in turn had always been acknowledged as second only to him. If the relationship of these two full brothers was comparable to that of 'Ali Quli and Khusrau, about which information has survived – and there is no indication of the intense rivalry between Ilkhani and Imam Quli which characterized so many other brother relationships – the subordinate brother accepted his role, regarded his senior brother's sons as his own, and in terms of political succession favored them over his own sons. By *c.* 1881 Imam Quli's eldest son, Muhammad Husain Khan, who was approximately Isfandiyar's age or even slightly older, was commanding the Bakhtiyari cavalry contingent in the Vali'ahd's guard. He broke with his father and became one of two centers of opposition to Ilkhani. Muhammad Husain probably realized that his father would support Isfandiyar's claim to the ilkhaniship at his expense, and in addition Isfandiyar was more highly regarded within the Bakhtiyari, he was perceived as the model khan, and his designation as successor had been recognized in Tehran.

The Vali'ahd, Muzaffar al-Din Mirza, himself probably encouraged and supported Muhammad Husain in his opposition, because he feared a challenge by his own elder brother Mas'ud Mirza Zill al-Sultan for succession to their father's throne.

Zill al-Sultan's jealousy of his younger brother, the Vali'ahd, was known; he was also suspicious of anyone who had close ties with him. This included Amin al-Sultan, one of Nasir al-Din Shah's prime ministers, who later became known as Atabak A'zam; he is frequently referred to as Sadr A'zam (prime minister). Amin al-Sultan had established a close relationship with Ilkhani, and in 1881 had secretly invited him to Tehran.[77] Zill al-Sultan was also suspicious of Ilkhani's growing power; under his rule of some thirty years the Bakhtiyari had achieved a semblance of stability which had increased Ilkhani's wealth, which, in turn, had enabled him to extend his influence and purchase villages in Chahar Mahall and in northeastern 'Arabistan. Najm al-Mulk, on his visit to 'Arabistan in 1881, referred to the Bakhtiyari khans as being "firmly established" and receiving a good income from their property there.[78]

Ilkhani, though he had earlier enjoyed good relations with the Vali'ahd, was perceived by his enemies among the Qajars, especially Farhad Mirza, Mu'tamid al-Daulah, governor of Fars, as encouraging Zill al-Sultan in this dispute. Muhammad Husain, attendant on the Vali'ahd, was both a source of information for the Qajars on Ilkhani's affairs and privy to court intrigue and rumors. Since Ilkhani was regarded by this time as a major power and even a serious threat to the central government, Muhammad Husain Khan saw an opportunity to gain power in the Bakhtiyari at his uncle's and cousin's expense. He did not disguise his independence and opposition, for – according to tradition – on one significant occasion he dared to ride in front of Ilkhani mounted on a white horse, accompanied by his bastagan. The great khan merely shrugged off this affront and breach of manners.

Ilbaigi, the other family conspirator to cooperate with the Qajars, also saw a limited future for himself and his sons unless a change were brought about before Ilkhani's natural death. He, too, could not hope to challenge a combination of Imam Quli Khan and Isfandiyar Khan, assuming they had some support at court. By 1882, but not earlier than 1878, Ilbaigi had allied with the Qajars against Ilkhani. The basis for Qajar misgivings included the following factors: Ilkhani's perceived challenge to the governor of Fars, which included his dispute with him over Falard and his grant of refuge to the Darashuri section of the Qashqa'i; his dominance in 'Arabistan, as reported and possibly exaggerated by Najm al-Mulk; his possible ties with the British – Walter Baring and Captain Wells had recently completed a reconnaissance of the Bakhtiyari for the Government of India, and Ilkhani had just placed an arms order with G.S. McKenzie of Grey, Paul and Co.;[79] and the possible direct threat to the throne if Ilkhani were to combine forces with Zill al-Sultan. Possibly to prove his loyalty to his father and the Vali'ahd, Zill al-Sultan was forced to break with and then kill Ilkhani.

Benam al-Mulk, one of Zill al-Sultan's agents, noted the alliance between uncle and nephew, Riza Quli and Muhammad Husain, and described them as great intriguers.[80] Traditionally, Ilkani accompanied the tribe on its annual migration, and after arriving in the summer pastures he would go to Isfahan to pay the annual tax to the governor; the tax for that portion of the Bakhtiyari under the governor of 'Arabistan was paid before the departure of the tribe, although the total was most often paid in Isfahan because Zill al-Sultan was the governor of the whole southwest. In 1882, when paying this tax, Ilkhani was seized and strangled by Zill al-Sultan, and Isfandiyar and 'Ali Quli were imprisoned. Whether it was due to the suggestions of Farhad Mirza or to the fears and ambitions of Zill al-Sultan, is not known, but an order was probably given by the shah for his death. In his memoirs, *Tarikh Sar Guzasht Mas'udi*,[81] Zill al-Sultan vehemently denies that he was the source, claiming that he was only carrying out his father's command; however, this book was lithographed in 1907, when Ilkhani's sons and nephews were beginning to play a major role in national politics. I'timad al-Saltanah reports the following in his voluminous and informative diary: "Husain Quli Khan Bakhtiyari of the Haft Lang, who was very respected and one of the great, powerful, wealthy, and mighty chiefs of Iran, had died in Isfahan. It is known that Zill al-Sultan poisoned [in fact strangled] him."[82] And, later, he continues: "The Prince [Zill al-Sultan] paid a lot of attention to me. He confidentially showed me the order in which the Shah had insisted upon the necessity of killing Husain Quli Khan Bakhtiyari."[83] Benam al-Mulk noted:

After the death of Husain Kuli Khan the Prince evinced kindness and consideration towards Mohammed Husain Khan, whom he sent to the Bakhtiari country.
He appointed the Ilkhani's brother, Haji Imam Kuli Khan, to the Chieftainship of
the Bakhtiari and Reza Kuli Khan to the Ilbegiship. All the allowances, honours,
and the administration of the Bakhtiari cavalry were divided between the late
Chief's two brothers and Mohammed Husain Khan. By these means the Prince
maintained his authority amongst the Bakhtiaris.[84]

The precipitous end of Ilkhani's long rule once again plunged the
Bakhtiyari into a prolonged dispute over the question of succession and
inheritance.

Although an expected and feared general uprising of the Bakhtiyari did
not result, disorder was manifest among the tribes for the next twelve
years as the three factions formed various combinations in attempts to gain
pre-eminence. There was no question that the office of ilkhani would be
filled by candidates from this group of Ilkhani, Hajji Ilkhani, and Ilbaigi
khans, for during Ilkhani's rule of some thirty years authority had become
even more firmly identified with his descent group, their wealth had so
increased that none of the khans from other lineages could hope to
compete, and ties within the Bakhtiyari and with all factions of the Qajars
were so encompassing that short of mass imprisonment and confiscation of
estates–which did occur in the 1930s under Riza Shah, but from which
Nasir al-Din Shah shrank out of fear of Bakhtiyari power[85] – all other
Bakhtiyari leaders were removed from contention.

Ilkhani's legacy – in addition to his power, wealth, and lands – included
a Bakhtiyari of some 30,000 families, or 150,000–180,000 individuals, and
an estimated 3,000,000 animals; tribal taxes of 14,000 tumans, and
probably 22,000 tumans for Chahar Mahall, submitted and cleared; 200
cavalry in imperial service;[86] increased agricultural productivity; improved communications of roads and bridges for migration and
marketing; and order and unity – disrupted, of course, by his execution.

The legacy of Ilkhani, the man, however, is more difficult to discern.
Physically, Husain Quli Khan must have made an imposing presence.
From a photograph – probably taken in either Isfahan or Tehran *c.*
1879 – he appears taller than average in stature, perhaps six feet, and quite
obviously the khan in command; he alone is seated and is shown as alert,
poised, and pressing a rifle to one thigh and grasping his sword at
midscabbard on the other – to him, symbols of his authority. In the only
other extant photograph, perhaps taken on the same occasion – and
probably in Tehran, for he is wearing court dress, including the tall Qajar
astrakhan and khal'at – Ilkhani has the same confident bearing.

His reputation as a great khan must have been reinforced by his striking
appearance, for his contemporaries held him in great awe. Two English-

men were equally impressed. G.S. McKenzie of Grey, Paul and Co., who visited him in 1875 and again in 1878, noted both his commanding presence and his openness to the idea of trade, bridges, roads, etc. And Walter Baring, seeing Ilkhani in November 1881, only six months before he was killed, wrote:

Hursein [*sic*] Kuli Khan is a fine stalwart man of about 60 or 62, the very picture of rude health. As I have said he was most civil, but one could not help seeing that he was also a trifle suspicious, and though eager to talk about Russia and Afghanistan, Kuldja, and every other conceivable political topic, he was somewhat reticent about the affairs of his own tribe. It puzzled him to understand what could have brought us there, as of course like every other oriental, he simply scouted the idea of any sane person travelling for travelling's sake.

He is in favour of the opening of the Karoun to free navigation, but would not be altogether pleased to see a good road made through his mountains, as it would naturally weaken his now very independent position.

It was easy to see what a power the Eelkhani is among the tribe, as the veneration and respect with which he was treated by all was quite remarkable.[87]

Ilkhani's dignity, guarded manner, and reserve are seen, too, in his "Kitabchah", in whose pages he rarely reveals a glimpse of his personal feelings. He shows great interest in his favorite sons, Isfandiyar and 'Ali Quli, through his frequent mention of them (his endearments are stock ones), but he also demonstrates some affection for young Khusrau in expressing concern for his broken elbow. Ilkhani's obsession with horses and his prowess as a great hunter are not unexpected for a tribal leader, but his agricultural pursuits of bringing scions to transplant in orchards, of sending for an elixir to attract starlings to eat the locusts, or of building irrigation systems constitute something of a surprise and an added dimension to an increasingly complex picture of the man. He notes earthquakes and evinces concern about the effects of drought. His admiration for heroic effort ending in death – in the crossing of the chasm – suggests a very human response. But he also notes the death of someone, and then immediately turns to an unrelated matter. This naturalness and lack of pretense are additional human factors in his personality. His response to Qajar ruthlessness is almost a sense of relief that he is not yet their victim; although Ilkhani shows pride in and dismay at the expense of having Zill al-Sultan as a guest in Bakhtiyari, and he finds satisfaction and pleasure in accompanying the shah hunting and in bestowing coins on the retinue in honor of the shah's skill in marksmanship.

Ilkhani expects deference from his inferiors and proves his own to the shah and the Qajar princes, but he also expresses his exasperation at having to bear Qajar intrigue, which interferes with his efficiency as tribal leader and military and civil administrator. This sense of himself, and what he regards as the appropriate conduct for his roles, distinguishes Ilkhani's character. Some of the qualities important to him are obvious and relate to his family and the Bakhtiyari: leader, hunter, horseman and breeder, judge, arbitrator, host, and military commander. Others, however, are less obvious and demonstrate an additional trait in his makeup, an awareness of what was appropriate outside the Bakhtiyari context: poet and journal keeper, patron of religious shrines, and antiquarian (in preserving his own and his family's documents). An example of this last quality can be seen in his placement of an inscription at the site of a water reservoir at Dasht Gul – now deep in the lake behind a great dam: "By order of the Great Khaqan, Husain Quli Khan, Ilkhani of the Bakhtiyari, the work of the reservoir and waterway was completed, 1292[/1875]."[88] This notion of what is expected from a ruler – a stone inscription – and a sense of completion, in permanently associating his name with one of his projects, demonstrates his perception of professionalism and awareness of what was the appropriate conduct of not only a Bakhtiyari but an Iranian leader. His success, and perhaps this sense, contributed to his downfall: potentially, he was a leader of nineteenth-century Iran.

Ilkhani, in addition to expressing his exasperation with the Qajars, is aware of his limits when he notes, in his letter to Nasir al-Din Shah, that his brothers and sons can take his place and carry on, that he is not indispensable. From subsequent Bakhtiyari perception, however, he was indispensable. The death of this patriarchal figure marked the end of thirty years of relative Bakhtiyari unity and stability, and the contrast – even with the re-establishment of his family's dominance – led to posthumous charisma. Bakhtiyari have stated that there has been only one ilkhani in their history; the memory of Ilkhani as the ideal was the mark to which subsequent holders of that office would be held.

Chapter VI

The post-1882 Bakhtiyari

Ilkhani's death underscored the weakness of the Bakhtiyari when confronted by a determined central government which, even though traditional and decentralized, had the ability to manipulate internal divisions.

Ilkhani had regarded the Bakhtiyari as autonomous but recognized the shah as sovereign, generally obyed his orders, and accepted his awards of land and incomes. Nasir al-Din Shah on his part never sent a military force to challenge Ilkhani's autonomy; nor did he take military action in Ilkhani's sphere of influence, the territories immediately adjacent to the Bakhtiyari – i.e., Chahar Mahall and northeast 'Arabistan – without Ilkhani's assistance. Furthermore, Ilkhani was assassinated in Isfahan and not among the Bakhtiyari, where the Qajars feared an uprising.

The Qajars had earlier challenged strong Bakhtiyari leaders such as Muhammad Taqi Khan Chahar Lang. Why then did they allow Husain Quli Khan Ilkhani's power so to develop that by 1882 he seemed to pose a threat to their suzerainty? First, Ilkhani only gradually increased his power, always maintaining close ties with the Qajars and their ministers and governors. He performed services and cooperated with Qajar governors and was instrumental in the suppression of revolts, especially in 'Arabistan, thus winning confidence. He appears also to have been an effective governor of the Bakhtiyari, both maintaining order and remitting taxes to the imperial government. But finally, the Qajars assumed, and rightly, that they possessed greater power, that they had British and Russian support, and that they could appropriately reward allies or depose rivals.

The Qajar shahs, like their predecessors, attempted to uphold their authority, maintain their power, and limit tribal threats to their sovereignty through the retention of hostages at court, the resettlement of tribal populations, the division of tribal leadership, and the awarding of grants and favors. An equally important factor in limiting the power of the khans, however, was the internal tribal social and political structure. Even had the Bakhtiyari tribes, or their ruling families, been united, the state would have sought Ilkhani's removal, and – given its greater power – would have succeeded.

Following Ilkhani's death in 1882 and the formation of the three factions, the Ilkhani, the Hajji Ilkhani, and the Ilbaigi, it became possible for tribesmen to express disagreement by giving their support to one of the three rival power centers. In subsequent generations the potential number of khans eligible for the highest tribal positions increased dramatically. In each of these factions a significant factor, with political and economic ramifications, was increased rivalry in the elaboration of the bastagan system. The growth in the number of bastagan and in the number of khans eligible for the ilkhaniship resulted in increasing Bakhtiyari instability as the khans sought both the economic and the political means – within and outside the Bakhtiyari – to emulate Ilkhani and to accede to that office. In the disorder of 1882–94, the office of ilkhani moved from one faction to another as each maneuvered for imperial support. Bakhtiyari khans outside the Ilkani, Hajji Ilkhani, and Ilbaigi lineages, lacking their accrued political and economic advantages, were in no position to compete. Finally, in 1894, the Ilkhani and Hajji Ilkhani, with the support of Nasir al-Din Shah, drew up an agreement excluding the Ilbaigi faction and choosing the eldest from the former two families for the positions of ilkhani and ilbaigi.[1] This division was recognized by the shah's government and then by the British in the 1898 contract for the Bakhtiyari road; it was reconfirmed in the oil agreement of 1905 and in subsequent Bakhtiyari and British accords. All incomes, whether from tolls on the Bakhtiyari–Lynch road, tribal dues, guard service, or oil shares, were divided between the Ilkhani and the Hajji Ilkhani. Again in 1909, in a secret agreement between the two ruling factions, anticipated incomes and governorships from the successful outcome of the Constitutional Revolution were to be divided on the same basis. In 1912, by the conclusion of yet another agreement – but this time with British support – Sardar Jang was designated ilkhani for a five-year term. By this time the British legation had supplanted the shah's government as the most significant power in southwest Iran, and British support was to be sought in the same manner as the shah's had been in earlier periods.[2]

The framework for the resolution of leadership problems, increased incomes from British ties, and the southwest expansion of land holding into 'Arabistan allowed the khans to play increasingly national roles. This added to the number of variables necessary for power in the Bakhtiyari – position in the family, tribal base, land and incomes for retainers, and ties to the central government, the British, neighboring tribes, and urban centers. Ironically, instability at the highest level increased, but at the tayafah level there was increasing stability as those units aligned more or less permanently with either the Ilkhani or the Hajji Ilkhani factions.[3] The British presence allowed the khans a greater degree of flexibility – it was

97

possible for them to play Britain off against Tehran, other tribes, or even family rivals – but the expansion of British power in southwest Iran also exacerbated intertribal rivalry between the Bakhtiyari and the Arabs, the Qashqa'i, the Khamsah, and the tribes of Kuhgiluyah.

Three internal factors aggravating competition within the Bakhtiyari leadership and linking the great khans' rivalry to their national ambitions appeared early in this century as well. The first was the removal of the senior great khans either to Tehran or to one of the provincial capitals. Second, responsibility for governing the Bakhtiyari was left in the hands of their sons, two of whom were designated acting ilkhani and ilbaigi. Major decisions, however, were still made by the senior khans, who utilized the telegraph or messengers to convey them. The pool of junior khans from which these acting officials could be chosen had grown considerably, placing a strain on economic resources and intensifying rivalry on the local level. Finally, there was the opposition of the other tribes, especially the Qashqa'i, of Shaikh Khaz'al, the paramount Arab tribal leader in 'Arabistan, and of the urban population in Iran to the increasing role of the Bakhtiyari khans on a national level. The denouement to this process of alienation of the khans' tribal base was to be given by Riza Shah.

The 1894 agreement

In the twelve years following Ilkhani's death, 1882–94, the rivalry between the three factions – Ilkhani, Hajji Ilkhani, and Ilbaigi – reached crisis proportions and affected not only the Bakhtiyari but, increasingly, adjacent regions. After Ilkhani's death, his eldest son, Isfandiyar Khan, and a younger son, Hajji 'Ali Quli Khan, were imprisoned by the Zill al-Sultan, and Imam Quli Khan and Riza Quli Khan were appointed ilkhani and ilbaigi and remained in these positions for the next six years. But their appointments were now linked with the Zill al-Sultan's ability to maintain his ascending position in relation to Muzaffar al-Din Mirza Vali-'ahd and 'Ali Asghar Khan Amin al-Sultan (in effect prime minister but without that title).

Mas'ud Mirza Zill al-Sultan was a formidable power in the last decades of the nineteenth century, and until the end of February 1888 he governed all of Iran south of Kashan and west of Kerman except for coastal cities that were under the Amin al-Sultan. There were countless rumors that Zill al-Sultan was planning the overthrow of his father or that he would oppose the accession of the Vali'ahd at the death of Nasir al-Din Shah. This was credible to the shah for the following reasons: the British were soliciting Zill al-Sultan's support for a railway concession in the south and for the opening of the Karun river to international trade, and it appeared that Britain might be prepared to back Zill al-Sultan's claim to southern Iran on the death of the shah; Zill al-Sultan was jealous of his younger brother, who had been designated Vali'ahd because of his "royal" mother; Zill al-Sultan had a scale of living almost comparable to the shah's, which was extremely expensive to maintain; and he had the largest and best-equipped military unit in Iran. The animosity between Amin al-Sultan and Zill al-Sultan neared breaking point when Amin al-Sultan learned of the prince's attempt to buy off Malik al-Tujjar of Bushihr, who farmed the government and customs of the Fars littoral from Amin al-Sultan. When the shah refused Zill al-Sultan's request for the governorship of Kerman, Zill al-Sultan immediately resigned all of his governorships, not expecting his father to accept the resignations. But probably acting under the influence of Amin al-Sultan, the shah accepted all the resignations except for that of the governorship of Isfahan. This set off a chain reaction in central and southwestern Iran, as Amin al-Sultan immediately began to consolidate his power. The governors and leaders appointed by Zill al-Sultan fell with him and were replaced by Amin al-Sultan's supporters. Now Amin al-Sultan appointed Riza Quli Khan as ilkhani in place of Imam Quli and named Isfandiyar Khan as ilbaigi. Amin al-Sultan knew that this would immediately split the Bakhtiyari into warring factions, and he would be compelled to commission forces to restore order not only in Bakhtiyari but in 'Arabistan. He, too, wished to divide the Bakhtiyari and weaken their power. One of these armies was led by the newly appointed governor of 'Arabistan, Nizam al-Saltanah, who was accompanied by his brother, Sa'd al-Mulk, the newly appointed governor of Bushihr; they marched into Bakhtiyari against Imam Quli Khan and into 'Arabistan, in an attempt to impose the authority of the central government and to seize Shaikh Miz'al Khan of Muhammarah. Great Britain viewed this with a concern that was to echo through the first quarter of the twentieth century.

Were the Persians to acquire direct authority over the Arabs of Arabistan, and substitute Persian governors over the hereditary Chiefs of Mohammerah, our [British] influence and political power in these parts would be inconveniently affected. Sheikh Mizal Khan, like his father, Hajji Jabir Khan, has always placed his information and authority at the disposal of this agency [the consulate at Basrah], and he would at once, if called upon, hold himself and his tribe at the orders of the British Government. While he is the Chief, the position and resources of Mohammerah are potentially under British control for the extension of commerce or other purposes; and it is possibly a knowledge of this that has at the present juncture occasioned the desire of the Persian Government to depose him.[4]

With the Bakhtiyari in revolt and with the threatened removal of Shaikh

Miz'al Khan, all of southwestern Iran was in a state of unrest, and fighting
broke out as groups struggled for power within their own tribes or against
government forces in the area. By July, Nizam al-Saltanah brought a
semblance of order to 'Arabistan. For his aid in this Isfandiyar Khan was
given the title of Samsam al-Saltanah, but the revolt in the Bakhtiyari
continued for the next seven years. Shaikh Miz'al Khan was not seized,
but afterwards he was cautious to the point of refusing to enter the Persian
government vessel on the Karun lest he be detained.

The animosity between the new ilkhani, Riza Quli Khan, assisted by
Isfandiyar Khan, and the former ilkhani, Imam Quli Khan, resulted in a
number of battles, raids on each other's property, and thefts of the animals
of each other's supporters. Nizam al-Saltanah arranged a truce and an
unknown settlement, and it was during this truce that he used a Bakhtiyari
force, under Isfandiyar Khan's leadership, to secure peace in 'Arabistan
and to impress the authority of the central government on Shaikh Miz'al.

Then in 1890, at Nau Ruz (the new year, which in Iran is observed at
the beginning of the vernal equinox) Imam Quli Khan was reinstated as
ilkhani, Isfandiyar Khan remained as ilbaigi, and Riza Quli Khan once
again became governor of Chahar Mahall.[5] In 1892, before the tribe left
'Arabistan for its summer pastures, Imam Quli Khan and Riza Quli Khan
were imprisoned in Shushtar by the governor of 'Arabistan, and Isfandiyar
was designated ilkhani. The imprisoned khans then made an appeal to
Amin al-Sultan through Aqa Najafi, one of the leading religious figures of
Isfahan. Next the younger khans in the shah's service in Tehran joined
their brothers in the Bakhtiyari and began attacking and raiding their
cousins. Riza Quli Khan settled this for the time. Early in 1893 the
Bakhtiyari and Chahar Mahall were returned to the jurisdiction of Zill
al-Sultan, who had been newly reappointed governor of Isfahan.

The first act of His Royal Highness on receiving the appointment was to appoint
Imam Kuli Khan Ilkhani of the Bakhtiari and Reza Kuli Khan Governor of
Chahar Mahal . . .

The Sadr Azam at first insisted that Isfendiyar Khan should be kept in office,
and although the Zil-us-Sultan strongly objected as he had already telegraphed the
appointment of Imam Kuli Khan, he was induced by the firmness of the Sadr
Azam to offer the post to Isfendiyar Khan, who, however, positively declined to be
under His Royal Highness's authority, and the appointments made by the
Zil-us-Sultan were sanctioned . . .

The Sadr Azam, to whom I have spoken on the subject, tells me that he is
powerless to find a remedy for the state of things which exists in the Bakhtiari
country. The proper policy to pursue would be to attempt to conciliate the
different sections of the tribe, instead of which the Zil-us-Sultan apparently sought
to stir up strife between them. The constant fights which took place were a disaster

for the country which was thereby rendered insecure, while the villages in which the fighting took place were utterly ruined. The loss of a certain number of Bakhtiaris was perhaps no great matter, but the policy of the Zil-us-Sultan to foster enmity among the different sections of the tribe in order to prevent it from becoming too powerful, was, the Sadr Azam was convinced, a mistaken one and one which would probably lead to further trouble.[6]

By the end of 1893 Chahar Mahall and Bakhtiyari continued to be unsettled, and the tribesmen were raiding villages and caravans that were traveling between Isfahan and cities to the north. Isfandiyar Khan was in Tehran as a refugee in Amin al-Sultan's house, and Zill al-Sultan was demanding that he come to Isfahan to make his submission.

Meanwhile, Zill al-Sultan had so devastated the villages and property of Najaf Quli Khan, a younger brother of Isfandiyar Khan, that Najaf Quli was threatening to kill Zill al-Sultan. Consul Preece of Isfahan also reported that Riza Quli Khan paid Zill al-Sultan 70,000 tumans for past revenues due and 30,000 tumans as a present. (This would appear to be an exaggerated figure, unless this amount represents the assessment for three years, because in 1890 the tax paid to the governor of Isfahan was 22,000 tumans and the amount paid to the governor of Khuzistan 15,000 tumans.[7])

Apparently many of the Bakhtiyari had been opposed to Riza Quli Khan, who had been oppressive and rapacious. In 1893, as governor of Chahar Mahall, he seized 200 houses and businesses in Urujan and expelled their owners for failure to pay the tax that he demanded, and these people then appealed to Zill al-Sultan and to Aqa Najafi for redress; the latter telegraphed the Amin al-Sultan on their behalf. Finally, in 1894 – according to Sardar Zafar, who provides the only account of this critical development – the sons of Husain Quli Khan and Imam Quli Khan took steps to restore order and to remove all vestiges of power from Riza Quli Khan, who was sabotaging their positions not only as tribal leaders but as landlords. Central to the conflict were the Mizdij estates of the khans, some of which were tuyul for the maintenance of Bakhtiyari troops and the rest of which were claimed individually by the khans. (Part of this problem may have stemmed from the private portions of Mizdij that had been held jointly by Ilkhani and his brothers, and, with Ilkhani's unexpected death, no division had yet been made.) To resolve this matter, Nasir al-Din Shah, through Amin al-Sultan, appointed Zill al-Sultan as arbitrator. It was decided that those khans who had individual claims to the purchased portions of Mizdij would own them individually, and that the remainder would be divided between the governorship of the Bakhtiyari and the governorship of Chahar Mahall.[8] It was also agreed that the flock tax (gallahdari) was to be divided into three shares among the following three khans (probably for distribution among the three families they represented): to Hajji Ilkhani as the representative of his family; to Hajji 'Ali Quli Khan for the Ilkhani; and to Hajji Ibrahim Khan, who was Ilbaigi's eldest son, as the representative of the Ilbaigi.[9]

Shortly after this settlement – and again according to Sardar Zafar, who was one of the participants – Muhammad Husain Khan Sipahdar (later entitled Sardar Mufakham), Hajji Ilkhani's eldest son, proposed that the Ilkhani and Hajji Ilkhani branches exclude the Ilbaigi faction from the Bakhtiyari government. (Possibly they were assisted by Amin al-Sultan in this venture.) It was accepted and also agreed upon that the eldest member of the family would be the ilkhani and the next in age would serve as his ilbaigi, that after each khan had taken his personal share in Mizdij the remainder would be considered the common property of all, and that the central government should indemnify Najaf Quli Khan for his losses suffered in fighting. Before this agreement there had existed only the vague principle that any male in the khans' lineage was eligible to be ilkhani; during Ilkhani's long tenure in office, this was modified so that only those in his family or his brother's family would be candidates for his office. This was now more narrowly defined – the two families would share in the governing of the Bakhtiyari and the eldest of one family would be ilkhani and the eldest of the other, ilbaigi. Numerous skirmishes occurred between Ilkhani/Hajji Ilkhani and Ilbaigi forces, but the Ilbaigi family never regained its loss and its members were relegated to peripheral roles. (This basic principle of the sharing of power between the two families, although modified again, remained until 1936, when Riza Shah placed the Bakhtiyari under civil administrators.) To reinforce the initial agreement Isfandiyar Khan of the Ilkhani married the daughter of Muhammad Husain Khan of the Hajji Ilkhani, and Muhammad Husain married Isfandiyar's daughter. As further evidence of this new amity a representative from each of the families went together to Tehran to lead the Bakhtiyari in the shah's guard.[10]

Furthermore, in this last decade of the nineteenth century the khans were able to extend their influence as far south as Ram Hurmuz, where Amin al-Sultan sold them khalisah (crown property) at what the khans considered a low price, 10,000 tumans. (However, they also had to pay Nizam al-Saltanah 13,000 tumans, because part of Ram Hurmuz had been given him by the central government in payment for a loan.) This property was divided equally between Ilkhani and Hajji Ilkhani families, but there were disputes within each family as to how its half should be divided. Ilbaigi and his son Hajji Ibrahim Khan went to Tehran hoping to be included in this but were unsuccessful.[11] On the eastern side of the Bakhtiyari in Chahar Mahall the khans continued to be embroiled with

Zill al-Sultan, who was not only governor but also a large landowner in that district of his province.

The British and the Bakhtiyari

Also in that critical last decade the British – both government and private firms – began to play increasing roles in southwest Iran and the Bakhtiyari. Layard's earlier Bakhtiyari visit of 1843 had come to nothing, and Sawyer's military reconnaissance for the Government of India in 1891 would now be brought to fruition. Britain's nineteenth-century eastern policy was motivated by fears of Russian expansion through Central Asia, Afghanistan, and Iran to the borders of India. In Iran, Great Britain hoped to halt Russian advancement by adopting the principle of strengthening and reforming the Qajar government so that greater control could be exercised over that country. Consequently, in 1856–7, when Lieutenant-General Sir James Outram requested a change in his orders, which forbade him to deal directly with the semi-autonomous tribes in the southwest, permission was not granted.[12] At the end of the century, when there were fears lest Russian influence penetrate to the head of the Persian Gulf, Britain modified its policy in view of the Qajars' continued inability to rule.

Changes in the British policy of maintaining central authority, at least in regard to southwest Iran and the Bakhtiyari, were suggested by Lord Curzon, viceroy of India, when he wrote:

Whatever be the prospect of opening up . . . the country that lies northward of the Karun River, and this is inhabited by the Lurs and other nomad tribes, it is certain that British influence has obtained a material foothold in that corner of the Shah's dominions, through which the Karun flows in its middle and lower course, and where the road now being constructed through the Bakhtiari country, by contract between the Bakhtiari Chiefs and Messrs. Lynch, should open an alternative and almost exclusively British door of commercial access to Ispahan . . . We think that no opportunity should be lost of strengthening our influence with the Arab, Bakhtiari and Lur tribes . . . .[13]

Although Curzon's suggestions were initially sidetracked and ignored in the Foreign Office,[14] his ideas on strengthening British relations with tribal leaders gained support and paralleled similar notions in the Foreign Office, and were implemented in the first two decades of the twentieth century. With their strategic requirements in southern Iran and the Persian Gulf for the defense of India and their growing commercial relations in southwestern Iran, particularly after the discovery of oil in large quantities and the switch over to oil as the fuel for the fleet (1913), the British, even more than before, attempted to impose a stability on 'Arabistan and the Bakhtiyari that the Iranian government had seldom tried, let alone achieved. The British increased their commitments to Shaikh Khaz'al, the paramount Arab leader in 'Arabistan, dealt directly with the Bakhtiyari, and attempted to influence their affairs. With the shaikh the British were successful because they were dealing with one dominant leader. With the Bakhtiyari, however, they were less successful, but nevertheless attempted to bring the various tribal factions together in support of the ilkhani so that they could work with a single authority rather than with what they styled the "many-headed hydra of Bakhtiyari leadership". These policies prevailed until Riza Shah put an end to the autonomy of both the shaikh and the Bakhtiyari at the end of the first quarter of the twentieth century.

The Bakhtiyari road

The possibility of a road through the Bakhtiyari had long been discussed,[15] but at the same time the khans had certain reservations about it. They especially feared that the government might use it to control them. After the 1888 opening of the Karun river to commerce it was to the advantage of British political and commercial interests to push for a route there.

In 1895 J.R. Preece, consul-general of Isfahan, was sent into the Bakhtiyari to question the khans about the possibility of a road.

I [Preece] had one or two private talks with Isfendiar Khan together with Hajji Ali Kuli Khan . . .

   In the first case the conversation turned on the question of making the road from Ispahan to Shuster. They said that they were quite willing and anxious to do anything that they could to facilitate such an end, it was what they all wanted. They quite saw how it would open up their country and improve the prospects of the tribes, and generally help to the much wished-for end of taking the tribesmen out of their wild state and civilize them. This was a traditional idea with the Khans. The little things I pointed out could be easily done, they said, the only one difficult question was the bridge, that to them was the stumbling block. Although Hajji Ali Kuli Khan had taken this on himself, and for the tribe's sake was anxious to do something, yet he did not see what he could do. If they built a bridge, got from England, the Government would immediately assume that they were in an opulent state, and would increase their taxes. This was a question in which they wanted help. (A present of such a bridge as was necessary would be good policy, I think, if Her Majesty's Government are willing to help the Bakhtiari . . .)[16]

In these same talks with Preece the khans said that if they could have the right to levy a tax on the road they would guarantee the safety of the road, build caravanserais, keep the road in good repair, and place their own mules and muleteers on it. They went on to express fears that Great Britain might use the Bakhtiyari as a base and the road as a means of attacking the north or even of annexing 'Arabistan.

(The khans' fears were not groundless, because only five years earlier the Government of India had sent Major H.A. Sawyer on a military survey mission in the Bakhtiyari. Furthermore, Preece's report insisted upon British support for the ilkhani, Isfandiyar Khan, in his rivalry with the Zill al-Sultan. In later years he encouraged support for the factions of the khans who might be more cooperative with the British. And the stage had been set from the very beginning for British involvement in tribal matters.)

The concession for the Bakhtiyari road was apparently drawn up by Colonel Picot, British military attaché in the Tehran legation. Modifications were incorporated at the suggestion of the signatories: Mushir al-Daulah for the Iranian government and Isfandiyar Khan Sardar As'ad, Muhammad Husain Khan Sipahdar, and Hajji 'Ali Quli Khan for the two governing branches of the Bakhtiyari. The agreement was signed by them on 23 April 1897.[17]

During the negotiations for the concession and the agreement with Lynch, the Bakhtiyari khans were fearful lest the Iranian government find cause for intervention or that the British government, or Lynch Brothers, might obtain some advantage or control over them and their territory. At no time during the first fifteen years of the agreement were the khans to allow their tribesmen to have friendly contact with Lynch employees; the khans were to be intermediaries, and they maintained a hostile position toward them analogous to the one they maintained to neighboring tribes. Hajji 'Ali Quli Khan was the spokesman for the khans; although he was not always present at negotiations, no agreement was ever signed without his approval. It appears from the sources that he alone of all the khans was aware of the implications of these agreements, and he was always adamant, to Preece's chagrin, in guarding the Bakhtiyari's independent position in relation to Tehran, to the British legation, and to British firms. The khans profited from this venture, not only from the tolls that were collected but because the bridges served as collection points for the annual gallahdari as the tribes were migrating to the yailaq, and there was less opportunity to miscount or to evade the tax altogether, unless other migration routes were followed.

Lynch Brothers were primarily concerned with their investment. During the negotiations, when it became evident that a concession would be given not to them but to the khans, they did not object so long as there would be guarantees given by the Iranian government that, first, the

Bakhtiyari khans would carry out their end of the agreement, and that, second, in the event of their failure to do so the Iranian government would fulfill it. This hurdle was cleared when the government issued the following (19 October 1897):

The Persian Government having taken cognizance of the Agreement made between the Bakhtiari Chiefs on the one side, and Messrs. Lynch on the other, for the construction of a road from Ahwaz to Ispahan, and from Shuster to Ispahan, give an assurance that the aforementioned Bakhtiari Chiefs, or such Chief as may be appointed by the Persian Government in their place at the head of the tribe, will be made to carry out the terms of the said Agreement, and one of the conditions of the Chieftainship of the Bakhtiari tribe will be that the terms of this Agreement shall be carried out.[18]

This proclamation was significant because the government officially recognized the agreement between the khans and Lynch. In the event that the ilkhani and ilbaigi, two of the signatories, were deposed, the Iranian government would require the new leaders to execute the terms of the agreement. Lynch had not foreseen this problem arising.

In 1901, when Isfandiyar Khan Sardar As'ad Ilkhani and Muhammad Husain Khan Sipahdar Ilbaigi, two of the three Bakhtiyari witnesses to the Bakhtiyari–Lynch agreement, were called to Tehran, it was rumored that they were to be dismissed as tribal rulers. Their Tehran agent sought support from the British minister, Sir Arthur Hardinge, asking him to obtain a promise from the Atabak A'zam, the prime minister, that no change would be made while they were absent from the Bakhtiyari. Hardinge declined to commit British support to that extent, but he told the Atabak that any intended changes in the Bakhtiyari leadership might affect British commerce and that no change should be made while the two paramount khans were in Tehran.[19] This the Atabak promised.[20]

Tehran was more reluctant to agree to Lynch's reservation concerning guaranteed payments because the Iranian government believed that there was no direct gain for itself and that in its continuing financial crisis it could not take on any new responsibilities. It finally agreed, however, and on 19 December 1897 declared: "The Persian Government promises that in the event of the Bakhtiari Princes and Chiefs not paying the interest and yearly instalments on the fixed dates, in accordance with their agreement and guarantee made with Messrs. Lynch, the officials of the Persian Government will be responsible for the collection and payment of this money."[21] With this Lynch was prepared to give up its demand that the administration and management of the road remain in its control, but when disputes arose over nonpayment this company appealed to the British legation and not directly to the Iranian government.

On 14 December 1899 the suspension bridge over the Karun was completed, the road was open, and Isfahan could be reached after a journey of fifteen to eighteen stages. From a commercial viewpoint the Bakhtiyari road was a success; from 1900 to 1909 tonnage increased from 102 to 1,485 tons.[22]

Lynch Brothers complained constantly about the shortage of pack animals; the expected animals and muleteers from the Bakhtiyari never materialized, and most of the muleteers were established on the older trade routes and were reluctant to change. Preece reported that the khans did not want to place their own animals on the road, becuse: "This they consider derogatory to their position as chiefs."[23] The khans on their part charged Lynch Brothers for their failure to abide by the agreement in overexpending by £3,000, by failing to complete work on the road bed, and by failing to build additional caravanserais. The decline in tonnage and tolls in 1903 and 1908 was the result of insecurity caused by Bakhtiyari and Kuhgiluyah raids, but in the first three or four years there were surprisingly few complaints by Lynch regarding security. According to the concession given to the khans by the central government, they were to be allowed to pursue raiders and thieves; however, the Kuhgiluyah were under the governor of Fars, who objected to or prohibited Bakhtiyari pursuit. The khans requested British support at Tehran for the proposal that the Kuhgiluyah be placed under their jurisdiction; or, alternatively, that they be allowed to pursue the Kuhgiluyah into Kuhgiluyah territory. Hajji 'Ali Quli Khan, perhaps as a means of forcing British support, suggested at one point that the road be closed. In 1912 the Kuhgiluyah were placed under Bakhtiyari government, but their raiding continued until the end of World War I, when the Bakhtiyari with British assistance defeated them.

In the recurring disputes between Lynch and the Bakhtiyari the British either favored or more often, actively supported the Bakhtiyari out of fear that they might move into the Russian camp or that Russia might pursue its plan to build a railway or pipeline to the head of the Persian Gulf and thus be in a position to put pressure on the tribes. The Bakhtiyari–Lynch agreement marks a turning point for British relations with the southwestern tribes. Before this agreement there had been contact but no official relationship, and now this was to expand further with the discovery of oil in 'Arabistan.

Oil

William Knox D'Arcy was awarded his famous oil concession by the shah on 29 May 1901.

Drilling first began in November 1902 at Chia Surkh near the Iraq–Iran border west of Kermanshah. Two years later there were two producing wells, but there was still the unsolved problem of shipment of the oil. Drilling was then shifted to another promising area, the Bakhtiyari garmsir, and in 1905 drilling began in Mamatin and in 1907 at Maidan Naftun. In April 1908 G.B. Reynolds, the engineer in charge, received a cable to cease work, but he waited until this was confirmed in writing. Before confirmation arrived, oil was struck on 26 May 1908.[24]

While Preece met the khans on matters relating to the Bakhtiyari road the question arose about an agreement with the D'Arcy Oil Syndicate. The khans claimed that their consent was necessary before drilling could begin on their territory. In the autumn of 1905 Preece returned to the Bakhtiyari expecting to dictate the terms of an agreement and to have it accepted with little question. A number of changes had occurred, however, since his last visit in the spring. Just as internal Bakhtiyari factors affected the Bakhtiyari road, these were to impinge on oil negotiations as well. Najaf Quli Khan Samsam al-Saltanah (II) was ilkhani, and Ghulam Husain Khan Shahab al-Saltanah was ilbaigi; however, a power struggle was in progress in which Hajji 'Ali Quli Khan (Samsam al-Saltanah's younger half-brother) was attempting to consolidate his position with the central government, with Shaikh Khaz'al, and possibly with the Russian legation so as to replace his brother as ilkhani. (Samsam al-Saltanah probably had the stronger position within the tribe but only on this issue.) Hajji 'Ali Quli Khan took an independent position, jeopardizing the negotiations. During earlier discussions the previous spring the khans had suggested a 10 percent share in the profits, but when Hajji 'Ali Quli Khan arrived two days after the negotiations had begun he demanded 20 percent.[25] (He was partially angered by the gifts of a watch and gun given to the ilkhani and ilbaigi by the British government.)

During the negotiations Shahab al-Saltanah was most compliant, but he had to leave because of an illness and then death in his family. Despite his absence and Hajji 'Ali Quli Khan's intransigence, an agreement was reached: it was proposed that the khans receive 5 percent of fully-paid-up ordinary shares of companies formed to work the oil in the Bakhtiyari plus a cash settlement. This was cabled to London, and while awaiting the response the other khans hoped to persuade Hajji 'Ali Quli Khan to accept these terms. The company rejected the proposal. The khans then asked for 5 percent of the shares up to 200,000 and 2.5 percent of the balance issued.[26]

Preece was attempting to obtain the best terms he could for the Oil Syndicate, and Hajji 'Ali Quli Khan was attempting to do the same for the Bakhtiyari. He seemed unduly recalcitrant, but it must be remembered that, first, he was making a play for power within Bakhtiyari and was attempting to place the ilkhani and ilbaigi in a weak position; and that, second, Bakhtiyari dealings with a Western firm, Lynch – or, as it was now called, the Persian Transport Company – had not been perceived by them as just, nor did the Bakhtiyari leaders altogether trust British motives. Sixty years before, British forces had landed in the south, and only seven years earlier, at the time that Shaikh Miz'al was assassinated, a British gunboat had been sent to Muhammarah to maintain order. Even if British intentions were honorable, there was still Russian pressure on these friends of the British as well as some from the rapidly disintegrating central government.

The agreement between the Concession Syndicate Limited (D'Arcy) and the Bakhtiyari khans was signed on 15 November 1905 by Samsam al-Saltanah Ilkhani; Shahab al-Saltanah Ilbaigi; Hajji 'Ali Quli Khan; Nasir Khan Saram al-Mulk; J.R. Preece, consul-general of Isfahan; and George B. Reynolds for D'Arcy. Essentially, D'Arcy was given five years to survey and drill and to build roads and pipelines. The khans were to provide land – at no cost if uncultivated – and guards, and in return were to be paid £2,000 per annum and an additional £1,000 for the guarding of the pipeline when it was completed.[27]

In only a few months both parties to the agreement became dissatisfied: the khans had had second thoughts and the concessionaires were angry because the khans failed to provide the necessary guards, whose absence threatened the drilling. This failure to furnish guards was the result of tribal disunity. Hajji 'Ali Quli Khan had been designated ilkhani by the Atabak A'zam in December (he had also been given his late brother's [Isfandiyar Khan's] title of Sardar As'ad). He and the opposing faction, composed of both the Ilkhani and Hajji Ilkhani families and led by the former ilkhani and ilbaigi, Samsam al-Saltanah and Shahab al-Saltanah, had incurred heavy expenses within the confederation and in Tehran in their dispute over these important positions. As a result of this infighting, there was no agreement as to who should select and pay the guards. There was also the continuing dispute with the Persian Transport Company, which was presenting claims for Kuhgiluyah robberies. Sardar As'ad for one realized that similar claims by the Oil Syndicate could be higher than the Bakhtiyari had anticipated during the negotiations. At one point the Oil Syndicate considered the possibility of stopping work because the number of guards was insufficient. When the khans, therefore, pressed for renegotiations the Oil Syndicate looked on this as an opportunity to bring up its complaints.

In the struggle for tribal leadership, between December 1905 and May 1906, contradictory orders were sent dismissing and reappointing guards at the drilling sites. There were also fears among the khans that the quarterly guard installments would be paid to their rivals. Grant Duff, the British chargé d'affaires in Tehran, cabled Sir Edward Grey, the foreign minister in London, for permission to support Samsam al-Saltanah and the ilbaigi, Shahab al-Saltanah, against Sardar As'ad.[28] As a further concession to the former two, and to uphold the 1894 agreement concerning division between the two Bakhtiyari factions, Grant Duff informed the Syndicate that it should pay the quarterly guard installment equally to each of the four signatories and not the total amount to one of them.

In addition to providing this direct support of the Samsam–Shahab faction, the British legation took active steps to have the agreement recognized by the central government. A copy of the Bakhtiyari agreement was given to Mushir al-Daulah, who replied that the government could not do as asked:

I have the honour to state that the article in question [3 of the 1901 concession] only refers to the lease or purchase of lands about which the concessionaires can come to terms with the owners, but the latter cannot, without the knowledge or approval of the Persian Government, make with any person an agreement, the stipulations of which affect the rights of the Government.

The Persian Government cannot accept the agreement which the Oil Syndicate propose to make with the Chiefs and when the draft was sent to the Foreign Office a reply was sent in writing saying the Persian Government could not accept and certify the agreement in question . . .[29]

The Oil Syndicate had hoped that official recognition would give them support in case of dispute with the khans, and perhaps it was the khans who persuaded the Iranian government not to recognize the agreement so that a new one would be negotiated.

This concern for the central government's recognition of the D'Arcy–Bakhtiyari agreement continued into 1907, at which time Cecil Spring-Rice, the British minister in Tehran, believed that its opposition might be due not only to its desire to assert suzerainty over the tribe but also to its fear that relations between the British and some of the Bakhtiyari might become too friendly. He did not want to object too strongly to the government's refusal, because this might bring it to the attention of the Majlis, or National Assembly, which would adopt the government's view.[30] It was also explained to the British that the official objection to the Bakhtiyari–Syndicate agreement was "on the ground that the scope of the contract includes some territory which would appear to belong to the Persian Government". Should they "ratify this contract, they would admit that the territory in question belonged to the Bakhtiyari tribe".[31] This memo goes on to explain that some Shushtar sayyids claimed that a portion of this land was *vaqf* (religious endowment).

Internal Bakhtiyari politics and rivalries complicated their relations with the British – both the legation and the Syndicate. Samsam al-Saltanah and Shahab al-Saltanah had been reinstated as ilkhani and ilbaigi, but then, in April 1907, Shahab al-Saltanah was designated ilkhani by the shah in place of Samsam al-Saltanah.

Order was not the result. There were armed clashes between Samsam al-Saltanah and Shahab al-Saltanah. Samsam ordered the removal of the oil field guards. Both sides appealed to Spring-Rice and, in an attempt to win his support, each emphasized the danger that the other was creating and the threat this posed to British lives and property. The shaikh of Muhammarah was pleased with the fall of Samsam al-Saltanah and hoped now to settle his own differences with the khans. Samsam was ordered to Tehran under the threat that retribution would fall on his only son Murtaza Quli Khan, who was in the capital. Delays favored Shahab, who was attempting to marshal his support from the central government. Percy Loraine, who was traveling through the Bakhtiyari at this time, noted that Samsam appeared to have widespread support among the tribesmen themselves.[32] Samsam al-Saltanah refused to follow the Atabak's orders to proceed to Tehran. His men attacked a British legation courier, Kuhgi-luyah raided the oil sites at his instigation, and robberies were perpetrated by his men on the Bakhtiyari road. The new ilkhani, Shahab al-Saltanah, was more restrained and attempted to fulfill his promises by sending guards to the drilling sites and restoring stolen goods to the Syndicate.[33] But then in June, Samsam was reinstated as ilkhani and Shahab as ilbaigi. This restoration was probably related to the former's strength within the Bakhtiyari, an arrangement with the Atabak, and the removal of Nizam al-Saltanah from the governorship of Isfahan to that of Fars.

Unrest continued in the Bakhtiyari, and insecurity and the guard problem continued to plague the Oil Syndicate. Samsam al-Saltanah had been unwilling earlier to reach an agreement on this with D.L.R. Lorimer, the British vice-consul of Muhammarah, and the latter had placed his hopes in Shahab al-Saltanah's becoming and then remaining ilkhani. Lorimer wrote bitterly to the British minister and said that he would continue to work with the khans,

. . . but at the best they are a broken reed . . .

The unsatisfactory state of affairs is perhaps not entirely due to ill-will on the part of the khans, but largely to their total lack of administrative capacity, their want of trustworthy underlings, and their domestic quarrels which make them afraid in many cases of alienating to a rival the support of tribesmen who look on any form of discipline with abhorrence . . .

I have been inclined to minimize the danger to European lives and property, and on the whole I have been justified by events. It is with reluctance that now, owing to the spirit I see spreading among the irresponsible tribesmen, I feel myself obliged to adopt a more apprehensive tone.[34]

To meet this threat and to solve the guarding problem, twenty men from the 18th Bengal Lancers, commanded by Lieutenant Arnold Talbot Wilson, were ordered to Iran in November 1907. (Both Lorimer and Wilson became very knowledgeable about the Bakhtiyari but never understood the ambiguous relationship of the great khans with the tribesmen.)

Drilling continued despite the disagreements with the khans and oil was struck in April 1908. When it was determined that there were sufficient quantities to make exploitation profitable two companies were formed to make this possible. On 13 April 1909 the Bakhtiyari Oil Company was incorporated with an issued capital of £300,000, and the khans were given 3 percent of its shares in accordance with their 1905 agreement. And on 14 April 1909:

The Anglo-Persian Oil Company was formed with a capital of £2,000,000, divided equally into ordinary and 8 percent preference shares. On April 15 the ordinary shares were transferred together with a cash payment of £380,250, to the three shareholders in the original companies . . . In exchange the Anglo-Persian Oil Company received all the rights granted in the D'Arcy Concession, all the issued shares in the Bakhtiari Oil Company, and all of the First Exploitation Company's shares with the exception of the £50,000 issued to the Shah and his ministers. The bulk of these were, however, purchased by the Anglo-Persian Oil Company a year or two later.[35]

On 6 May 1909 guarantees of autonomy were given to Shaikh Khaz'al by the British, and on 16 July the Anglo-Persian Oil Company leased one square mile of Abadan Island for a yearly rent of £650 for the first 10 years, to be increased to £1,500 in 10 years, and the shaikh was given a British government loan of £10,000.[36] In 1913 the Admiralty changed over to oil as its fuel for the fleet. The shares in the Anglo-Persian Oil Company were doubled, and the British government purchased them and became the controlling stockholder. Then a thirty-year contract was placed with the company for oil at a special rate. 'Arabistan and the Persian Gulf thus took on new importance and were no longer valued primarily for their commercial significance and for the defense of India.

The Constitutional Revolution

At the same time that the great khans were concluding oil agreements, their primary interests were shifting from the Bakhtiyari to the nation and the constitution. Until 1909 they had functioned as tribal chiefs, military leaders, landlords, governors, and tax collectors in their own or adjacent regions. After 1909 they were to add to these predominantly provincial roles those of prime minister and cabinet minister on the national level, as well as governorships outside their traditional areas of power. In earlier periods the shahs of Iran had been largely successful in checking tribal threats to central power by encouraging intertribal divisions, maintaining hostages, and relocating tribal populations. In the first decade of the twentieth century, however, a new threat was posed to Qajar power by increased general discontent growing out of hostility to Qajar misrule and foreign, particularly Russian, domination.

Nineteenth- and early-twentieth-century Iran was ruled by an absolute monarch, and under the Qajars power had been shared by the royal family and its ministers and by the bureaucracy associated with them, religious leaders, great landlords, tribal khans, and important merchants. Oppression, despotism, and injustice inflicted by one of these groups could be partially mitigated by appeal of the injured to one or more of the others for support. Increasingly throughout the nineteenth century and into the twentieth, foreign intervention, the call for internal reform, and the impact of Western liberalism were felt. The last two were frustrated by the first and by vested interests within Iran. The constitutional movement and its hoped-for reforms in the areas of governmental organization, education, justice, and the establishment of order were thwarted by self-interest, lack of cohesion, and ineffective leadership abetted by Anglo-Russian rivalry.

Membership on the part of the Bakhtiyari and the ulema in the coalition that brought about constitutional reforms in Iran in the first decade of the twentieth century is perhaps surprising. The ulema and the khans should have been opposed to this liberal movement because they represented traditional power groups and parochial interests, interests which would be curtailed by the governmental reforms implicit in constitutionalism. Analysis by Keddie[37] has shown that many members of the ulema supported constitutionalist aims and participated in the movement in order to limit the autocracy of the Qajar shahs and continued foreign encroachments. When the achievement of liberal and secular institutional reforms seemed attainable, many members of the ulema took a more conservative and traditional stance.

The Bakhtiyari could join this alliance because by this time the Ilkhani and Hajji Ilkhani khans had become confident of maintaining their dominant position in the tribal confederation. With this confidence and with the increased revenues and support available to them as a result of their agreements with British commercial firms and understandings with

British consular officers, the khans were in a position to take advantage of the increased discontent and to play a larger national role. As hostages in Tehran and as military leaders the khans had become aware of the growing dissatisfaction with the Qajars and of proposals to solve Iran's problems by reform and by adopting Western liberal ideas and institutions. Only Sardar As'ad, however, saw that by playing a dominant part in this movement, one which had a chance of success, the Bakhtiyari could have a larger voice in a new government.

Sardar As'ad alone among the Bakhtiyari was fitted for this role. He was not the eldest member of the Ilkhani branch; therefore, he could only hope to win the dominant tribal position by staging a coup against his half-brother Samsam al-Saltanah. Such an attempt failed in 1905 despite the support of the Atabak A'zam. Sardar As'ad suffered from failing eyesight, and this, too, was perhaps a factor in the decline of his position among the tribesmen and a factor in his development as the family man of letters. (When he became totally blind he had a secretary who read to him and took his dictation.) He not only was better read than his brothers and cousins but had traveled more extensively. While in Europe in 1908–9 he had had contact with nationalist and anti-Qajar Iranians there. By convincing the Bakhtiyari that they should support the nationalist cause and should march on Isfahan and then Tehran in support of it, Sardar As'ad could gain the power necessary to play an expanded national role and to shape the new government to his, or the Bakhtiyari's, advantage. This call for support of constitutional government to further tribal or traditional political goals is seen in Sardar As'ad's subsequent roles in the cabinet. For the other khans, however, the immediate goal was perhaps the opportunity for new incomes and the control of the nearest prize, the governorship of Isfahan.[38] Once a course was adopted, it had to be pursued lest the wrath of the restored Qajars – especially Zill al-Sultan, who considered Isfahan as his own fief – would fall on them. The initial limiting factors to these aspirations were internal Bakhtiyari disunity and the opposition of other southern tribal leaders.

The Bakhtiyari khans' apparent inability to unite in common action in the nineteenth century and the first years of the twentieth was overcome during the Constitutional Revolution, when all except two of the major khans resolved their differences, marched on Tehran with Bakhtiyari cavalry and militia, and joined the nationalists to overthrow Muhammad 'Ali Shah and to restore the Majlis. The outward appearance of unity and the leading role of the Bakhtiyari khans in the revolution seemed to assure them a predominant position in national affairs. In 1912 Bakhtiyari khans were governors of seven cities including Kerman, Isfahan, Yazd, and Kashan, and one khan was prime minister and another minister of war. It can be argued, however, that the Bakhtiyari, though seemingly at the height of their power in 1912, were in a weak position. For they were opposed by many of the traditional elites; by the nationalists; by important tribal leaders such as the vali of Pusht Kuh, Shaikh Khaz'al of Muhammarah, and Saulat al-Daulah, ilkhani of the Qashqa'i (whose brother was allied with the Bakhtiyari); and by the inhabitants of many major cities where the Bakhtiyari khans held post-revolution governorships. The Bakhtiyari were also opposed by the northern tribal confederation of Turkmans, Shahsavan, and Kurds, most of whom were still supporting the deposed shah or one of his brothers. The Bakhtiyari troops, who constituted a large portion of the Iranian "army", never exceeded 2,000 in number, and would have been of negligible value – because they were untrained and poorly armed – against a combination of "Yifram" Khan's forces (Ifraim Sa'id, a Turkish Armenian), the rejuvenated gendarmerie, and the Russian-trained and -officered Cossacks. Other than this support and the greatly exaggerated strength of available Bakhtiyari tribesmen, the Bakhtiyari khans could rely only on the Qavams, the leaders of the Khamsah confederation. It was also popularly believed that the British legation would support the Bakhtiyari under almost any circumstances. Although Sir Edward Grey wired the British ambassador in St Petersburg, Sir George Buchanan, that Britain would support a regency under Sardar As'ad,[39] the khans enjoyed considerably less than full British support. However, their Achilles heel lay not in the strength of the opposition but within themselves and their own political instability.

The Bakhtiyari entered in an important and dramatic way into national politics in the course of the Constitutional Revolution of 1905–11, but not until its later phase after 1909. The revolution began in December 1905 with the bastinado of some merchants and sayyids and the subsequent protests and closing of the bazaar. Opposition had built up over increased foreign loans and intervention; the powerful role of M. Naus, the Belgian customs director; the increased oppression by the government in the provinces; and the autocratic and oppressive rule of the prime minister, the 'Ain al-Daulah. At this time there was no mention of a constitution, but rather demands for the dismissal of certain government officials, including the 'Ain al-Daulah, and the establishment of an *'Adalat-khanah* (house of justice) which was to be made up of representatives selected by the clergy, merchants, and landlords and to be presided over by the shah. This institution's primary functions would have been to abolish favoritism and to make all subjects equal before the law. In January 1906 Muzaffar al-Din Shah eased the crisis by promising action; however, not until an even more serious crisis in the summer of 1906 did he accede to the demands – to which were now added the demands for a constitution and a representative National Assembly. In September the Electoral Law was promulgated, and in October the Majlis was opened. The Fundamental Laws were signed by Muzaffar al-Din Shah, and ascribed to by the Vali'ahd Muhammad 'Ali, on 30 December 1906. The shah died eight days later. He was succeeded by the Vali'ahd, who had attempted to suppress the constitutionalist movement in Tabriz, where he had been governor. Muhammad 'Ali Shah ushered in a period of reaction not only in Tehran but also in the provinces, where the governors of Rasht, Shiraz, Isfahan, and Zanjan attempted to crush the movement and prevent the election of provincial deputies. In March 1907 the Isfahanis revolted against the Zill al-Sultan (whose governorship of that city was in its thirty-eighth year), and he resigned.

Early in 1909 the Bakhtiyari began to play an active role in support of the constitution. By this time Muhammad 'Ali had abolished the Majlis, arrested nationalist leaders, and suppressed the press. Riots flared up across Iran, and in Tabriz the shah was declared deposed and armed revolutionaries held the city against royalist troops. Great Britain and Russia, who two years previously had partitioned Iran in the Anglo-Russian Convention of 1907, urged the shah to grant a constitution and to reinstate some form of representative government as a means of restoring order. In November 1908 the shah's army began the siege of Tabriz, and the shah declared that he would neither restore nor grant a constitution.

In the south, Muhamad 'Ali Shah sent the oppressive Iqbal al-Daulah as governor to Isfahan. The new governor attempted to suppress the constitutionalists, who now sought to enlist outside support; this included the Bakhtiyari. The leading khans hesitated because of their own internal rivalries and because they wanted to assess the shah's strength. Late in 1908, however, an agreement was reached with the Isfahanis, who promised to support the Bakhtiyari and to pay Bakhtiyari expenses in Isfahan.[40] In January 1909 Zargham al-Saltanah, the eldest son of Ilbaigi, entered Isfahan with Bakhtiyari troops and helped the citizens depose the governor. On 5 January Samsam al-Saltanah, with another force, arrived at the city and assumed the duties of governor. He asked the shah to confirm him in this position, and the shah refused. Samsam's half-brother Sardar As'ad, who had been in Europe for almost two years, where he had had contact with Iranian exiles and direct experience with Western liberalism, wrote the following letter to *The Times*:

In some issues articles were published and their purport was to attribute to the present constitutional movement in Persia and to its leaders aims of a self-seeking and personal nature.

Permit me to state, Sir, in the name of my brother, Samsam-as-Soltaneh, with whom I am in almost daily communication, that these statements and insinuations are entirely devoid of foundation. The sole object of my brother in going to Isfahan was to put an end to the disorders that had broken out in that city. His present object is to preserve the peace and remove any pretext for foreign intervention in Persia or for foreign control of our national affairs. When his Majesty, the Shah, shall have convoked the Mejlis and thus restored the legal form of Government, my brother will at once submit himself to that Government and consider his mission as at an end.[41]

Sardar As'ad returned from Europe in March to take over the leading role in Bakhtiyari preparations for the march on Tehran. Upon his return he telegraphed the shah expressing his loyalty and urging the re-establishment of the constitution.[42] (It will later be seen that he also sought the support of Shaikh Khaz'al and obtained a loan from him.)

Sardar As'ad's foreign travels possibly had a direct impact on the Bakhtiyari political system, too. Just after his return, the two families, Ilkhani and Hajji Ilkhani, concluded another written agreement, the Secret Agreement of 1909.[43] This was a further extension of the 1894 agreement, and was undoubtedly influenced by the Lynch and Oil Syndicate agreements and perhaps by Sardar As'ad's European journey. But it was also composed in anticipation of the wealth and power that might be gained if they were to help establish a constitutional government, and it stated that all wealth and power should be divided equally between the Ilkhani and Hajji Ilkhani factions. This 1909 agreement reveals the true motivation behind Bakhtiyari unity and their pragmatic approach to the revolution.

In the spring of 1909 there was continued opposition to Muhammad 'Ali Shah throughout Iran. In April, under the pretext of protecting Russian nationals and property, the Russians intervened and occupied Tabriz. With this occupation the center of resistance moved to Rasht and Isfahan. In the same month the British and Russian legations applied a sharp goad to the shah in the form of a note pointing out that the only area over which he had complete control was Tehran, and that the Powers would grant him a loan if he would restore the constitution, convoke a new Majlis which would have to give its assent to the loan, grant amnesty for all political offenses and permission for exiles to return, and dismiss certain reactionary leaders.

The Rasht nationalists under Sipahdar A'zam moved slowly toward Tehran, arriving at Qazvin on 5 May and then delaying to await the arrival of the Bakhtiyari from Isfahan. On 3 May Sardar As'ad and Samsam al-Saltanah

. . . telegraphed jointly to all the foreign Legations expressing their gratitude for the measures taken to save Tabriz, but asking at the same time that the Powers should now interfere no further in their internal affairs. They added, after protestations of loyalty to the Shah, that they and all other Nationalists were about to march on the capital to force on His Majesty the fulfilment of pledges to his people.[44]

Throughout May rumors circulated in Tehran that the Bakhtiyari were split into the customary opposing factions, but the tribesmen finally began their march toward the north. (Actually the major khans were united in this action except for Amir Mufakham, who was one of the leaders of the royalist army; under his title Sardar Ashja' he had served the shah, who at that time was Vali'ahd and governor of Azerbaijan, for seven years.)

Part of the delay was due to lack of funds. The khans were able to borrow £2,000 from Shaikh Khaz'al – as well as from other sources – and when it was asked why he made this loan his agent replied

... that the Shaikh wished to get hold of Ram Hormuz and that the latest loan was not formally secured on lands there, yet it would greatly assist the Shaikh to acquire them. He said that the Bakhtiari now owed the Shaikh 30,000 Tomāns and would soon owe more and that the result would be that part . . . of Ram Hormuz would soon fall into the Shaikh's hands.[45]

Shortly before leaving Isfahan, Sardar As'ad called on the British consul, and said that "he had spent much money. The Shah would never forgive him. He intended crippling His Majesty utterly, and were it not for the fear of Russian intervention he would dethrone him."[46] Six days after their departure from Isfahan, the Bakhtiyari reached Qum; they were followed by the British and Russian consuls from Isfahan, who because of the promises made by the shah for the restoration of the constitution attempted to halt the Bakhtiyari advance – but to no avail.

On 26 June a second detachment of Bakhtiyari left Isfahan, and a third was being mobilized; this was to bring Bakhtiyari strength to 2,000 men plus a few pieces of artillery. Early in July 1909 the Bakhtiyari moved north from Qum toward Tehran, with the royalist army retreating before them. The prime minister announced that he "does not believe either the Bakhtiari or the revolutionaries are keen on a fight, and thinks the Shah's troops sufficient to beat them".[47] The two Isfahan consuls continued in the wake of the Bakhtiyari, still hoping to stop them. According to Bakhtiyari tradition, the Bakhtiyari were secretly encouraged by the British to continue. Two thousand Russian troops arrived at Inzali on 8 July. Meanwhile Sipahdar, the leader of the Rasht force, declared an armistice of two days (4–6 July) during which the shah could act on nationalist demands. Additional Bakhtiyari reinforcements were sent from Isfahan despite the strong protests of the British and Russian legations. And the unusual unanimity among the Bakhtiyari khans continued.

On 11 July the Russian army reached Qazvin, and suddenly, on 13 July, the Bakhtiyari and the nationalists entered Tehran without fighting a major battle. Sipahdar and Sardar As'ad professed loyalty to the shah, stating that their forces had come only to insure the restoration of the constitution. "They would treat the Cossacks [the shah's brigade, whose officers were Russian] as friends, unless provoked to do otherwise. The leaders intimated that they would pay the greatest attention to the protection of the life and property of foreigners."[48] This they did.

Fighting with the Cossacks continued for four days. The shah refused to agree to a truce unless the nationalists surrendered, but on 16 July he abdicated and was granted asylum in the Russian legation, and Colonel Liakhoff and the Cossacks surrendered. That evening the nationalist leaders, the chief mujtahids, and many members of the first Majlis met at the Baharistan formally to depose Muhammad 'Ali and to choose his twelve-year-old son, Sultan Ahmad Mirza, as his successor under the regency of Azad al-Mulk, the head of the Qajar family.

The first Majlis of 1906 had been faced with four almost insurmountable problems: finances, unification of the country, foreign intervention, and the machinations of Muhammad 'Ali Shah. These same problems confronted the second Majlis, which opened on 15 November 1909.

The treasury was empty; the provincial administration was in a state of chaos; and Russian intervention threatened. Cabinet crises were frequent and the Assembly, divided into numerous small groups, was split by dissension. Russian troops, which had been introduced into Northern Persia ostensibly for a temporary occupation to defend foreign life and property, were not withdrawn.[49]

In the first cabinet, Sipahdar became prime minister and Sardar As'ad was designated minister of the interior. Regarding these two leaders, Sir George Barclay, British minister, wrote Sir Edward Grey:

It is largely due to the prestige of the two victorious revolutionary leaders – Sipahdar and Sardar Assad, now respectively Prime Minister and Minister of the Interior, that the Government is able to carry on with its insufficient funds, and it is questionable how far a Cabinet, of which they do not form a part, could maintain such authority as the Central Government now possesses.[50]

In this position Sardar As'ad was able to select provincial governors; he appointed his brothers and cousins to posts in the south and the brother, and enemy, of Saulat al-Daulah, ilkhani of the Qashqa'i, to the governorship of Shiraz. The position of Sardar As'ad and the unity and power of the Bakhtiyari were immediately threatened when he began to play such an important role in the new government, for in a short time the southern tribes were aroused, fearful of Bakhtiyari pre-eminence. There were rumors that Saulat al-Daulah was preparing to march on Tehran.

In April 1910 the southern tribal khans met to sign an agreement to limit Sardar As'ad's growing power, which they considered a potential menace to their power in the face of the widely divided Majlis. Shaikh Khaz'al assured the British that it would be "absolutely colourless, and shall commit him to no aggressive action".[51] The British threatened to withdraw their support if it did. The political resident in the Persian Gulf raised the question with the Tehran legation about the possibility of removing Sardar As'ad from the cabinet so as to prevent a crisis from developing in the south. Sir George Barclay, however, thought that Sardar As'ad was the sole stabilizing member of the cabinet.[52] Reports were coming in that Bakhtiyari cavalry were raiding and inciting the tribes in Fars and in 'Arabistan.

The British minister spoke with Sardar As'ad about giving assurances to the southern tribal leaders. He replied that he was about to resign and leave for Europe, but that the Bakhtiyari troops would remain in Tehran. He also stated that the Bakhtiyari were not in 'Arabistan, as rumored, but in Fars in operations against the Kuhgiluyah.[53]

Shaikh Khaz'al, Saulat al-Daulah, and the vali of Pusht Kuh reached an accord on 17 April 1910[54] known as the Southern Pact. In this agreement the three united to protect Iran, complete and strengthen the constitutional government, maintain security and facilitate trade, extend their friendship to other chiefs and nobles who desired unity, support and protect each other, and support and maintain the independence of the Majlis.

Shortly before the signing Sardar As'ad resigned his position as minister of the interior, and the cabinet fell. This occurred not as a result of southern opposition but as a result of the question of an Anglo-Russian loan and of Great Power opposition to a private loan the Iranian government was secretly negotiating with a private British firm. The cabinet was reorganized, and Sardar As'ad became minister of war and Sipahdar, minister of the interior;[55] this change in no way limited the former's ability to select southern governors.

Late in the spring of 1911 Sardar As'ad had announced his intention to journey to Europe for eye treatment when the Khamsah tribal confederation leaders and Bakhtiyari allies, Qavam al-Mulk and his brother Nasr al-Daulah, were arrested. Sardar As'ad then threatened to join the opposition in the Majlis to force the cabinet to fall unless these men were released. There was general fear that the government would be unable to maintain order unless Sardar As'ad were propitiated, because he controlled some 1,000 Bakhtiyari cavalrymen in the capital. Without waiting for the settlement of the Qavam question and their conflict with the governor of Fars, however, Sardar As'ad left for Europe at the beginning of June.

The Bakhtiyari government

In the summer of 1911 a Bakhtiyari once again became a member of the cabinet when the threatened return of Muhammad 'Ali brought about a coalition cabinet which included Samsam al-Saltanah as minister of war. A state of siege was declared by the Majlis, which gave extraordinary powers to this minister. Samsam al-Saltanah then ordered 2,000 Bakhtiyari to prepare to march from Isfahan, and Morgan Shuster, the American who served as financial adviser, provided the funds. The Majlis was asked to place a price of 100,000 tumans on the head of the ex-shah, and Samsam al-Saltanah "was so enthusiastic over the idea that he declared his willingness to raise the money from his personal estate if the Majlis felt any hesitancy on that score".[56]

On July 26 a new cabinet was formed as the result of a loss of confidence in Sipahdar, whose loyalties were clearly suspect. Samsam al-Saltanah was selected as prime minister with the portfolio of minister of war. At the same time Bakhtiyari cavalry under Ja'far Quli Khan Sardar Bahadur, the eldest son of Sardar As'ad and later the third holder of this title, were distinguishing themselves against the attempted restoration of Muhammad 'Ali. In the west, against Salar al-Daulah, other Bakhtiyari distinguished themselves more by looting and retreat. As the Bakhtiyari, who had been mobilized by Samsam, began to arrive in Tehran, their khans made such exorbitant demands for funds that Shuster threatened to resign.[57]

Despite Bakhtiyari proclivities toward self-aggrandizement, Russia and Great Britain regarded the Bakhtiyari presence in the government necessary to maintain order. They were also felt to be a balance to the more militant nationalists. Although the Bakhtiyari leaders moved back and forth among the various political factions, they most often sided with the traditional pre-revolutionary elite. Despite qualified support from the Powers, the Bakhtiyari were generally execrated by the populace for their misrule, extortion, and misconduct.

The Bakhtiyari have generally been described as being venal and inept in governing Iran, especially following the coup of December 1911, but the question might well be raised as to the ability of any person or group to solve Iran's problems in the face of Russian occupation, Russian and British domination, internal divisions in the Majlis and country, continuing problems of financial solvency, repeated attempts to return Muhammad 'Ali to the throne, the absence of a body of people with administrative and governmental experience, and the breakdown of order. As minister of war, however, Sardar As'ad had initiated significant reforms in the Iranian army.[58] (Except for the Russian-trained and

-officered Cossacks, the army did not become an effective force until the advent of Riza Shah.)

Certain administrative reforms in the various ministries[59] were carried out in the period of the so-called "Bakhtiyari Domination"[60] of July 1911 to January 1913, but the program presented by Samsam al-Saltanah's cabinet has been more accurately described as "a program designed to forestall liberal and patriotic protests".[61] The first months of Samsam's premiership occurred while Sardar As'ad was in Europe. During this time an international crisis was precipitated in October 1911 when Shuster and the Treasury gendarmes confiscated the property of Shu'a' al-Saltanah for arrears in taxes, and later when it was decided to appoint Mr Lecoffre – a British subject who had worked for the Imperial Bank – financial inspector in Tabriz. These moves were considered detrimental to Russian interests in its sphere of influence. On 2 November, as a result of the abovementioned affronts, the first Russian ultimatum was presented demanding the removal of Treasury gendarmes from Shu'a' al-Saltanah's property and their replacement by the Cossacks and an apology by the foreign minister. The Iranian government answered with a promise to submit the question to an impartial investigation. There were then reports of Russian preparations to occupy the north. Despite British advice to accept the Russian demands the cabinet vacillated, relations were broken off with Russia, and a new cabinet was formed again under Samsam al-Saltanah. The order was then given for the removal of the Treasury gendarmerie from Shu'a' al-Saltanah's garden, and the new foreign minister Vusuq al-Daulah apologized to the Russian legation. On 21 November, two days before the presentation of this apology, Samsam al-Saltanah and other khans sought Sir George Barclay's response to a proposed *coup d'état*,[62] as well as the response of the Russians.[63]

Sir Edward Grey replied to Barclay: "We certainly cannot encourage *coup d'état*, but have no more intention of interfering with a Bakhtiari *coup d'état* in Persia. Attitude of both Powers should be one of neutrality to these internal movements so long as their interests are respected."[64]

The Russian minister in Tehran, Stanislaw Poklewski-Koziell, was instructed to work with Barclay and "he was to make sure 'not to repulse the Bakhtiaries and not to impel them to give up energetic actions against Shuster and the Majlis desirable from our point of view'".[65]

The Iranian government, complying with the first Russian ultimatum, expected a withdrawal of Russian forces, but three more battalions arrived, and six days later the Russians presented a second ultimatum demanding Shuster's dismissal within forty-eight hours, an agreement not to employ any foreign advisers without the prior approval of the British and Russian legations, and payment of an indemnity to defray the cost of sending Russian troops into Iran. The Majlis, against the cabinet's wishes, rejected this ultimatum, but the regent did not accept the cabinet's resignation.

The second ultimatum unified the country in opposition to Russia. Sardar As'ad was momentarily expected to return, and according to Barclay the other khans were trying to delay his arrival, which "may modify any plans which his brothers and cousins may have made in the meantime, as he is reported to be hand-in-glove with the Ultra-Nationalists or Democratic party".[66] Poklewski noted that Sardar As'ad's views would be crucial.[67] Unexpectedly, then, upon his return at the beginning of December, Sardar As'ad opted for moderation and supported submission to the Russian demands.[68] At this same time Sir Edward Grey sent the following message to Sir George Buchanan, British ambassador in St Petersburg, who had been discussing the problems of the regency and the government in Iran with A.A. Neratov, the Russian assistant minister of foreign affairs: "We should raise no objections to Sardar Assad becoming Regent should events in Persia necessitate such a change."[69] The Russians were willing to utilize the Bakhtiyari against Shuster and for a new government in Iran; however, they could not rely completely on the khans because of their close relationship with Britain and British commercial interests, and, as Kazemzadeh notes, "The Russians feared that Sardar As'ad might attempt to usurp the throne, a contingency 'most undesirable' in the eyes of Russia, whose government was firmly committed to the Qajars."[70] The Bakhtiyari sought Russian advice and support; they went so far as to offer to withdraw their opposition to Muhammad 'Ali if their own safety could be guaranteed by the Russian minister.[71] This hoped-for support was not unlike the support they expected from Great Britain during World War I should they take a position contrary to that taken by the central government.

On 15 December Russia threatened to move its troops from Qazvin to Tehran unless the ultimatum conditions were met. Sardar As'ad attempted to conciliate the Russians, and even the Democrats were willing to conclude some type of agreement with Russia, but insisted upon keeping Shuster, whom they believed the only one capable of stopping the sack of the Treasury. The Majlis voted, 39 to 19, to establish a committee of five to consult with the cabinet to come to a settlement with Russia.

The committee was appointed, the principal member being Sardar Assad, and at a meeting with the Cabinet on the 21st instant at the Palace, under the presidency of the Regent, the committee, under the strongest pressure from Sardar Assad – as Yefrem [Khan] . . . described it, "with Mauser pistols at their heads" – gave their consent to the Government's accepting the Russian demands.[72]

On 24 December the regent, Nasir al-Mulk, and the cabinet, with gendarmes and the Bakhtiyari cavalry, forced the dissolution of the Majlis, which was not to be reconvened until 7 July 1914. Shuster observed that only the 2,000 Bakhtiyari in Tehran and the presence of Russian troops 80 miles away at Qazvin kept the populace from attacking the regent and the cabinet.[73] To allay suspicions of a Bakhtiyari regency, Sardar As'ad sent the following telegram to H.F.B. Lynch on 24 December:

I desire to give every assurance that myself and my family do not in the least think of acquiring the Regency or of establishing a Bakhtiari dynasty. We shall serve responsible and Constitutional Government alone, and no other regime. Rumours of dissent between the Regent and myself are without foundation, as are all other rumours which mischief makers are spreading against myself and the Cabinet. The Cabinet is most trustworthy, and deserves the fullest confidence; it is inspired with only patriotic feelings. You can fully assure the friends of Persia in this respect.[74]

That Sardar As'ad did not succeed in being designated regent in place of Nasir al-Mulk was due not only to possible opposition from Russia and Iranian nationalists but also to traditional elements in Iran, especially Shaikh Khaz'al and the ilkhani of the Qashqa'i, and members of his own family who were fearful of the power that he might amass.

From the *coup d'état* of 24 December 1911 until January 1913 Samsam al-Saltanah was prime minister, but according to Yahya Daulatabadi[75] the real source of power was Sardar As'ad. Iran's sovereignty was all but lost because Russia continued with its military and diplomatic intervention, the cabinet recognized the 1907 Anglo-Russian Convention,[76] and Britain strengthened the autonomous position of Shaikh Khaz'al of Muhammarah with additional promises. Nepotism was the order of the day; Sardar Muhtasham, of the Hajji Ilkhani faction, was added to the cabinet, and other khans enjoyed provincial governorships. In June the regent left the country, and once again Sardar As'ad was accused of plotting for the regency when he called a meeting at his home to discuss the possibility of reconvening the Majlis – the only legal means of making a change in the regency. The Majlis was also needed to ratify a loan for the Treasury, which continued to be empty, but Russia was opposed to the seating of another Majlis.

In October Samsam al-Saltanah telegraphed the reactionary and exiled Sa'd al-Daulah to return for a possible premiership; however, this was opposed by the people of Tehran. Finally, in January 1913, Samsam al-Saltanah and Sardar Muhtasham both resigned from the cabinet, and 'Ala al-Saltanah formed a new one without any Bakhtiyari; however, this was not the end of Bakhtiyari power, since the presence of a large number of armed tribesmen in the capital always held out the threat of a coup. In

July 1913 the Bakhtiyari troops skirmished with the gendarmerie, and desultory fighting with occasional loss of life continued into August. Finally, bowing to pressure from the British legation, the Swedish officers of the gendarmerie, and the cabinet, the khans agreed to follow the British minister Sir Walter Townley's directives, which specified that all armed Bakhtiyari except for small escorts for each of the khans had to return to the Zagros. Without this military advantage, which often amounted to little more than nuisance value but was nonetheless disruptive, and with increased opposition to their misrule, the Bakhtiyari khans lost their superiority and were reduced to the level of other power groups. They also lost important provincial governorships except for that of Isfahan.

The Bakhtiyari khans rose to national power because of their military resources, and because the traditional leaders – first the Qajars themselves and then the elite, such as Sipahdar – became discredited as a result of their ineffectiveness. The Bakhtiyari lost power in the same way – they became discredited and their military strength was counterbalanced by the new gendarmerie. Traditional leaders, including Samsam al-Saltanah and Sardar As'ad, were unable, in the period between 1906 and the outbreak of World War I, to deal with Iran's financial difficulties, internal disorder, Russian occupation and intervention, and British acquiescence to Russian schemes. Iranian nationalists hoped that constitutional and parliamentary government and administrative reforms, especially those begun by Morgan Shuster in the Treasury, would strengthen Iran and allow it to deal with internal problems and foreign domination. Nationalist aspirations were crushed by Russian moves and by the traditional leaders, who, like the Russians, opposed a strengthened and centralized government, which would limit their access to political and financial gain. Sardar As'ad was more sympathetic toward nationalist and reformist aims; nevertheless, the Bakhtiyari and the governments in which they participated fell far short of achieving these aims. They were handicapped by their own lack of experience and the enormity of the problems with which they had to deal, by their own traditional attitudes and ties, and especially by divisions within their own families. Few decisions could be implemented without regard both for the division of power and wealth between the Ilkhani and Hajji Ilkhani and for the opposition of southern tribal leaders, who feared Bakhtiyari encroachment on their prerogatives.

Internal Bakhtiyari developments

The Ilkhani/Hajji Ilkhani agreement of 1894 had restricted paramountcy within the Bakhtiyari confederation to the two eldest males of those two families. The first part of this principle, selection of the ilkhani and ilbaigi from these two families, was observed until Riza Shah removed the ilkhaniship from the Bakhtiyari and placed it under his direct administration, and the second part, selection by primacy of age, was followed, with two exceptions, until 1912; however, in both these cases, Sardar As'ad in 1906 and Shahab al-Saltanah in 1907 – the claimants to the position of ilkhani – had the backing of the central government but not that of the tribe, and their tenure lasted only a few months. Since 1895 Isfandiyar Khan Sardar As'ad (Ilkhani faction) had been ilkhani, and upon his death in 1903 his cousin and ilbaigi, Muhammad Husain Khan Sipahdar (Hajji Ilkhani faction), became ilkhani, and Najaf Quli Khan, the eldest of the Ilkhani, became ilbaigi. The latter became ilkhani upon the death of Sipahdar in 1905, and Ghulam Husain Khan Shahab al-Saltanah, the next in the Hajji Ilkhani branch, was designated ilbaigi. In 1910 an acting ilkhani and ilbaigi were selected because the senior great khans were active in national affairs, and they delegated their authority to their sons. Thus the principles established in the 1895 agreement were essentially honored. This was strengthened by the Secret Agreement of 1909, which clarified the division of power between the two factions and specified that the hoped-for spoils of the revolution would be shared.

The 1909 Secret Agreement was signed by the Ilkhani and Hajji Ilkhani factions after Sardar As'ad's return from Europe on 3 April 1909 and ratified in June. It begins by stating that it is for the purpose of "promoting the national movement, strengthening the constitutional cause, and promoting good feelings between the abovementioned families [Ilkhani and Hajji Ilkhani]". It continues by stipulating that Zargham al-Saltanah (head of the Ilbaigi faction) is to be excluded from all Bakhtiyari affairs. All benefits and distinctions obtained from the government or nation and all taxes and income, whether from the Bakhtiyari, Chahar Mahall, Isfahan, or other parts of Iran, will be divided equally. (Necessary expenses and the maintenance of militia at Isfahan will be deducted from the Isfahan income before the division is made.) Sardar As'ad for the Ilkhani and Salar Ashraf for the Hajji Ilkhani will discipline any member of the family who is yaghi (a rebel). It adds:

If the constitutional Government is established and the members of the Hussein Kulli family obtain any Government posts, further if the said new Government shall wish to remove the Sardar Muhtesham [formerly Shahab al-Saltanah] and the Salar Asharaf from the administration of the Bakhtiari and the Chahar Mahal, and should wish to give the said administration to the members of one family, having dispossessed the other, those in office shall not accept, except on the condition that the said administration is equally divided.[77]

Also, Sardar As'ad promises to prevent his brothers Samsam al-Saltanah and Sardar Zafar (Hajji Khusrau Khan, formerly Salar Arfaʿ) from fighting with Sardar Muhtasham and Salar Ashraf. Another item concerns Amir Mufakham (formerly Shujaʿ al-Sultan) and Sardar Jang, two khans who were supporting the shah: the property, horses, and guns of any of their followers who return to the Bakhtiyari are to belong to Sardar Muhtasham. The agreement was witnessed by Aqa Nurullah (an Isfahan mujtahid).

In June subsidiary agreements promising support of the main document were signed.[78] (The preamble to the agreement includes the name "Salar Hishmat" with the Ilkhani faction. This probably refers to Imamallah Khan Sardar Hishmat, brother of Zargham al-Saltanah, and, therefore, an Ilbaigi. Sardar Hishmat had married one of Sardar Asʿad's daughters.[79]) But clause 1 refers to only the two families, which means Ilkhani and Hajji Ilkhani.

The 1909 agreement makes no mention of tribal responsibilities or division of duties. A third agreement dated 10 July 1912, written under British legation supervision, spells these out in some detail and makes more basic changes in the Bakhtiyari system. This was a move on the part of the British to stabilize the Bakhtiyari after the senior great khans had left their territory in the hands of the younger khans. Dr M.Y. Young, an official of the oil company, wrote:

It has been our chief trouble during the past two years that there was no proper authority here to whom matters could be referred for immediate attention. Since the senior Khans have gone to Tehran and other towns, they have regarded the Governorship of their own country as of minor importance. Sirdar Ashja, in an outburst of confidence, said to me one day last winter: "The life of nomads is no longer a life for us and to rule the Lurs our children are good enough."[80]

The British, both the legation and the oil company, hoped that order and stability could be achieved by the appointment of an ilkhani for a definite period of five years, with a detailed agreement on responsibilities approved by the khans. An analysis of this document reveals many of the problem areas in the Bakhtiyari government. No mention is made in this third agreement of the shah's confirmation or "appointment" of the ilkhani; however, the Iranian government at this time had a Bakhtiyari, Samsam al-Saltanah, as prime minister, and his brother, Sardar Asʿad, was minister of war. The 1912 agreement[81] begins:

We, the undersigned, have, with complete confidence . . . by order of the Imperial Government and of our own family, appointed Serdar Jang [Nasir Khan] to the Governor in Chief of Bakhtiari, Chahar-mahl [sic], Kuhgluieh [sic] and Behbehan from the present year . . . [March 1912 to March 1917] which constitutes five complete years. He will independently and powerfully, with absolute authority, be independent "Ilkhani" of the Bakhtiari tribe . . .

Thus Sardar Jang is given sole power and authority to deal with problems in the Bakhtiyari and the other places mentioned. Kuhgiluyah had been removed from Fars with the expectation that Kuhgiluyah could become pacified. Since 1907 Bihbahan had been governed jointly by Shaikh Khaz'al and a Bakhtiyari governor, but in 1912 it was placed solely under the Bakhtiyari.

Not since the death of Ilkhani had any ilkhani been given such authority and – on paper – power. Previously a consensus of the great khans had been required before a decision could be carried out, which was difficult to achieve because of the factions and jealousies within the two families. In the immediately preceding period, when there had been deputy ilkhanis and ilbaigis, decisions were delayed until their seniors had deliberated in Tehran and had sent their recommendations back.

Article 1 extends the ilkhani's authority and allows him to select his own ilbaigi, but he must be chosen from the Ilkhani branch because Sardar Jang is Hajji Ilkhani. This conforms to the old principle of selecting the two leaders from each of the two families, but here the ilbaigi is chosen not on the basis of age but upon his ability to work with the ilkhani. Earlier there had been attempts by ilbaigis and their faction to sabotage the ilkhani's directives and position, and vice versa. It was hoped this would be ended. Sardar Jang's ilbaigi was to be one of the third-generation khans, Murtaza Quli Khan, Samsam al-Saltanah's eldest son.

Article 2 gives these two leaders jurisdiction over all the khans descended from Ja'far Quli Khan, Husain Quli Khan Ilkhani's father, which extends their control over the khans of the Ilbaigi faction as well. If necessary they can even expel troublesome khans from the Bakhtiyari.

If any of the sons (or descendants) of the late Jaafer Kuli Khan should disobey or rebel, they (the "Ilkhani" and "Ilbegi") will have the right to punish them severely with personal and tribal force. Should the affair become serious and should the disobedient person or his dependants sustain loss of property or of life no member of the family will have the right to complain.

Article 3 extends their jurisdiction to cover the khans of the other tayafahs, kalantars and kadkhudas, and Bakhtiyari tribesmen; they are given the right "to dismiss or appoint, and to grant or withhold salaries". Sardar Jang and the ilbaigi are empowered to collect all the Bakhtiyari and Chahar Mahall revenues – the gallahdari of Faridan and Chahar Mahall, the oil company guard money, and road tolls – and they are to make the necessary disbursements for the oil company guards and repairs on the roads and the bridges. "No member of the family will, on any account, have the right to interfere or to claim any share." Previously receipts had been divided equally, at least in theory, between the two families. Each family had had to pay out of its share for repairs, claims, guards, etc., but they could seldom agree on this and had usually delayed.

Article 5 covers the maliyat, taxes paid to the central government. Out of Bakhtiyari revenues the ilkhani is to pay the government allowances of the ilkhani, the ilbaigi, and the officers in charge of Bakhtiyari troops in the government's service, and also maintain them. He is also to make payments on the outstanding installments to the Persian Transport Company. "If there should be a small balance it is to be paid to the special Bakhtiari sowars [savars, or cavalrymen]. Should the Government claim the balance of the Bakhtiari 'maliat', the family must be responsible for it and Serdar Jang and Morteza Kuli Khan will not be answerable for the same."

As working capital, £8,000 had been borrowed for the ilkhani from the Imperial Bank of Persia, and article 6 states that it is his responsibility to make the proper payments, and that in the case of his dismissal or death it will be the responsibility of the next ilkhani. This £8,000 is to be used to pay arrears to Tehran, road guards, and the expenses for the impending expedition against the Kuhgiluyah. Article 7 requires the khans of the family who had already collected the various revenues to turn them over to Sardar Jang. Under article 8, those khans in Tehran or other provincial centers who require savars will have to pay Sardar Jang fifteen tumans for each one before he can dispatch them. The agreement was signed by the two senior members of each family, Samsam al-Saltanah and Sardar As'ad for the Ilkhani and Sardar Muhtasham and Amir Mufakham for the Hajji Ilkhani.

Alignments between factions in the Bakhtiyari and the neighboring tribes were important factors in internal Bakhtiyari politics. The most important of these were the Arab tribes under the suzerainty of Shaikh Khaz'al. Bakhtiyari relations with Shaikh Khaz'al fell into three categories: as landlords, as tribal leaders, and as political allies or enemies. The shaikh was initially a co-purchaser with Sardar Zafar, and probably with Sardar As'ad, of Zaitun, a rich agricultural district south of Bihbahan. But at the same time the shaikh was feuding with their elder half-brother, Najaf Quli Khan Samsam al-Saltanah.[82]

The Bakhtiyari road was another area involving a jurisdictional dispute between the khans and the shaikh. A small segment of the road fell within the limits of the shaikh's territory. Although the khans were responsible, according to their concession from the shah and the agreement, for the security of the road, they were hampered in the pursuit of raiders who fled from the Bakhtiyari into Fars and 'Arabistan. The British feared that

Bakhtiyari/Shaikh Khaz'al disputes might lead to a large-scale battle; this same potential was present in the problem of raids on the road. The Kuhgiluyah were the most frequent raiders, but there were also raids by Bakhtiyari, Arabs, and Qashqa'i. The British approached the shaikh on the question of assisting in the maintenance of the security at his end of the road, but he felt the road was an expense he should not have to bear; he could not afford to maintain guards on it or along his border with the Bakhtiyari, where similar incidents could conceivably arise.

The Kuhgiluyah were never able to pose a major threat to the Bakhtiyari in the same manner as the Arabs under Khaz'al and the Qashqa'i; like these two larger confederations, the various sections of the Kuhgiluyah had political and affinal ties with the two major factions in the Bakhtiyari. During internal crises in the Bakhtiyari and then during periods of national unrest – 1909, 1912, and 1915 – the Kuhgiluyah increased the intensity of their raids. The first serious attacks began occurring in the summer of 1905, when eighteen unladen and two laden mules were carried off.[83] Pressure was put on the khans and the central government to make full recovery, and by the following March Mushir al-Daulah reported to Grant Duff, the British chargé d'affaires, that the khans had recovered 2,615 tumans in cash, sixteen mules, and five donkeys with only 400 tumans still outstanding.[84] This was one of the occasions when the khans were successful in recovering stolen money and property. Although their concession from the shah authorized the Bakhtiyari to pursue raiders, the governors and tribal leaders were reluctant to have the Bakhtiyari savars moving through their territory: there was the danger of theft and damage and of fighting and resistance by local groups, as well as the fear that the Bakhtiyari might succeed in extending their own political influence and absorb new territory. It was this threat of Bakhtiyari power following their successful role in the Constitutional Revolution that brought three of their most powerful neighbors – Shaikh Khaz'al, Saulat al-Daulah, ilkhani of the Qashqa'i, and the vali of Pusht Kuh – together in the 1910 Southern Pact, in which they agreed to resist expansion of Bakhtiyari power to the national level.

The events in 1910[85] in the Bakhtiyari point up the essential problems in their political system. The khans were split into two major descent groups: the sons and grandsons of Ilkhani versus the sons and grandsons of Hajji Ilkhani. (Sardar Hishmat, a son of Ilbaigi and a partisan of the Ilkhani faction, was attempting to be included in the power system. Sardar Hishmat married one of Sardar As'ad's daughters as well as one of Samsam al-Saltanah's, and three of his full brothers also married either daughters of Samsam al-Saltanah or daughters of Sardar Zafar.). In 1910 alignments followed these family lines, but on earlier occasions, such as the 1905 struggle for the ilkhaniship between Samsam al-Saltanah and Sardar As'ad (half-brothers), the Hajji Ilkhani faction supported Samsam, but later there were some defections to Sardar As'ad. The British recognized and worked within the basic framework of the two divisions. For the Bakhtiyari road the khans first divided their shares into two and then as follows:[86]

Ilkhani	*Hajji Ilkhani*
(1) Hajji 'Ali Quli Khan Sardar As'ad	(1) Ghulam Husain Khan Sardar Muhtasham
(2) Najaf Quli Khan Samsam al-Saltanah	(2) Nasir Khan Sardar Jang
(3) Yusif Khan	(3) Sultan Muhammad Khan
(4) Khusrau Khan Salar Arfa'	(4) Lutf 'Ali Khan [?]
(5) and (6) sons of Isfandiyar Khan	(5) and (6) [?]

A similar division of oil company shares – 11,670 in the Bakhtiyari Oil Company and 15,540 in the First Exploitation Company – was observed by the two families. One-half were issued jointly to Ghulam Husain Khan Sardar Muhtasham and Nasir Khan Sardar Jang and one-half jointly to Najaf Quli Khan Samsam al-Saltanah and Hajji 'Ali Quli Khan Sardar As'ad. Each half was then divided into thirds and these thirds were shared, with one exception, by full brothers: (1) the sons of Isfandiyar, Najaf Quli and Yusif, and 'Ali Quli and Khusrau; and (2) the sons of Muhammad Husain and 'Ali Akbar and Muhammad Riza (this is the exception), Ghulam Husain and Sultan Muhammad, and Lutf 'Ali and Nasir. Similarly the parties to the various agreements among themselves or with the British followed the two divisions.

The Bakhtiyari struggle in 1910 also illustrates the various mechanisms at work to check tribal disunity and the power of the khans: the withdrawal of support of the tayafahs of the tribe, the formation of intertribal alliances, and mediation by urban religious leaders, the central government, and the British legation. The recognition of the shah's government, and subsequently the British legation, was required to maintain the ilkhani in his position. When Sardar As'ad temporarily succeeded in deposing Samsam al-Saltanah (1905), the Amin al-Sultan sent him the following telegram:

As it is His Majesty's desire to see the welfare of the Bakhtiari, its proper organization, and tranquil order, the office of Ilkhani and Ilbagi is being permanently granted to you, for which the confirmatory Commission will duly follow.

You will hereafter attend to organize, order the tribal affairs, punish and reward those who deserve. You will in future deal strictly with those who cause disturbance, and at any rate future order must be assured. If any of your relations cause disorganization among the "ils" his estate must at once be confiscated, and he will thereupon be dealt with as Government's betrayer.

You are placed in a position to control the affairs of the Bakhtiari tribes and you will thereupon be held responsible. On the contrary to the past and previous years, order and organization must be restored.

The necessary telegraphic orders are being sent to the Governor-General of Arabistan to render you any assistance you may stand in need of for organization of your affairs.[87]

It was through his personal relationship with the Atabak that Sardar As'ad was given this position, and it was through Shahab al-Saltanah's ties to Muhammad 'Ali Shah that he was awarded this position in 1908. But in both cases, Bakhtiyari tradition and alliances were the ultimate electors, and Samsam al-Saltanah was reinstated.

The shah's recognition provided the ilkhani with power, with prestige, and with the possibility of military and economic support from one of the governors, either of Isfahan or of 'Arabistan. As early as 1903 the khans had sought the prestige and support of the British legation, and they similarly looked to the British as a potential mediator in their disputes, particularly with Shaikh Khaz'al.

Finally, in 1912, Sir Walter Townley could dispatch a consular corps of twenty-one men so that: "It will be made quite clear to the minor khans, who are inclined to give trouble, that Sardar Jang enjoys the moral support of His Majesty's Legation, and I hope that the new ilkhani will thus be enabled so to strengthen his position as to render himself paramount."[88] The instability in Bakhtiyari leadership that necessitated these various agreements followed a pattern: a force would be assembled for battle, both sides would square off, and, after a few feints, terms for a withdrawal would be arranged. Only occasionally did these encounters result in substantial loss of life, but they were attempts to gain an advantage and to pursue it during the negotiations for a settlement. After an agreement had been reached the disadvantaged party would wait for a more opportune occasion, reassemble its support, and resume hostilities. But the most important mediating factor was the Bakhtiyari polymorphic structure, in which economic, social, and political interests and unity were the focus of small units within the tribe. Any threat to the goals of these small units was met by the transfer of support to a rival party to balance the effects of concentration of power. To assure broad tribal support and to work the system to their own advantage, khans established networks of relationships based on social ties, marriage and blood; economic bonds, pastures and booty; and political links and alliances. Implicit in this problem is also the question of an outside enforcing authority. The use of sealed Qur'ans or the witness of religious dignitaries were attempts to appeal to some higher authority for recognition of agreements; on the secular side, the central government and the British legation played a similar role. In this period the central government was seldom in a position to enforce these agreements, but rather exploited the existing disunity to its own advantage. British aspirations for five years of stability under Sardar Jang were not realized. The Ilkhani faction was jealous of his power, Sardar Jang felt that he was not receiving his share of the incomes, and the British themselves withdrew their backing because of his amorphous position in regard to World War I crises – those involving Shaikh Khaz'al, Wassmuss, and Iranian neutrality. And the British with their failure to bring unity and stability to the Bakhtiyari resorted to direct payments and military support.

The Bakhtiyari and World War I

After World War I broke out Iran declared itself neutral (1 November 1914); nevertheless, it was to be the scene of a number of major battles. As Russian troops still occupied northern Iran, and as Turkey was allied with the Central Powers, it was inevitable that Iranian Azerbaijan should see some of this conflict. There were strong pro-German as well as pro-Turkish sentiments in Iran, the former out of distrust of the British and Russian roles in Iran, and the latter out of sympathy for co-religionists. German military missions, especially the one led by Wassmuss, the "German Lawrence", were working among the southern tribes, particularly in Fars. In January 1915 Wassmuss appeared in Shushtar, and religious leaders were preaching jihad. The younger Bakhtiyari khans had been restive and wanted to play a more dominant role in Bakhtiyari and national affairs. The war gave three of them the opportunity to express this by joining Turkish forces near Kermanshah, and one of the leading bibis, Bibi Maryam, was to lead a troop of German soldiers through the Bakhtiyari. Bakhtiyari unity and government were once again strained. Sardar Jang had had heavy expenses in attempting to put down Kuhgi-luyah raids, to control the younger khans, to protect the oil sites and Bakhtiyari road, and to maintain general order. The ilkhani also thought that the other khans, especially Samsam al-Saltanah, now governor of Isfahan, were giving him neither support nor his share of their incomes from governorships as promised in the 1912 agreement. In recognition, however, of the comparative stability maintained by Sardar Jang, Sir

Walter Townley suggested that he be awarded a K.C.M.G., and also that a K.C.I.E. be given to Sardar As'ad so as not to slight the other factions.[89]

By this time Abadan was exporting 25,000 barrels of oil a month. In February 1915 the pipeline was cut. Then it was reported that Sardar Jang had assisted Wassmuss through the Bakhtiyari. Dr Young vouched for Sardar Jang's loyalty and wrote: "the Sirdar had his own Mullahs to reckon with".[90] He also reported that the pipeline was sabotaged not by the Bakhtiyari but by the shaikh's Bavi tribesmen who were in rebellion. Despite Young's assurances there were misgivings about the loyalty of the Bakhtiyari khans. As a result of the unsettled religious and political conditions in 'Arabistan, Shaikh Khaz'al, with British support, asked Sardar Jang for cooperation in guarding the pipeline and in dispatching Bakhtiyari troops to Ahvaz.

Sardar Jang's equivocal response to the shaikh prompted the British to begin withdrawal of some of their support for him. The viceroy of India informed London that because of Sardar Jang's assistance to the Germans and reply to Khaz'al, he would be opposed to the awards of honor being given to the khans.[91] Townley concurred, but added: "I am convinced that Jang's good-will can best be secured by money. Khans have lost their influence, and could be made to accept any arrangement made with Jang and Bahadur."[92] (Ja'far Quli Khan Sardar Bahadur, later Sardar As'ad [III] and Riza Shah's minister of war, was Sardar As'ad's eldest son and now his spokesman, because Sardar As'ad was by now blind.) Sir Percy Cox was authorized to meet Sardar Jang and Sardar Bahadur; however, Cox reported: "Sirdar Jang's attitude . . . iri regard to incursion of Turkish troops, fanatical rising in Shuster, safe conduct of Wassmuss, and rising in Arabistan has been most equivocal, and even his staunch adherent Dr. Young, wired on 27th April that Sirdar's present attitude excited his grave suspicion."[93] Cox went on to list the demands to be presented to the khans: that they (1) refuse to take up arms against the British, discourage jihad generally, and suppress it in their own territory; (2) maintain internal order, secure the escort for the oil fields and Bakhtiyari road, and, in Isfahan, protect British subjects and maintain security of the road and telegraph lines up to the Fars boundary; and (3) come to a permanent friendly understanding with the shaikh and cooperate with him in 'Arabistan by refusing asylum to refugees and by maintaining peace on their borders. Bakhtiyari governors in southern Iran had also to agree to suppress fanaticism and to protect British subjects and interests.

In return for this we should undertake on conclusion of war to preserve Bakhtiari country with its present limits for tribe and give Khans local autonomy to deal with their own tribesmen in their own way under our aegis. We should agree to keep Bakhtiari Governor at Ispahan under our guidance and be prepared to consider Bakhtiari candidates among others for other governorships in sphere controlled by us. We should be prepared later on to consider sympathetically any workable proposal they might put for obtaining access to ports on Persian Gulf.

On receiving undertaking to the effect required from recognized representatives of two families we would pay each branch £5,000 now, and £10,000 each at end of war if they carry out their part of bargain effectively.[94]

The viceroy authorized Cox to begin negotiating along these lines, but a minute paper noted that Britain might not be in a position to fulfill certain of these conditions. Part of the Bakhtiyari was within the Russian sphere of influence, according to the 1907 Anglo-Russian Convention, and Isfahan was in the Russian sphere and Russia would insist on its own candidates. Also, regarding the promise of governorships in the British sphere, "it must be remembered that the Bakhtiaris are not loved outside their own country, for their rapacity is inordinate even according to Persian standards".[95] There was also the fear that if the Bakhtiyari were given access to the Persian Gulf, they might in the future come under Russian influence and provide Russia with an access that to this time had been denied. One reason for Townley's actively pro-Bakhtiyari position in 1911–12 was this fear that a Bakhtiyari–Russian wedge might be driven to the Gulf. This minute paper also adds: "The proposals will not strengthen the Central Government, but it is more than doubtful whether it can ever again be anything but an ineffective shadow, and we can make a condition of our support (as in the case of Mohammera) that the Bakhtiaris shall remain loyal to the Central Government."[96]

Meanwhile, also in 1915, the Anglo-Russian Convention of 1907 underwent some modifications. The "Constantinople Agreement", a series of diplomatic exchanges in February–April 1915, gave the neutral zone, except for certain areas near Isfahan, Yazd, and the Afghan border which were added to the Russian sphere, to Great Britain.[97] Consequently, the threat of a Russian presence in southwestern Iran was greatly lessened and the prospects of a Bakhtiyari–Russian accord diminished.

Sir Walter Townley was replaced by Sir Charles Marling as the British minister in Tehran. Marling had new reservations about Cox's suggestion for the lines the discussions with the khans should take. He mentioned that guarantees of autonomy were meaningless because the khans already considered themselves autonomous, and a guarantee of their territory would be considered by them as a restriction to their future expansion. Also, promises of governorships might prove embarrassing, and he suggested that the best course to follow would be to keep the khans "loyal to us by secret (?) service inducements".[98] Marling also raised the question whether

Ilkhani and Ilbegi would not have the power to negotiate compact (of?) [*sic*] this kind even if definite appointments were made; their authority is limited in practice to internal affairs of tribe and pact of kind suggested would have to be submitted to committee of senior Khans, and their assent would have to be obtained. Much time would be lost in discussions between Khans as at this time Khans are scattered.[99]

In 1915 the India Office, London, noted that the Bakhtiyari khans had thus far fulfilled all of their responsibilities in regard to the protection of the oil fields. But negotiations for an agreement were becoming crucial, because of the uncertainty of Iran's position in relation to Britain and Russia; it was feared that a break might be imminent. Cox met the ilkhani and ilbaigi in late May to arrange a temporary agreement, and to obtain from them the promise that if Iran were to enter the war against Britain and if because of this they could no longer give the necessary protection to the oil company, the Bakhtiyari khans would give the company twenty days' notice in advance and protect the company's employees during this period. Cox reported his meeting as follows:

I met the Bakhtiaris, Sirdar Jang and Bahadur and had full discussion with them on 23rd and 24th May . . .
   Negotiations ended in the two Khans mentioned giving me a writ to the following effect: "They cannot believe that Persia will be drawn into war. In any case they will express their painful convictions to the ruling Ministers, and will do their utmost to dissuade them. If, however, Persia should join our enemies they themselves undertake to protect the employees and the property of the Company and to maintain order along the Bakhtiari borders to the utmost of their power. Should affairs develop so unfavourably as to make them doubt whether they can afford effective [protection?] any longer they will give 20 days warning in order to enable the Company to consider and arrange other measures. During these 20 days they will continue to be personally responsible for the safety of the Oil Co.'s British community."
   In consideration of the above and of the fact that they have remained down [in the garmsir] a month longer than usual and assist in maintaining normal conditions at the oil fields I have given them £1,000 each.
   As far as these two Khans are concerned I am convinced that in the event of war it is their *bona fide* intention to do their best to secure that the Oil Co. does not suffer harm in their territory; but some of the junior Khans have been admitting (?) irresponsible and pro-German views, and the fact that these two Khans are quite unable to answer for the tribes or any of the senior Khans warrants the suspicion that some of them have been squared by German agents.[100]

Not since 1903, when the khans were paid £700 because they had completed four caravanserais and Lynch had refused to discount two years' interest, had the British government made a known direct "payment" to the Bakhtiyari.

Throughout the summer there were conflicting reports regarding the loyalty of the khans; the great khans appeared to be pro-British, but a number of the younger khans were not. 'Arabistan was in an uncertain state, as was the central government. There were fears that unless an agreement were reached the khans might be influenced by pro-German factions in Tehran, so it was imperative that all the major khans sign a pact. Correspondence moved back and forth from the Persian Gulf to London, Tehran, and India, and finally on 13 December 1915 an agreement was signed in the garmsir by the ilkhani, the ilbaigi, and Amir Jang, and with the assent of some of the junior khans. Two months after, on 15 February 1916, it was also agreed upon and signed by the senior khans living in Tehran and by the British minister. In the garmsir another £1,500 was given to the ilkhani and £1,000 to the ilbaigi.[101] The holders of these positions were now Ghulam Husain Khan Sardar Muhtasham and Yusif Khan Amir Mujahad.

This Anglo-Bakhtiyari agreement of 1915 was concluded with the following obligations accepted by the khans: (1) to maintain security in the Bakhtiyari territory and to protect the oil fields; (2) not to encroach upon districts adjacent to their present southern borders *"except by order of the Persian Government"* and especially not to encroach upon the district of Liravi; (3) to maintain friendly relations with the shaikh and not to give asylum to refugees from his territory, nor was he to give asylum to any Bakhtiyari; (4) to discourage agitation and disturbances in the Bakhtiyari; (5) neither to take arms against Great Britain or her allies nor to furnish supplies or transport to those who might oppose Britain, but only *"so long as amity exists between Great Britain and Persia"*; (6) if hostilities were to spread to Iran, to prevent members of the tribe from taking part and to maintain order along the Bakhtiyari road and to protect British lives and property, it being understood that if any khan who signed should fail in this "his share in the Oil Company will be forfeited to the British Government and His Majesty's Government will have every right to take such further measures as they think necessary to show their displeasure"; and (7) if Iran were to conclude a treaty of alliance with Great Britain, to place all of their forces at the disposal of the allies of Iran and *"to assist as far as they can"*. In article 8, Britain undertook to maintain their traditional friendly relationship, and "to help them in their difficulties as far as they properly can, whether [between] the Persian Government or between themselves. This assistance will include as in the past the consideration of Bakhtiari candidates for Governorships in provinces where British interest are paramount."[102] The significance of this agreement is that it represents the culmination of Anglo-Bakhtiyari relations. Although the agreement was not generally known in Iran, its existence was assumed; all Iranian nationalists came to regard Bakhtiyari leaders as British clients.

Of equal significance for the Bakhtiyari confederation was the request, made by the ilkhani and ilbaigi to Sir Percy Cox several months later, in which they sought direct British military support in upholding the authority of their positions in the Bakhtiyari; in the past this had been the function of the central government. "Khans apprehend that on return to Chahar Mahal they will be confronted with a great deal of hostility and obstruction from the disaffected member of the hierarchy and will only [be able] to maintain their position as Ilkhani and Ilbegi provided that they enjoy manifest backing from us, as Sardar Jang did."[103]

They asked, first, that vice-consul E. Noel of Isfahan and his consular force be allowed to join them in Chahar Mahall; and, second, that a letter be given them in which the British stated their support and approval of the ilkhani and ilbaigi and that: "It is incumbent on the other Khans to support their authority and that any Khan opposing or intriguing against them will be regarded by us as disloyal to Central Government and hostile to British interests and will incur our active displeasure."[104]

The Bakhtiyari and Riza Shah

Iran's many problems were exacerbated by World War I. With the collapse of Czarist Russia, the rejection of the Anglo-Persian agreement by the fourth Majlis in 1921, and the disillusionment following the failures of constitutionalism, the groundwork was laid for the *coup d'état* of 1921 led by Riza Khan, later Riza Shah. He successfully suppressed separatist movements in Gilan, Khurasan, Kurdistan, and 'Arabistan and revolts in the other provinces, gained control over the Majlis, blunted the opposition of the ulema, and set out to unify Iran and to break the power of the tribal leaders who might pose a threat to his attempts to centralize power and the government. He accomplished this with the backing of the urban centers and a small but Western-trained and -armed military force. His moves against the Bakhtiyari and the other tribes did not consist of a frontal attack but a series of military, economic, and administrative maneuvers extended over a period of time. The intensity of this campaign, the singlemindedness of Riza Shah, and his Western-type army were forces that had never before confronted the Bakhtiyari khans.

In June 1922 the "Shalil Incident" occurred, in which the Bakhtiyari were provoked into attacking a small Iranian force that was being sent by

Riza Khan through the Bakhtiyari to 'Arabistan. This attack aroused nationalist sentiments in Tehran and enabled Riza Khan to impose an economically crushing indemnity on the Bakhtiyari, one which could not be evaded by traditional means. In 1921 and 1922 the Bakhtiyari khans lost their governorships of Kerman, Yazd, and Isfahan. In 1923, Riza Khan withdrew their right to be accompanied by military retainers and removed the Chahar Lang from the authority of the ilkhani. This was followed by appointment of Iranian governors within the Bakhtiyari itself. In 1928, the Anglo-Persian Oil Company was instructed to lease land through the governor of Khuzistan and not from the khans. A delayed revolt occurred in 1929, and following a Bakhtiyari defeat three khans were executed. In 1933, the positions of ilkhani and ilbaigi were abolished; however, Murtaza Quli Khan, the ilbaigi at the time, was appointed governor, and, in 1936, the Bakhtiyari territory was divided and placed in two separate administrative districts, Isfahan and Khuzistan, under civil administrators. In 1934, three important khans were imprisoned and executed, including Ja'far Quli Khan Sardar As'ad (III), Riza Shah's minister of war. And in 1938–9, Riza Shah exacted his last due from the khans by forcing them to sell villages and their oil shares to the central government.[105] In this same period a similar campaign was conducted against the other tribes. There was opposition in the tribes to this expansion of the center's power, but only desultory resistance. The khans themselves were only too aware of what was happening, but they failed to present a unified front to this attack.

Postscript: The Bakhtiyari and Muhammad Riza Shah

The denouement to the Duraki great khans' tribal power was administered by Riza Shah's centralization of power through the establishment of the nation–state and a modern army. Significantly too for the Bakhtiyari, Britain, in the critical stage of the early 1920s, chose not to support them or Shaikh Khaz'al but Riza Khan.[106] Following Riza Shah's abdication, in the period of World War II and before the re-establishment of Pahlavi autocracy, the great khans – Amir Mufakham and Sardar Muhtasham of the old generation were still living – and their sons and grandsons did not seek to recover their roles as tribal leaders. Rather, they sought restoration of property seized by Riza Shah: estates and indemnification were granted to some.

Particular family concerns lay at the heart of great khan politics, and increasingly this had expressed itself outside the Bakhtiyari. The new generation of khans were no longer even trained there but were educated in Europe. Sardar Muhtasham could remark with some irony: "We

Bakhtiaris . . . used to be great fellows for horses and women and hunting, but now our boys are becoming tennis champions instead."[107]

Internal competition among the great khan families intensified as their numbers increased, not only under Riza Shah's centralization and divide and rule policies but in the decentralization following his abdication in 1941. Even before it, leadership from the tayafah level had emerged to challenge and further divide the great khans. Given inherent family rivalries, decreased incomes and increasing demands on them, and uncertainty in relations with both the central government and the tayafahs, the great khan families either lacked or were unwilling to commit their assets to re-arming the Bakhtiyari and re-establishing a political role for themselves from a tribal base. In addition, a re-armed Bakhtiyari would have been no match for the resources of the nation–state and the army without Great Power support, which was probably not forthcoming. These families, like the nontribal elite, then sought to maintain their standing – and many did not succeed – through wealth and social standing based on land and, increasingly in the 1950s and 1960s, investments, education and training, and political acumen and service in the military, bureaucracy, court, or the oil industry. Some of the most notable examples of this continuing transition are to be found in the careers of Soraya Isfandiyari, the shah's second wife; Timur Bakhtiyar, SAVAK's first chief; and Aqa Khan Bakhtiyar, the head of the National Iranian Oil Company.

Shahpour Bakhtiar, however, best exemplifies this process. His father, Muhammad Riza Khan Sardar Fatih – a younger son of Imam Quli Khan Hajji Ilkhani – was one of those khans executed by Riza Shah in 1934. Even had a traditional Bakhtiyari structure been maintained, the early death of Sardar Fatih and the fact that he was but one of a number of young khans and not pre-eminent meant that his son Shahpour – and he had only one other son – could not have played a significant role within the Bakhtiyari. Nevertheless, Shahpour studied law in Paris, served in Mosaddegh's government, helped lead the opposition to the shah's autocracy, and emerged as the shah's last prime minister only to be rejected by Khomeini as a collaborator and as a Western liberal. Indeed, he was probably more at home in the liberal West than in 1979 Tehran – certainly more so than in the Bakhtiyari.

The Bakhtiyari tayafahs were also affected by Riza Shah's abdication and the policies adopted by Muhammad Riza Shah. The former's policy of forced sedentarization was abandoned. A Bakhtiyari administrative entity, along with Chahar Mahall, was created in 1943,[108] and its first governor was Murtaza Quli Khan. His appointment exacerbated Ilkhani and Hajji Ilkhani great khan rivalries but helped perpetuate the Ilkhani/Hajji

Ilkhani framework for tayafah alignments. Although the great khan families were no longer directly involved in tayafah politics, leading members of these families acted as power brokers in Tehran, Isfahan, or Khuzistan for Bakhtiyari when they were involved with the government or urban society.

The central government provided little support for the pastoral nomadic sector, but its general economic and social policies, especially after 1962, had a major impact on the Bakhtiyari. Voluntary sedentarization proceeded at a faster rate, with Bakhtiyari settling on land opened up by land reform, working in the oil fields or Kuwait, or laboring as unskilled workers on the many construction projects in urban centers. There has been greater integration not only into the national economy but into society as a whole through the military and education.

Little information is yet obtainable on the Bakhtiyari in post-Pahlavi Iran, but with Khomeini's return a delegation from each of the Ilkhani and Hajji Ilkhani factions of the tayafahs appeared before him.[109] And in the summer of 1980 ten Bakhtiyari were executed, charged with fomenting an anti-Khomeini coup.[110] Others have been imprisoned or are living in exile.

The answer to the question of the khans' failure to unite in response to Pahlavi policies, especially those of Riza Shah, is to be found in certain social and political factors of the Bakhtiyari, some of which are common to other Near Eastern societies, which contributed to the development of disunity or the upsetting of the equilibrium of Bakhtiyari society. The underlying basis of the camping unit of the pastoral nomadic tribes in the Zagros is cooperation in the exploitation of pastures and water resources. Each camping unit is in economic competition with other camping units, a competition expressing itself in economic and political rivalry and resulting in segmentation along "genealogical" lines. However, these camping units also coalesce and cooperate according to a lineage principle at the next higher level of organization, to protect and insure their pasture rights. It is at this level, whether it be called il, tayafah, or tirah, that land rights are held and the khan assigns them. Theoretically, if a comparison may be drawn from other Near Eastern pastoral nomads (i.e., the Kurds and the bedouins of the Arab world), the need to protect tribal territory from the sedentary world, as well as from other nomads, is the chief factor in fusion or unification; the mechanism for accomplishing this is genealogical identification, either genuine or fictive.

In the smallest element of Bakhtiyari society, the family, there is this same potential for fusion and fission: fusion in defense of the family's interests, and fission in disputes over inheritance and position within the family. Frequent mention has been made of conflict between brothers, and there are also examples of son fighting against father and uncle (father's brother). This is partially a result of Islamic inheritance practices. Theoretically all sons inherit equally, but the execution of the division of an estate as well as the practice of anticipatory inheritance contribute to factionalism in a family. This in turn is related to the question of authority, not only within the family, but also in larger political and social groups, where the need for alliances places a leader in a position where he is reluctant to alienate possible supporters. A khan might be the only one who can make decisions affecting another tent and also the only one who holds coercive power, but his ability to command ultimately rests upon the support given to him by his family or followers.

The need for allies is further illustrated in marriage practices. The preferred marriage in the Islamic Near East is patrilateral cousin marriage (marriage with father's brother's daughter). This "plays a prominent role in solidifying the minimal lineage as a corporate group in a factional struggle".[111] This type of preferential marriage reinforces fissional tendencies by narrowing the group that can be expected to provide support. Not unexpectedly the khans of the Ilkhani and Hajji Ilkhani factions have a larger proportion of exogamous marriages, which has the opposite effect and provides ties with other lineages that will give them political support. (Sardar Zafar's first wife was his father's brother's daughter, Bibi Sakinah, the daughter of Hajji Ilkhani, but five of his other six wives were daughters of important but lesser khans within the Bakhtiyari.)

Another problem related to authority and to inheritance is that of accession to power. This was a problem not only for the Bakhtiyari but also for Iran as a whole. There was no principle of primogeniture, though the eldest son frequently acceded to power, but only the broad principle that any male from certain families could be elected leader. Most often election was accomplished by military support and the extermination of all rivals or their removal, either by exile or by confinement. In nineteenth-century Iran, following the Treaty of Turkmanchai in 1828, in which Russia guaranteed the accession of 'Abbas Mirza and his descendants to the Iranian throne, the Great Powers played an important role in selection of the ruler. Britain performed a similar function in the Bakhtiyari after 1912. Prior to the 1894 agreement between the Ilkhani and Hajji Ilkhani factions, military conflict and assassination of rivals was the rule in the Bakhtiyari. The 1894 agreement divided the power and wealth between the two paramount families, and this division was reinforced in their subsequent agreements and their relations with the Iranian government and the British; however, the basic problem of disunity remained and competition among themselves continued.

The khans were not only tribal leaders but also landowners. And their resources from their land holdings were used to gain political ascendancy within the tribe and in Iran, and from these positions, as ilkhani or a provincial governor or as a leader of a military contingent, the khans could obtain more land. Lambton underscores the importance of land ownership when she writes:

Possession of land conferred a not inconsiderable economic benefit upon the holder. It enabled him to keep a body of armed retainers. This in turn gave him considerable power. In effect, it meant that the government had often to defer to the large landowner in the areas in which he held land. This again gave the landowner social prestige as well as political power.[112]

Both as tribal leaders and as landlords and officials in Iran these khans were in competition with their brothers, uncles, and cousins. In the larger framework of Iran they were in a competitive position first for suzerainty and alliances with those people on their borders, and second for power in the provinces and at the capital, either for favor with the leaders holding high positions or for the attainment of these positions, and within the tribe they sought power so as to be able to attain national positions and power.

This disunity was a factor shaping family and tribal politics and, ultimately, the history of Iran. The khans were heirs of a socio-economic system and a historical tradition which together allowed little maneuverability when they were confronted with new forces. First, they were leaders in a polymorphic social and economic system whose essential relationships were defined by competition for limited resources, but whose units were also loosely bound together when there were overriding needs such as direction and coordination of the migration, adjudication of disputes, or integration into the larger economy and society of Iran. Tribal identity encompassed a common tradition and ideals, specially recognized lineages, and the Bakhtiyari dialect, and this identity was demonstrated by political allegiance to certain khans. These leaders were selected out of chiefly lineages and, although they held primary coercive power in the tribe, they had access to far greater economic resources and could thus maintain retainers to enforce their power. The very nature of Bakhtiyari society provided a check against abuse of its use by the mechanism of withdrawal of political allegiance.

Secondly, the Bakhtiyari khans were not only leaders of pastoral nomads but were also important landlords and in some cases leaders in sedentary society. As a bridge between the two societies – for the pastoralists political leaders and integrators into the national fabric and for sedentary society tax collectors, conscriptors, landlords, and military and civil leaders – the khans were able to use this dual role for their own advantage. After 1909 the Bakhtiyari khans played an increasingly important role in Iranian society, and the chief khans left the day-to-day management of tribal affairs to the younger khans and only intervened on matters of major policy. As national leaders they spent their energies on the traditional aim of aggrandizement. They were aided in the pursuit of this by the increased incomes and power brought about by the opening of trade routes through the Bakhtiyari; by the discovery of oil on tribal lands and, hence, by the increased strategic importance of their area for the British; and by their decisive role in the Constitutional Revolution. British representatives in Iran hoped to unify the khans' authority as a means of promoting Great Britain's imperial interests. The chief obstacle to the fulfillment of this goal, and to the hope of some khans regarding rule of Iran itself, was the existence of traditional power groups which especially included dissident members of their own families and other tribal leaders, such as the Qashqa'i khans and Shaikh Khaz'al, who were fearful lest their power be encroached upon by increasing Bakhtiyari power. With these internal and external checks, the absence of complete British support, and the development of a national unified and centralized state under Riza Shah and then Muhammad Riza Shah, there was little hope for adaptation of these semiautonomous tribal leaders. The khans had not had previous experience with such a unified power in Tehran, and because of their own political heritage of disequilibrium were unable to cope with it.

"Kitabchah" (translation)

Husain Quli Khan Ilkhani's "Kitabchah" (1290/1873–1299/1882) was kept in an unprepossessing little volume – octodecimo (c. 4 in. × 6¼ in.) – with a mottled dark blue cover and violet end papers. Ilkhani utilized only 112 of its pages and covered them with an almost illegible shikastah script. The first page, as well as part of page 113 and pages 114–16, contains notes entered, also in shikastah, by Hajji Khusrau Khan Sardar Zafar, one of Ilkhani's sons. On pages 113–16 Sardar Zafar describes Ilkhani's death, and on the very first he notes that Zill al-Sultan seized the "Kitabchah" at the same time he had Ilkhani assassinated in 1882; he adds that the "Kitabchah" found its way into the library of Saram al-Daulah, one of Zill al-Sultan's sons, who in turn gave it to Sardar Zafar. Sardar Zafar had antiquarian and historical interests and, with his death, the "Kitabchah" came into the hands of his favorite and like-minded son, the late Senator Amir Husain Khan Zafar-Bakhtiyari, and then finally to his son, Malikshah Zafar-Bakhtiyari. The "Kitabchah" is – or was – in Malikshah's library in Tehran.

Not only does Husain Quli Khan fit the romantic image of a khan, but his actual role and attitudes are revealed in his personal and official documents, which help the reader to gain a better understanding of Bakhtiyari and Iranian history. Husain Quli Khan was largely responsible for the unification of the Bakhtiyari tribes into a confederation in the third quarter of the nineteenth century, and the Qajars greatly feared his power.

Qajar apprehensions of a united Bakhtiyari were justified, because a generation later, in 1909, the Bakhtiyari functioned as a confederation under the leadership of Hajji 'Ali Quli Khan Sardar As'ad (II), Husain Quli's son, and participated in the deposition of Muhammad 'Ali Shah and the reinstitution of constitutional government.

Historians, who tend to be more familiar with the constitutional period than with nineteenth-century Iran, have taken the importance and power of the Bakhtiyari for granted and have assumed their key role in the Constitutional Revolution to be yet another example of tribal or confederational solidarity. Moreover, Husain Quli Khan has been regarded as the paradigmatic pastoral nomadic leader. Questions may well be raised, however, as to whether the Bakhtiyari had functioned as a confederation earlier; as to the nature of Husain Quli Khan's role, especially in comparison with that of earlier Bakhtiyari leaders; and as to the nature of his relationship to his confederation and the central government.

These historical perceptions regarding the Bakhtiyari and other tribes have been determined by uncritical assumptions and by the absence of sources. The use of Western terms and concepts – including the very terms "tribe" and "confederation", the latter implying corporate interests and the willingness to act on them – assumes that Iranian units are compatible with Western notions. Moreover, specific misunderstandings regarding the Bakhtiyari can be traced directly to two books – Layard's fascinating and important *Early Adventures in Persia, Susiana, and Babylonia* (1887) and Curzon's monumental and invaluable *Persia and the Persian Question* (1892). Sir Henry Layard spent the months of October 1840 through August 1841 in the Bakhtiyari as the guest of Muhammad Taqi Khan, the leading khan of the Chahar Lang (the other moiety of the Bakhtiyari and rival to Husain Quli's Haft Lang), and Muhammad Taqi Khan gave Layard the impression that he was the paramount Bakhtiyari. At that time there was neither a dominant khan recognized by the Bakhtiyari nor a single official representing the central government. Layard did not publish his account until 1887, by which time the office of paramount khan of all the Bakhtiyari, that of the ilkhani, had been created by imperial decree. The assumption was subsequently made by Curzon, who relied heavily on Layard as a source about the Bakhtiyari, that such an office and its attendant political relationships and structures had characterized earlier historical periods.

Nasir al-Din Shah granted Husain Quli Khan the title of ilkhani in 1867; thereafter Husain Quli was always known by that designation. Persian and Western sources alike note the esteem and respect commanded by his name, and fear of Ilkhani's growing power compelled the shah and his son, Mas'ud Mirza Zill al-Sultan, governor of Isfahan and Ilkhani's suzerain, to kill him. Not only was Ilkhani one of Iran's most important khans, because of his political, diplomatic, and military skills, but he also excelled as a provincial administrator, landlord, hunter, and horse breeder.

Given these qualities, none of which presupposes literary interests, and given his lack of formal education, it is perhaps noteworthy that Ilkhani should have kept a diary – or, perhaps more accurately, a notebook containing some annual jottings – henceforth referred to as the "Kitabchah" (lit. notebook). Ilkhani's literary pretensions were not confined to the "Kitabchah"; a portion of his poetry, written under the pen name "Sayyarah", remains. According to family tradition, Ilkhani always carried with him a Qur'an, this "Kitabchah", and an accounts book. Unfortunately the latter has yet to be located. He maintained a number of *munshis* (agent–secretaries) in his service to note decisions and to represent him. In addition there were other Bakhtiyari in his attendance known as *mullas* – a title that carried no religious connotation, but merely indicated that the bearer was literate – who could also have kept records. Ilkhani also had access to the urban ulema, especially in Isfahan, for drawing up contracts and agreements, and close ties existed between leading Isfahan mujtahids and his family. Certainly Ilkhani's munshis and mullas could have provided him with a written account of a year's events, supplemented by the legal record, had that been what he wanted.

Why then should he have kept his "Kitabchah" for the last ten years of his life? To correct the record? For posterity? To imitate Qajar courtiers such as the aforementioned I'timad al-Saltanah? Or for some private satisfaction? As a record his "Kitabchah" offers only fascinating glimpses of events in the decade from 1872 to 1882. In it Ilkhani made no attempt to provide detailed information; the sole exception is his record of his visit to Tehran and the court in 1879, and even this is a bareboned account except for his description of a hunting trip with Nasir al-Din Shah. Had his purpose been to present his version of a dispute, he certainly could have clarified his major conflicts with Farhad Mirza Mu'tamid al-Daulah, governor of Fars, especially concerning the disputed jurisdiction of the Darashuri subsection of Qashqa'i and the community of Falard. Implicit in the "Kitabchah" is the assumption that anyone who might read it would know not only the outline but the details of these incidents. Ilkhani's entries are always matter-of-fact, and nowhere does he consciously assert a specific view. These two points – assumption of knowledge and the "Kitabchah's" matter-of-factness – would seem to rule out the desire to preserve a record for his sons, which is the explicit purpose of Sardar Zafar's "Tarikh Bakhtiyari".

We are left with the possibility that Ilkhani, who lived in a society that accorded the man of letters great honor and who was probably aware that Qajar courtiers kept diaries, derived personal satisfaction from recording the events of the year – raids, weather, interaction with Qashqa'i and Arabs, agricultural projects, relations with the shah and his government, taxes, land acquisitions, horses and horse breeding, hunting trips and family marriages and incidents. Initially entries are fragmented and are expressed in a straightforward manner; however, later ones are less episodic and more sustained, almost as if Ilkhani now felt at ease making entries that he considered important in his "Kitabchah". Regardless of the motivation for keeping such an account, Ilkhani's "Kitabchah" is a significant document, because, to date, it is the sole source for the activities and perceptions of a major nineteenth-century khan.

"KITABCHAH" TEXT

The state and condition of the provinces and other things in *The Year of the Cock, 1290.*[1]

I sent a group against the Arab Bani 'Abd al-Khan.[2] Aqa Susan, the brother of Aqa Bandar,[3] was killed, [but] the Arabs were plundered.

Aqa Parviz[4] bought the Sharak[5] mare [for me] for 250 tumans. A Zaghiyah mare was taken by Mirza 'Ali Baz[6] from the Arabs and was brought [to me]. In this year [alone I obtained] a total of 40 head of mares; some were purchased and some were gifts.

We came to yailaq, where I made a wedding for my beloved son, 'Ali Quli,[7] and they brought the daughter of Khajah Khalil[8] from Gumbadan[9] [as his bride].

Saham al-Mulk was in Ganduman[10] with three regiments. The Shah had gone on a journey to Europe.[11] Isfandiyar[12] went from Tehran with

[Bakhtiyari] cavalry. Those Hajjivand[13] plundered the tayafah of the Shahi.[14]

I came to Malamir.[15] I sent my dear [brother] Aqa Riza Quli[16] with a group against the Bahmah'i,[17] and they took the upper fortress[18] and destroyed the Bahmah'i.

There were very high prices, indeed famine: wheat could not be found for four qirans a mann[19] in the Bakhtiyari. I gave a place to Muhammad Husain Khan, the son of Khuda Karam Khan,[20] and he had remained in Falard.[21]

[During the year] an earthquake struck Chaqakhur,[22] and the buildings, and the fortress, were completely destroyed. I sent Hajji Muhammad Karim[23] to Karbala Mu'ala[24] to decorate the Haram with mirror mosaic. I gave him 3,000 tumans, and he left and began work. We shall see how much he will spend before the end of the work.

I went to Malamir for several days hunting wild boar. We killed 250 head of wild boar. The group that went against the Bahmah'i killed 460 boar in two days at Gulgir[25] on Kuh Asmari.[26] In this year, these events, which have been recorded [here], took place.

The following took place in *The Year of the Dog, 1291.*[27]

[I received] one of Hajji Sayyid Musa's Vaznah mares and one of 'Ali Riza Khan's[28] Jalfah mares, which I took from Aqa Riza Mustaufi,[29] and bought a Saglavi[30] mare from one of the royal princes.

[When] we reached the summer pastures, I sent Mirza 'Ali Baz to Shiraz to Husam al-Saltanah,[31] who put right the affair of Muhammad Husain Khan, the [aforementioned] son of Khuda Karam Khan. They turned Khuda Karam Khan out from Qal'ah Valayat.

Out of necessity Ja'far Khan Bahmah'i came to Chaqakhur. I took care of his problems. Saham al-Mulk came to Ganduman and then went to Shiraz.

Suhrab Khan Qashqa'i[32] appeared before Husam al-Saltanah, who seized him and cut off his head.

Mirza 'Ali Baz brought from Fars Muhammad Shah's revenue list[33] [authorizing the collection of taxes of the tayafah of the] 'Ali Shaikh [which had long since gone into the Qashqa'i].

There are daily earthquakes in Chaqakhur. Day, 1291.[34] There has been much snow and rain this year. I bought the remainder of Sudanjan[35] [and now own all of it]. I [also] purchased two dangs of the village of Sirak[36] belonging to those Charmini.[37] Zill al-Sultan[38] became the governor of Isfahan. Isfandiyar received a farman[39] from Tehran; the villages of

Mizdij[40] along with the other villages I had were removed from the Isfahan revenue assessment. Aqa Imam Quli[41] remained in yailaq with his family while I and Aqa Riza Quli came to garmsir, and spent two months in Malamir and Kuh Asmari. Thanks to God, the time passed very happily. At Asmari we killed 200 head of game.

Shaikh 'Abd al-Rashid, son of Shaikh Sultan,[42] came to Asmari with all the Arabs and kadkhudas of Ram Hurmuz for two nights. I gave him two mules and one tent, and he left. Aqa Riza Quli sent a man for a Nisban mare belonging to Aqa Fath 'Ali, son of 'Ali Riza Khan.[43] He paid 200 tumans for it, and they brought it.

We came to Andakah,[44] and in *The Year of the Hog, 1292*,[45] a Sharak chestnut mare foaled a filly by an 'Ajil stallion with four white fetlocks. A Jalfah mare belonging to Aqa Riza Quli threw a colt, and they brought a third mare with a foal at foot which they let roam with the herd to be covered.

I sent Najaf Quli[46] among the Mamivand[47] to finish the matter of 'Abdallah Khan [chief of the ?] Fuladvand.[48] The Nasiyan Fahl stallion died. This year the following have died: Aqa Sa'id Murad of the Ahmad Khusravi[49] and Aqa Ghulam 'Ali, son of Khalil Khan of the Bahmah'i Lajmir Aurak.[50] Aqa 'Ali Quli took the daughter of Aqa Talib of the Kahkash[51] [as his bride]. Amir Tupkhanah died.

I went to 'Arabistan, where H.H. Hishmat al-Daulah[52] quarreled with the Cha'b[53] scoundrels. They fired off 50 cannon rounds; it did not do any good. After several days I went and brought the son of Shaikh Lutfah Khan and the son of Shaikh Muhammad Khan as hostages. Camp was broken and moved toward Ahvaz, and we went to Havizah. I myself left for Muhammarah and then by steamboat as far as Fao at the beginning of the sea.

In this year I gave a mare of Zayir Khiyab, along with a Vaznah mare belonging to Shaikh As'ad, to Aqa Iskandar Ahmad Khusravi [to look after?], and the 'Abayah Sharak[54] mare of Mir Falfal and the Kuhalan[55] mare to Aqa Nasrallah Ahmad Khusravi. I had three three-year-old colts, Vaznah, 'Abayah, and 'Ajil, nimah[56] with Hajji Sayyid Musa. We divided them, and I gave him 330 tumans and took the three we had owned jointly.

H.H. Hishmat al-Daulah was dismissed, and H.E. Mu'izz al-Daulah[57] became governor. H.E. Ziya' al-Mulk, too, had become vizier. In this year H.H. Husam al-Saltanah was dismissed from [his governorship of] Fars, and H.H. Mu'tamid al-Mulk became governor. I dismissed Khajah Timur Khan Mugu'i and appointed Khajah Khan Jan Khan and Khajah Najaf Quli Khan as governors [of the Mugu'i].

Hajji Mahdi Chadur-push finished five tents. He completed them for

300 tumans. Goods in Isfahan and the districts are very cheap. In Chahar Mahall[58] nobody is buying a kharvar[59] [of wheat?] even at two tumans.

H.H. Zill al-Sultan, governor of Isfahan, came as our guest to Mizdij for five days. As a pishkash[60] gift I gave him the Kuhalan mare of Aqa Nasrallah Ahmad Khusravi with the Hamdani[61] mare of Amir Quli. The expenses [of his visit] totaled 1,500 tumans.

Muhammad Husain Khan, the son of Khuda Karam Khan, encircled his father's fortress and imprisoned him.

I built the bridge Pul Karah and the expenses totaled 1,400 tumans. Rustam Khan Janiki[62] was in charge of work at the bridge.

Khan Baba Darashuri[63] came into the Bakhtiyari with 30 families. I bought three three-year-old colts from Aqa Habiballah Babadi Kashah[64] for 200 tumans; a half share of two of them had belonged to me. From Aqa Muhammad Taqi Babadi Kashah, I also bought one horse; half of it had been mine so I paid him 60 tumans for his half.

I went to the mountains for five days' hunting, and we killed 20 head of game. We returned and Isfandiyar and 'Ali Quli went to Tehran to be H.I.M. the Shah's attendants. This year Isfandiyar became a sartip.[65] The Faridan and Chahar Mahall regiment had a fight with Saham al-Daulah[66] and caused an uproar. Shaikh 'Abdallah, son of Shaikh Sultan, brought his proofs. The son of Shaikh Miz'al[67] and the son of Hajji Jabir Khan[68] expelled him [Shaikh 'Abdallah] from Ram Hurmuz. Muhammad Husain Khan Bahmah'i, son of Khalil Khan, came to Chaqakhur this year. Khusrau[69] fell and dislocated his elbow; he still has not recovered.

'Imad al-Daulah, governor of Kermanshahan, died. Darab Khan Qashqa'i[70] went to Tehran and was appointed ilbaigi of the Qashqa'i, and he returned.

Iskandar Khan Aurak died.

We repaired the fortress of Ab Bid[71] and its buildings. I sent for the qanat builders of Paradumbah[72] to work on three branches of Ab Bid qanats.

Khajah Timur went and threw Khajah Khan Jan Khan out from Qal'ah Huma. Khajah Timur has turned away from me.

Aqa Imam Quli left with his family for the garmsir. I, too, God willing, will go to Malamir the day after tomorrow, the 25th of the month of Shavval.[73]

Mirza Aqa and the 'Alivand broke with 'Ali Riza Khan and came to yailaq. I gave Mirza Aqa a yellow cashmere robe of honor that had belonged to Zill al-Sultan.

'Ali Riza died this year.

Ziya' al-Mulk was with H.E. Mu'izz al-Daulah, who was governor of 'Arabistan. Ziya' al-Mulk took three regiments and four artillery pieces to the gates of Havizah [to attack] the Mihavi Arabs, [but] the Mihavi Arabs defeated the soldiers and the artillery. When I heard this, I took 1,500 savars and infantry and went to Shushtar so that I could go to [their aid at] Havizah. A note arrived from Ziya' al-Mulk, and peace was concluded with the Mihavi. I gave my men permission to go home.

[The events of] *The Year of the Mouse, 1293.*[74]

Aqa Imam Quli and Aqa Riza came to Ab Bid to hunt. I was in Dizful hunting gazelles, and we killed many.

I appointed Aqa Imam Quli's beloved son, Muhammad Husain,[75] governor of Ram Hurmuz and sent him there. I [also] made Mirza Aqa[76] governor of Janiki.

The Vaznah mare of 'Ali Quli gave birth to a filly as did Aqa Riza Quli's Jalfah mare.

H.E. Mu'izz al-Daulah was dismissed, and a telegraphic command arrived giving Ziya' al-Mulk charge over guarding the roads. [Mu'izz?] al-Daulah left by the Luristan road.

I came to yailaq. Nasrallah Khan brought the Sharak mare, and we went to Gharab, where we spent two days looking at the mares. I [then] went to Ardal.[77]

H.H. Zill al-Sultan gave Chahar Mahall to me. This year a difference arose between 'Ali Quli Khan Qashqa'i[78] [and] Darab Khan Qashqa'i; they had a slight quarrel. 'Ali Quli Khan left with a tayafah of the Darashuri and went toward the Buir Ahmad. Darab Khan remained at Khusrau Shirin.

Some Qashqa'i thieves killed my Vaznah horse out from under Aqa Zaman.[79]

Ziya' al-Mulk was given permission to leave Dizful and came [to the Bakhtiyari] by way of Bazuft.[80] He stayed four nights in Ardal and departed for Tehran.

In this year I again dismissed Khajah Timur, and appointed Khajah Najaf Quli Khan governor of the Mugu'i. H.H. Hishmat al-Daulah became governor of 'Arabistan [and] Luristan, and he came to Khurrama-bad. I sent Aqa Parviz to the Prince's residence with a beautiful gold-framed timepiece and one length of a white cashmere shawl as pishkash. Mirza Sayyid Ahmad became [his] vizier, so I also sent him a shawl.

With the help of God I laid the foundation for the Daupulan[81] bridge, and, God willing, with lime and brick it will be completed.

H.H. Mu'tamid al-Daulah[82] became governor of Fars, and Mu'tamid al-Mulk was dismissed.

I took the stallion of Aqa 'Ali Akbar that was nimah with me [and after paying him] 200 tumans [for his nimah], I sent it to the Shah. [In addition] I took the dun-colored Vaznah mare of Mulla Sultan 'Ali Shamarvand that was my nimah and sent it to Tabriz for the Vali'ahd.[83]

Khusrau left for pilgrimage at Mashhad Aqaddas with his mother. I sent Najaf Quli with 100 savars to accompany them. They went to Burburud[84] to the house of Bahram Khan, son of 'Ali Aqa Khan. I took his sister [as a bride] for my beloved son, Isfandiyar. They went and returned with her. With the grace of God, the others continued to Tehran, where 'Ali Quli is to remain in the service of the Shah. Isfandiyar will take the family on pilgrimage.

Also, during this year we married another dear son, Amir Quli,[85] to the daughter of Rustam Khan Janiki.

This year, too, H.H. Zill al-Sultan, the son of the Shah, entrusted Chahar Mahall to me. I was very kind to the peasants of Chahar Mahall and showed them consideration; and I gathered a good tax, too.

In this year Hajji Muhammad Karim finished the mirror mosaic in the Haram of Sayyid al-Shuhadah, upon whom be peace. He returned and the expenses totaled 6,000 tumans.

Khalil Khan [Bahmah'i] died. The family of my kind brother, Aqa Imam Quli, left for Mecca Mu'azamah. Aqa Bandar, Mulla Mirza, and Mulla Sultan, 'Ali Shamarvand also accompanied them.

I spent Ramazan[86] in Ardal. H.I.M. the Shah,[87] who wanted to talk with me, sent a telegram from Tehran, and summoned me to the Isfahan telegraph office to hear what he had to say.

We completed the public buildings and rooms of Ardal.

H.H. Mu'tamid al-Daulah took Mushir al-Mulk[88] of Fars, and fined him 100,000 tumans. Darab Khan Qashqa'i seized all the kadkhudas of the Darashuri, and finished them off.

H.I.M. the Shah [again] called me to Isfahan to the telegraph office and offered me Bakhtiyari Burujird, that is the [area of the] Zaliqi and the Mamivand with the tayafah of the Sarlak. Since they were in bad condition, I did not accept and excused myself. I remained in Isfahan one month with the Zill al-Sultan, son of the Shah and governor of Isfahan, and he showed much favor [to me]. On the 4th of the month of Zi al-Qa'dah[89] I was finally given permission to depart from Isfahan and allowed to return to Ardal.

Aqa Murad Sahuni died. H.E. Zill al-Sultan took my bond for the taxes of Chahar Mahall.

On the 2nd of the month of Zi al-Qa'dah[90] we entered Malamir. H.H. Hishmat al-Daulah went to Havizah with four regiments of infantry and fought with the Mihavi of the Bani Turuf.[91] Many were wounded and killed on both sides. For the Mihavi there was no remedy.

During this year a difference arose between Mirza Aqa and Aqa Fath 'Ali. Mirza Aqa captured Aqa Fath 'Ali and Muhammad 'Ali Mirza. Aqa Rahim 'Alivand, after letting Aqa Fath 'Ali go, came to Malamir. Then I took Fath 'Ali's horses and weapons, which Mirza Aqa had seized, and returned them. They took whatever Aqa Rahim had. They were allowed to go. Vazir Farajallah and Aqa Mulla were blinded. I appointed Chiragh 'Ali Khan as agent, and he went to the 'Abdalvand Bushaq to collect the 'alafchah[92] due from them.

In this year, too, I sent 30 qanat builders to Ab Bid to work on the qanat. I left Malamir for hunting at Kuh Asmari, where we killed 200 head of game. From there we went to Gulgir and then [again] to Kuh [?] above Sar [?] and Darah Bid [?]. We spent three nights hunting and came toward Andakah. Chiragh 'Ali Khan came, brought the money from the 'Abdalvand Bushaq, and handed it over. H.H. Hishmat al-Daulah brought the Mihavi to his camp on sworn treaty, arrested them, and sent them on to Tehran.

[The events of] *The Year 1294.*[93]

I went from Andakah to Ab Bid, where I remained several nights. Every day we hunted gazelle, and of course every time we rode out we killed 50 head of gazelle. My dear brothers, Aqa Imam Quli and Aqa Riza Quli, also accompanied us.

I sent Mirza Parviz Khan to Fallahiyah to H.H. Hishmat al-Daulah – may my soul be his sacrifice – so that he would grant us permission to be dismissed and to go to yailaq. He wrote a very gracious letter in reply requesting our brief appearance before him, after which we could leave. I went to his camp in Khazinah near Fallahiyah with 50 savars. I appeared before His Highness, who spoke with great kindness and gave me permission to sit near him. The next day he sent me an 'Abayah mare he had purchased in Fallahiyah in lieu of 300 tumans due in taxes. He sent me a very fine cashmere shawl and a double-barreled rifle, pin-firing. I moved out and left for Ahvaz.

It was decided that H.H. Hishmat al-Daulah would go to Muhammarah, and he wanted to take me with him, but I did not want to accompany him because the weather was very warm and it was harvest time. [Regardless of] whatever I did, the Prince would not dismiss me, and I was forced to accompany him. We went by boat with 20 servants to Muhammarah. We left our beloved nephew, Muhammad Husain, the son of Aqa Imam Quli, at Ahvaz at the head of the savars. I, myself, with the 20 servants [without horses], continued by boat to Muhammarah. It took 12 hours from Ahvaz to Muhammarah.

H.H. Hishmat al-Daulah bought a mare for 400 tumans in Fallahiyah, and whenever I offered to buy this mare the Prince said I must pay 2,000 tumans. Finally, after much wrangling, I bought half of it from the Prince for 300 tumans; the mare was worth 600 tumans. I sent the mare for my brother Aqa Riza Quli. The Prince sent me two good Arab mares when I left Muhammarah. I also bought three head from him for 150 tumans. I also purchased a Havizah Halafah mare from the shaikh of the Bani Salih for 260 tumans. The Prince gave half of a good mare (nimah) to Mirza Parviz Khan. During this trip I bought a total of 10 head of good mares. We were in the heat of Muhammarah for 40 days suffering from the insects, torrid temperatures, and bad water. All the infantry, cavalry, and servants fell sick, and 100 died. After 40 days we were finally dismissed, and we came by steamboat to Ahvaz with 'Abdallah Mirza, the son of the Prince's brother. Then we took the boat on to Shushtar and then went to Gutvand[94] [by land].

This year I wrote H.H. Zill al-Sultan to seize and imprison Khajah Timur.

Anyhow we rode from Gutvand and traveled by night for 10 days until we reached Bazuft. And in one more day of travel we arrived at Chaqakhur.

Hajji Nasrallah Khan Qashqa'i, son of the Ilkhani Buzurg, who was the son of the daughter of As'ad Khan Bakhtiyari,[95] was appointed ilbaigi by H.H. Mu'tamid al-Daulah, governor of Shiraz. The latter had dismissed Darab Khan. Hajji Nasrallah and all the Qashqa'i kalantars came to Chaqakhur, where they were our guests for five nights. There were 500 persons in the party. I gave Hajji Nasrallah two good mares as gifts (ta'aruf),[96] and a good send-off.

Afterwards H.H. Zill al-Sultan sent word from Isfahan that "I am coming to Chaqakhur to be your guest." I went to Burujin to welcome him when he arrived. He was our guest for 14–15 nights. All the expenses, whether at Chaqakhur or in Mizdij, for entertaining the Prince amounted to 5,000 tumans. As a pishkash gift I presented him with five mares, 1,200 tumans cash, and two very fine and long shawls. The balance of the [aforementioned total] expenses were for the personal attendants in his entourage.

During this year Ihtisham al-Daulah, son of Mu'tamid al-Daulah, governor of Fars, sent a contingent of Qashqa'i and a regiment of infantry and regular cavalry to Kuhgiluyah after Muhammad Husain Khan, son of Khuda Karam Khan. He fled with his tayafah to Janiki on account of the Qashqa'i. The soldiers came to Falard and caused much damage. A petition was sent to the central government . Orders have been given that an agent should come from Tehran, see the damage in Falard, and give his judgment concerning it. But the Bakhtiyari will take vengeance a thousand times from the Qashqa'i in compensation. We shall see what God's will is.[97]

At this time I sent Aqa Mulla Rahim Samani to Tehran with 40 representatives from Chahar Mahall, after I had received confirmation from Zill al-Sultan that Chahar Mahall is ruined. Our beloved son, Isfandiyar, who had been in Tehran, helped them. He borrowed 2,000 tumans from Aqa Dadash Turk for the Chahar Mahalli and gave it to them for their expenses at court. They were given a tax reduction of 3,200 tumans from the ministers. [This was confirmed in] a farman[98] they received; and they returned.

For this year the taxes of the Haft Lang, Dinarani, Mahmud Salih, and the Mugu'i[99] have been paid up to today, the 2nd of the month of Shavval in the year 1294.[100] Since the tax of Janiki Garmsir, which is the responsibility of Mirza Aqa Khan, has not yet been collected, God willing, on the 2nd of the month of Zi al-Qa'dah[101] I shall go to Malamir to collect it.

This year I sent 10 head of horses to Tehran so that our beloved son, Isfandiyar, may give them to high government officials. Our other beloved son, 'Ali Quli, has also taken the 'Abayan 'Ajil mare as a pishkash gift for the Shah. As 'Ali Quli left with Bakhtiyari cavalry from Ardal for Tehran, I went toward Malamir.

Iskandar Khan Sarhang, whom they sent out from Tehran to assess the damage caused by the savars and soldiers in Falard and Janiki, arrived. He went and saw and confirmed in writing to Tehran that he had seen the destruction in the Bakhtiyari and truth is with Ilkhani. Iskandar Khan [next] went to Dih Kurd[102] with our dear brother, Aqa Riza Quli, to complete the payment of the taxes of Chahar Mahall. 'Ali Quli went to Isfahan to Zill al-Sultan to get his signature on the farman[103] for the reduction [of taxes] of Chahar Mahall. He sent it [to me] and left for Tehran.

I arrived at Malamir, and Mirza Aqa Khan came with all the kadkhudas of Janiki. I settled their affairs, and the kadkhudas left. Mirza Aqa Khan, Aqa Fath 'Ali, and Khuda Karam, all the brothers, came.

The weather of Malamir is very cold. Aqa Imam Quli also arrived from Andakah, and he had two falcons, one a talan and the other a qizil. They went to Saidi territory to hunt. The qizil falcon went in pursuit of a francolin, and amidst the bushes a wild cat seized the falcon and killed it. They killed 30 francolin and brought them back. Since it was the cold time of winter and the meat was not going to spoil, I gave the 30 birds to two men on foot to take to Ab Bid to Aqa Riza so he could send them to Zill al-Sultan in Isfahan.

Shaikh Pabarah, shaikh of the Al Khamis,[104] who had killed his own brother, Shaikh 'Ubaidallah, and who had brought all the kadkhudas of Ram Hurmuz with him, came to Malamir. He offered me a very fine chestnut mare as a gift (ta'aruf). He remained several nights. I, in turn, gave him a gabardine sardari[105] and, to those accompanying him, broadcloth sardaris. They left.

I ordered Aqa Fath 'Ali to be in Malamir [as governor of Janiki] and Mirza Aqa Khan to be governor of Qal'ah Tul.

During the year I brought several teams of qanat workers, God willing, and with the aid of the Lord of the Universe, I will make several qanats in Malamir. Half the Malamir qanats will belong to me and half will belong to the sons of the late 'Ali Riza Khan. I sent Mashhadi 'Abbas, who is entrusted with the mules, to Fallahiyah to H.H. 'Abdallah Mirza, who had gone there with a regiment to collect the taxes. I sent tobacco, cheese, some Isfahan gaz,[106] and other gifts with him for the Prince. He, on his part, sent me an 'Ambar chestnut mare Shaikh Lutfah Khan had given him as pishkash. Mashhadi 'Abbas brought it; it is a good horse with no faults except that it is 10 or 12 years old.

This year, too, Aqa Imam Quli sent and brought Ustad Khudadad Farsani to fix the dam of the Ab [Ch]alu. God willing, this year they will plant 100 shah manns of rice in Mashgiri. The second pool of Dasht Gul[107] had faults, and I told Ustad Khudadad to come and work to reconstruct the pool.

The Ottoman government is fighting with Russia this year. Russia has taken much territory from the Ottomans, and no one knows how it will end.

This year 20 Paradumbah qanat workers are laboring on the qanat of Ab Bid. The qal'ah of Ab Bid was finished this year. This summer its upper rooms are being finished.

I sent my beloved son, Najaf Quli, from Malamir to get the pasture ('alafchah) tax from the Mamivand that they customarily pay annually. We are at Malamir.

[The events of] *The Year 1295.*

The 1st of the month of Muharram 1295[108] we left from Malamir. The savars and baggage went to Andakah by way of Gudar Barduqmachi, while I, myself, went by the Izah road to make a pilgrimage to [the shrine of] Aqa Sultan Ibrahim. It rained and we were detained four nights in the Imamzadah. Finally, we became desperate. They set up the charah,[109] and we came up to the charah, I and my companions crossed. Shaikh Kazim, kadkhuda of the Shihan, sent everyone across on the charah. Then he sat in the seat and fastened the rope to his waist. He took the son of Chiragh 'Ali Malmuli, who was nine years old, in his arms, and grasped the rope in his hands at the same time to cross. In the middle of the crossing the connecting strap to the rope slipped from his waist, and all the weight was on his hands and arms. With all his strength, and with the son of Chiragh 'Ali Malmuli still in his arms, he moved along the rope. The boy clung on. The rope slipped off his waist, too, and the strength of Shaikh Kazim's arms gave out, and they both fell into the water. With God's help, the eight- or nine-year-old son of Chiragh 'Ali was washed up on the banks, but Shaikh Kazim drowned. They found his body after one month at Gudar Barduqmachi.

In any case, we went to Andakah, where we spent four nights at Aqa Imam Quli's. Barley and straw could not be found.

Out of necessity I went to Gutvand. Hasan Khan, an imperial rifleman, had come with an order for me either to reassure Muhammad Husain Khan Buir Ahmad and send him to Tehran, or to take him by force. I sealed a Qur'an and sent it [as my oath] to Muhammad Husain Khan Buir Ahmad. He mounted and went to Tehran. Praise God, everything turned out all right.

From Gutvand I rode to Dizful to H.H. Hishmat al-Daulah, may my soul be his sacrifice. So many tax agents had been sent that he was in difficulty; as the result of taxes and other matters he was very ill at ease. I brought him a bit of good news and cheered him up. I was in Dizful 10 nights.

The Prince went toward Muhammarah, and I, because of the matter of Muhammad Husain, did not accompany him but went instead to Ab Bid and planted the gardens there. I brought rooted trees from Dizful to Ab Bid. The garden was completed in 20 days. In those 20 days, I gave orders to the tribes to bring stones, and I sent for lime from Dizful, which they brought, so that the water mill of Ab Bid could be finished.

The 'Abd al-Khan, a tayafah of the Bin Lam, who are notorious thieves, attacked Shushtar and set fire to the thatched huts of the Shushtari; a total of 50 children were burned in their cradles. In addition, they burned Dizful and killed Sayyid Fathallah. They took a lot of plunder from Shushtar and Dizful. An order came from Tehran to attack and kill them, and the Prince told me to send cavalry to punish them.

Our dear ones, Muhammad Husain, son of Aqa Imam Quli, Najaf Quli, and 'Abbas Quli,[110] were sent with 100 savars after the Bani 'Abd al-Khan. The Bani 'Abd al-Khan got word of this and disappeared into the waste that is known as 'Abd al-Nabi Island. Shaikh Rashid, the son of

Shaikh Khamas, who supported them, let them pass, and they went among the Quli Chapi Arabs. They numbered about 1,500. The island had but one [entrance] road, and on the island side of it they constructed a breastwork. Their headquarters were in the center of the island. The cavalry arrived late in the afternoon and saw the strong fortifications at the entrance to the island. As night fell, they put up their tents to stay.

From our side, I sent our beloved Farajallah with riflemen to a point opposite the island, and I had told him not to allow savars to ride into the brush [in the dark], but if they were drawn into the brush to go on foot to enter it. I told all the tayafahs, too, not to enter it. Morning came quickly, and all the savars left their horses in the camp and went on foot. Those taking part in this battle were the Bakhtiyarvand, Mahmud Salih, and the Babadi Raki[111] were also present; they were led by Najaf Quli. The Duraki were separate and 100 savars [led by] Muhammad Husain were drawn up behind the riflemen with the flags. They moved off, and when they arrived the battle began. The Bakhtiyari charged, and however much [the Arabs] fired they did not retreat. The fortifications were entered, and they defeated the Arabs. The island was reached and the savars joined in. I gave orders that, since all were to be partners in plunder, no one was to take anything until all the Arabs were killed.

His Eminence Aqa Shaikh Ja'far Shushtari had written to me, if you kill all the tayafahs of the Bani 'Abd al-Khan, the reward will be greater than that for killing pagans, Jews, Christians, and Turkmen. I, too, told them that if you seize them you may kill them by Shar'[112] authority.

When the battle was over, 150 of the Arabs had been killed, but not one [Bakhtiyari] savar had been killed because of God's help; and none had been wounded. All [the rest of the Arabs] were taken captive, with the result that the wealth they held was so much that these 1,000 savars did not have strength to carry away any more. The Bakhtiyari brought the following: 30,000 sheep, 4,000 cattle, 60 mares with [?] colts, and 500 camels. But as they returned home with these animals there were many losses. I kept for myself all the camels, mares, and colts. The remainder was divided among the savars. On account of the raid I gave H.H. the Prince 2,500 tumans cash.[113]

After [the fighting] Shaikh Rashid, fearful of being killed, took refuge at my house in Ab Bid, where I showed him great respect. I saved him and gave him a robe of honor and 30 camels. He left for his own tents. Morning came and he was near the tents of the sons of Shaikh Baniyan. The sons of Shaikh Baniyan killed Shaikh Rashid, but left his women and children in the tents and went. Then I petitioned Hishmat al-Daulah to make Shaikh Shahid, the brother of Shaikh Rashid, shaikh, and he did.

Next the Prince returned from Muhammarah and sent for me. I

mounted and left for Ahvaz and the Prince. Hajji Jabir Khan, Nusrat al-Mulk, sent an 'Abayan Sharak stallion to me as a stud for my mares. Shaikh Rashid, when he came to Ab Bid, brought a very fine Hafkiyah mare for me. I accompanied the Prince to Dizful, and I was with him for several days. I was dismissed and came to Chaqakhur. After I had left, the sons of Shaikh Muhammad Khan killed their uncle, Shaikh Lutfah Khan, in the evening at dinner. They also killed his sons.

In this same year H.I.M. Nasir al-Din Shah and 20 members of the inner court, and Sipahsalar A'zam,[114] went to Europe.

Khajah Najaf 'Ali Khan Mugu'i, with Khajah Khan Jan Khan, his uncle, and all the khajahs,[115] who are at odds with one another, came to Chaqakhur for me to settle their differences. I made Khajah Najaf Quli governor of Mugu'i, and he left. I told the rest to go to Faridan.

Zill al-Sultan, son of the Shah, sent for me to go to Isfahan. Najaf Quli, khan of the Kashkuli,[116] Hajji Baba, khan of the Darashuri, and Ja'far Quli Baig, khan of the Farsi Madan, fled with 2,000 tents or families. H.H. Mu'tamid al-Daulah made Darab Khan Qashqa'i governor of Qashqa'i. These tayafahs, out of fear for their lives, sought refuge, and I gave them places from Mizdij to Dih Kurd. I told these tayafahs to stay, and I sent their kadkhudas to Tehran.

H.I.M. the Shah returned from Europe.

The Qashqa'i leaders went to Tehran and found sanctuary in the Shah's stable. H.I.M. gave them a farman which allowed them to go to 'Arabistan to be entrusted to me.

In this year our beloved son, 'Ali Quli, under God's care, left with his mother for pilgrimage to Mecca Mu'azamah. I went to Isfahan to the Zill al-Sultan, son of the Shah, and spent 40 days there. The time passed very happily.

During this year I built Pul Kaj. I also sent five master builders and 15 stonecutters from Hafshkan and Doubara to work on Pul Ab Dugh, which passes over a wide river. I also dispatched our dear Aqa Sulaiman, son of the late Mahdi Quli Khan, to the bridge. They worked two months to complete the footings. I told them not to do more work until it had become dry. I added, God willing, that the vaults could be built in the coming year and the work finished.

After thinking it over the Shah ordered the Qashqa'i to go to their own territory in Fars. His Majesty appointed Najaf Quli Khan Sarhang as agent, and brought him with me to Malamir. I sent for, and they brought, Hajji Baba Khan Darashuri and Najaf Quli Khan Kashkuli. I entrusted them to Najaf Quli Khan the commissioner; he took them and they departed. They went to Bihbahan to H.H. Ihtisham al-Daulah, son of Mu'tamid al-Daulah, who assured them of their safety.

Again the commissioner came to take Khuda Karam Khan to Shiraz. Khuda Karam Khan did not want to go to Shiraz [so] I sent him to Tehran with Muhammad Husain Khan, his son. At Shah 'Abd al-'Azim[117] they swore an oath and made peace. They were taken to the Shah, who graciously received them, and sent them to Shiraz to have their affairs settled and then to come and gather the tayafahs of the Buir Ahmadi.

In Malamir this year I brought several teams of qanat workers to work on the qanats of Imam Riza, Hara, and Baluq Ab. God willing this year's rice harvest will be good. This year rain did not come until 10 days after Chillah [the winter solstice] passed; 20 days after Chillah it had not yet rained. After that when the rain came, it did not amount to much. Countless locusts came to 'Arabistan. In all 'Arabistan and the Bakhtiyari mountains, they bred. I sent someone to Qazvin to bring back ab sar.[118] God willing, if the sar [starlings] come, perhaps they will eat all the young locusts. Until today, that is 10 days before Aid Nau Ruz, there is not grass enough in all 'Arabistan and the Bakhtiyari for the sheep to eat their fill. Everything is very expensive; a kharvar of wheat cannot be had for five tumans. God have mercy on us.

[The events of] *The Year 1296.*[119]

The Qapuchi-Bashi of the Shah's son was delegated to come and get something in the name of the notables of Shushtar, who were seeking compensation on account of the plundering of the Bani 'Abd al-Khan. It was finally arranged that I give [them] 2,500 tumans, and another 2,500 tumans that the Prince had already taken. [Thus] they received 5,000 tumans out of the plunder.[120]

Hajji Jabir Khan Nusrat al-Mulk became ill and went to Bombay.

This was the year of sheep dying, and many sheep in all the Bakhtiyari and other places have perished.

Shaikh 'Ali Al Kasir offered me (ta'aruf) a three-year-old 'Abayan mare; its value was 300 tumans. I bought it together with mares and a double-barreled breech-loading pin-firing rifle for 150 tumans. I sent them with a wild ass to Tabriz as a pishkash for the Vali'ahd. 'Abd al-Karim Baig Juzdani took them. I also sent Muhammad Husain, son of Aqa Imam Quli, to Tabriz to H.R.H. the Vali'ahd.[121]

This year [too] many locusts came to 'Arabistan, and have hatched many young. God knows how it will end.

H.H. Hishmat al-Daulah gave me the Hamdani mare Shaikh Rahmat Khan had brought and given him as pishkash as well as a European pin-firing rifle and a good telescope.

A lot of water came; it carried away the footing of Pul Ab Dugh. Now,

God willing, I want to reconstruct the bridge across the river at a different location.

Praise to God, my beloved son, Hajji 'Ali Quli, has returned from Mecca Mu'azamah with his mother and companions in perfect health. They have entered Shushtar, having come from Muhammarah to Ahvaz by Hajji Jabir Khan's steamboat; and from Ahvaz they came on horseback. The baggage mules went and brought them. The coming of Hajji 'Ali Quli has created the desire in me to go to Mecca Mu'azamah myself. I had begun preparations for it, but the government has raised obstacles. Finally, H.I.M. the Shah telegraphed for me to come to Tehran to obtain leave to go to Mecca. And Hajji 'Ali Quli was ordered to enter the service of the Vali'ahd and by the telegram he was granted the rank of adjutancy of the present.

When I was in Isfahan Aqa Najaf Quli, son of Mirza 'Avaz 'Alianvar, came to see me; he was sick and died.

I sent 1,000 grafted trees from Isfahan with 800 vine scions to be planted in the garden of Ab Bid; all grew. Ustad Khudadad, this year, has done a good job constructing the second pool. God willing, no faults will appear in it.

I gave 1,500 tumans to Mirza 'Ali Baz to go to Dizful to buy 50 head of mules from the Sagvand[122] for H.H. Zill al-Sultan, son of the Shah and governor of Isfahan. I am also going to take 100 head from the Bakhtiyari. At the beginning of summer I must send Zill al-Sultan 150 mules. He gave me 5,000 tumans to buy them. Mirza 'Ali Baz bought 85 head of mules for 2,500 tumans.

We came by way of Malamir to Ardal. In Malamir I received the bond for the taxes of the Janiki from Mirza Aqa Khan. I settled his affairs and came to Ardal.

H.H. Zill al-Sultan sent some of his retainers [tax collectors] to Mizdij. They took possession of Burujin[123] and caused a lot of damage. Until I came to Ardal myself, I sent a man with a petition; they recalled these tax collectors and bestowed on me a robe of honor and a raqam[124] for Chahar Mahall. Hajji Mahdi brought them.

In the yailaqs this year there is no spring rain for the grass. It will be a hard year; God protect us.

God willing I intend to go to Tehran at the beginning of autumn to gain leave from the Shah to make the pilgrimage to Mecca Mu'azamah.

This year, too, I ordered the construction of the vaults of Pul Malik, and they were finished.

At the beginning of autumn I left Chaqakhur for Tehran. I sent 22 very fine horses to Tehran a month before I left. They were led there by 20 men, and 'Abd al-Karim Baig Juzdani was in charge. They took and stabled them at Shah 'Abd al-'Azim. I, myself, went from Chaqakhur to Isfahan, where I remained 25 days with H.H. Zill al-Sultan, son of the Shah. I left for Tehran arriving on the 8th of the month of Zi al-Hijjah. [125] On that same evening I went to His Excellency Sipahsalar A'zam and he treated me with utter kindness.

Early in the morning I went to see Mustaufi al-Mamalik. The next day, which was Aid Qurban,[126] I went to the [royal] Salam, where I stood behind His Excellency Sipahsalar. The Salam came to an end, and H.I.M. the Shah came down and sat in a chair placed in front of Shams al-'Amarat.[127] [When] I was called to be in his Blessed Presence, I went. He asked when I had come and by which road, he inquired about the tayafahs, and he treated me with great favor.

In the meantime the regiments came to parade for His Majesty, and I went and stood near Sipahsalar A'zam. The review lasted two hours until the regiments left, and the Shah went in to the andirun. Everyone left for his own lodging.

Three days later Sipahsalar A'zam conducted me to a private audience with the Shah, where I spent one hour in the Blessed Presence and said what I had to say. He showed me great kindness. I sent three horses and 500 ashrafis[128] as pishkash to His Majesty. To all the high officials of the government I also sent horses, money, tarmah, shawls, and very fine cashmere shawls.

H.I.M. the Shah left for hunting at Jajrud.[129] I and Amir Husain Khan Shuja' al-Daulah Quchani of Khurasan were in the Shah's hunting party at Jajrud. When we passed Dushan Tapah,[130] we left our carriages and mounted horses. I and Amir Husain Khan were summoned to ride with the Shah.

First he spoke a little in Turkish with Amir Husain, and then with me; he asked about 'Arabistan, the battle with the Bani 'Abd al-Khan, and talked agreeably about many things. The [time] passed pleasantly. We saw much game in every valley; there were up to ten herds of wild ewes and rams, and too many to count. The Shah shot a very fine ram.

When we reached the tents, I and Amir Husain Khan shared one together; we were the guests of the Prince, Vajiallah Mirza. Since it was winter and cold, they put up tent covers and set up kursis.[131] And I passed the time very pleasantly with Amir Husain. We sent 100 ashrafi pieces [struck with the Shah's] image in honor of the hunt's trophies. We spent one more day with the Shah's hunting party.

As we left the camp the Shah summoned me and Amir Husain Khan and asked how we were. A little of the conversation with Amir Husain Khan was in Turkish and for the rest in Persian with me on all sorts of subjects. He treated us with great kindness and favor.

When we were among the game he only asked the following to accompany him: Master of the Hunt (Amir Shikar); Mahdi Quli Khan; his brother, Mirza 'Abdallah Khan Pishkidmat; Nuvvab Vajiallah Mirza; Ibrahim Khan, Deputy of the Stables (Nayib Istabl); and four others. Then we reached the game, so the Shah might fire a shot, and they stampeded, and the Shah ordered the freeing of the salukis. They were released and raced after the game.

I, Amir Husain Khan, Ibrahim Khan Nayib, and three others stayed with the Shah. The Shah was in a bad humor. The way went down, and we traveled a little and found a flock of game. They came toward the Shah, and we galloped our horses and headed the flock off. The game passed by. The Shah dismounted with his double-barreled breech-loading rifle and fired from about 400 paces. An eight-year-old ram fell, and retainers ran and cut its neck. The game fled to a rise that was 800 paces from the Shah. Again the Shah fired and hit another ram. They brought it too. The Shah was very pleased.

I, along with Amir Husain Khan [again] gave a servant 100 ashrafi pieces with images in honor of the hunt. All the riders gathered together. The Shah dismounted for namaz.[132] For the naz shust[133] he gave to each of his private attendants as well as to each dignitary one ashrafi. He announced that this money had been given by me and Amir Husain to him and cannot be given back to them. He took two ashrafis from his own blessed pocket and gave them to us; and, in so doing, showed us great favor.

We returned to our tents, where we spent five nights, at which time we were dismissed. The Shah returned to Tehran five days after us. He called me and Amir Husain to the palace buildings and showed us great kindness. In short, I was summoned ten times – including the times when we were riding – to the presence of H.I.M. the Shah, who showed his kindness.

H.H. Zill al-Sultan came to Tehran from Isfahan in the month of Safar[134] and the Shah showed him great favor.

[The events of] *the Year 1297*.[135]

The Shah granted him 'Arabistan, Luristan, and Iraq in addition to Isfahan, Yazd, and Burujird. Twenty days after Àid he honored H.H. Zill al-Sultan with a jeweled sword and a jeweled Quds order, and the latter left for Isfahan. I remained [in Tehran] on account of Falard, which Mu'tamid al-Daulah was claiming. Eight days after the Prince had left, the Shah honored me with a jeweled sword and dismissed me. I came by post to Isfahan, where I remained 16 days.

The Prince consigned Ja'far Quli Khan, Pishkidmat-Bashi, with a regiment to me, and dispatched it to 'Arabistan. Finally, with the help of God, I left Isfahan for the Bakhtiyari. Imam Quli from 'Arabistan and Aqa Riza Quli, who was in yailaq, came to Qahfarukh[136] to welcome me. Then we came to Naghan.[137] God willing, I shall go to 'Arabistan to bring order to its affairs. This trip to Tehran and the expenses of the past six months have totaled in cash, shawls, etc. 15,000 tumans. There is nothing else to be said.

I spent 15 days in Naghan. Chiragh 'Ali Khan, and the sons of the late Muhammad 'Ali Khan, came, and I gave orders regarding his problems. On the 27th of Jumadi [al-]Sani,[138] we departed from Naghan.

I notified 100 savars to come to 'Arabistan, and we came to Qal'ah Tul. Shaikh Jabarah and the kadkhudas of Ram Hurmuz all came to Qal'ah Tul. Ja'far Khan Bahmah'i also came to Qal'ah Tul. Ja'far Khan brought one of his good horses for me. Shaikh Jabarah also brought a good mare. In Bagh Malik[139] I gave both of them a robe of honor, presenting Ja'far Khan with a cashmere kalichah and a silver broadsword. I also gave cashmere kalichah and some Kirman kalichah twill to the notables from Ram Hurmuz; and they left.

I came to Ab Lashgar, then at the next stage reached Kurkur, and then we came to Shushtar. Ja'far Quli Khan, Nayib al-Hukumah, entered Dizful. I remained in Shushtar for two nights before we came to Dizful. 'Arabistan was in a very disorderly state. Every day caravans were attacked. An artilleryman was killed on the Shushtar road.

After I entered Dizful, I assembled all the shaikhs of 'Arabistan. [Those who] came included Mulla Mutallib Khan, vali of Havizah, and Shaikh Muhammad Khan, son of Hajji Jabir Khan. We settled the taxes for all. I sent Mirza Isma'il Khan, one of my own men, [who came] from Isfahan with a robe of honor and a decree from the Prince for Hajji Jabir Khan. He [then] submitted 10,000 tumans on account for his taxes. After several days I sent a 30,000-tuman installment to Isfahan.

The vali of Havizah brought two good mares for me, both Vaznah. Shaikh Muhammad Khan presented me with a Vaznah mare. Shaikh Farhan Al Kasir brought [yet another] Vaznah mare, as did Shaikh 'Ali Khan Jarim. I bought a Vaznah mare from Shaikh Khaz'al for 400 tumans. Ja'far Khan gave me a Halalah mare he got from Mir 'Abdallah. Shaikh Jarahi Ram Hurmuzi also brought me a good mare. In addition a total of 10 other head were brought from other places.

Praise to God, I brought order to 'Arabistan to the extent that the wolf may lie down with the sheep. Since I had never been in the heat of 'Arabistan, I was fearful but, thanks to God, it was not bad. I ordered a platform to be built in the middle of the river, where I spent my evenings. During the day, I moved into subterranean rooms. It was Ramazan, too.

Praise to God, it passed pleasantly. Their Excellencies Mulla Janab and Shaikh Muhammad Tahir, may God grant them health, telegraphed the Shah that we have never seen such order in 'Arabistan.

At the end of the month of Ramazan,[140] our dear brother, Hajji [*sic*] Imam Quli Khan, came with our sons, 'Abbas Quli, Ibrahim, and Khusrau, and they left for Mecca Mu'azamah. I wrote [asking] Hajji Jabir Khan to send them by his steamboat from Muhammarah to Ahvaz. On the 23rd of Shavval,[141] with our best wishes, they got on the boat for Muhammarah, where they spent 10 to 15 nights. They left for Mecca. May God watch over and protect them.

I was [still] in 'Arabistan [when] Mu'tamid al-Daulah, governor of Fars, dispatched Darab Khan Qashqa'i with a group of Qashqa'i. They came suddenly, raided the tents of Mirza [?], and plundered a small group of the al-Baigi Mal Ahmadi. They did not stay [but] went, and on their way found Aqa Habiballah, son of Asadallah Khan Kashah,[142] who fought them. They killed his horse and seized and carried him off. Several days after that H.H. Mu'tamid al-Daulah gave him a robe of honor and dismissed him.

Ihtisham al-Daulah strangled Muhammad Husain Khan, son of Khuda Karam Khan, with permission of Khuda Karam Khan himself, at night. Afterwards he said his horse had fallen and he had died, but it became known to everyone that Ihtisham al-Daulah had killed him. May God give [us] the opportunity to retaliate when the Qashqa'i come to the Sarhad.[143] Now I intend, with the help of God, to obtain good vengeance, but God's destiny will decide.

His Highness left Isfahan and came to Burujird, Iraq, Khunsar, and Gulpayigan, and then went to Khurramabad. After several days [his forces] captured Asad Khan Bairanvand and Sardar Khan Sagvand, along with five of their brothers, and executed all of them. They plundered their camp and seized their property, and those remaining fled and came to 'Arabistan to the Bin Lam. H.H. Zill al-Sultan wrote, for security's sake, send someone and bring in the guilty Sagvand and Bairanvand. I sent Mirza Parviz Khan Babadi with a Qur'an I sealed, and he brought them back. Then I gave him 500 tumans cash to cover their expenses.

The month of Muharram in *The Year 1298*.[144]

His Highness asked for pishkash so I sent Mirza Parviz Khan to Khurramabad with three very good horses and one Vaznah mare I had got for 200 tumans to Khan Hakim, and Ja'far Quli Khan also sent two mares and 500 [tumans] cash. His Highness also honored me with a robe of honor that was one of his own decorated sardaris.

My son Isfandiyar left Tehran with the corps of the late Hishmat al-Daulah, under orders [to put down] the rebellion of Shaikh 'Ubaidallah the Sunni [Kurd]. Hishmat al-Daulah became ill on the road and died. The corps went toward Mukri. 'Azizallah Khan Mirpanj, son of the brother of the late Amir Tupkhanah, with Shahsavan savars, and Isfandiyar with 70 Bakhtiyari, fought courageously and successfully. After they defeated the Kurds and destroyed them, Sipahsalar A'zam came with a big army and heaped praise on Isfandiyar and 'Azizallah Khan. They accompanied him to Tehran, where they made Isfandiyar first sartip, and they also gave the title Saram al-Mulk to 'Azizallah Khan.

At this time Ja'far Quli Khan[145] and I had a dispute, so I addressed a petition to His Highness that he be dismissed. I went again to Ahvaz and spent several days moving about Muhammarah. The governor, Mulla Mutallib Khan, offered a Rashidah mare to me. Shaikh Zuhrab Bavi offered a Nisban mare. Mir 'Abdallah sent four good mares from Hindijan and Diha Mulla. A Jarkah mare I had given my beloved son, Hajji Khusrau, was stolen in the territory of the Bani Lam. An 'Anafjah Arab stole it and brought it; I took it.

The Arab shaikhs gave as ta'aruf a total of 60 good mares and colts this trip, except for 10 head, which I bought from them. I sent Aqa Zaman Zarasvand[146] to 'Amarah, where he bought a Nisban stallion with another horse for 500 tumans. I bought several other horses, and the remainder were given as ta'aruf.

His Highness returned from Luristan and went to Tehran. The Shah showed him great generosity and favor by adding Fars and Kermanshah to his other provinces this year. Zill al-Sultan obtained leave from the Shah for Isfandiyar and his savars to depart, and brought them with him. H.E. Sahib Divan was made pishkar of Fars, and Jalal al-Daulah, son of Zill al-Sultan, was appointed governor of Fars. H.H. Mu'tamid al-Daulah was dismissed. 'Abdallah Khan, son of Khuda Karam Khan, who had taken sanctuary in the Shah's stable, came with Zill al-Sultan.

His Highness summoned me from 'Arabistan, and I came by post to Isfahan. Darab Khan Qashqa'i also came to Isfahan. However, His Highness wished to make peace between us. Because of Darab Khan's idiocy, however, I did not accept [this offer of reconciliation]. I told [Zill al-Sultan], were I to forget last year's Qashqa'i raid in the Bakhtiyari and not retaliate, he must dismiss Darab Khan and appoint Sultan Muhammad Khan as ilkhani with Hajji Nasrallah Khan as ilbaigi of the Qashqa'i. Zill al-Sultan accepted and dismissed Darab Khan. He made [Sultan Muhammad Khan] the ilkhani together with Hajji Nasrallah Khan the governor of Qashqa'i.

I also made requests regarding Vali Khan, son of Khuda Karam Khan, who had been seized by Mu'tamid al-Daulah. The Prince ordered his release and appointed him governor of Buir Ahmad. Khuda Karam Khan was expelled from the tribe.

'Abdallah Khan [and his retainers] came to Chaqakhur, and I gave him a [?] horse. Today, Friday, he was dismissed, and went off toward the Buir Ahmad. Hajji Baba Khan Darashuri came to Chaqakhur and is here now as I am writing.

I went to Isfahan and had Ja'far Quli Khan dismissed from 'Arabistan. His Highness, may my soul be his sacrifice, awarded 'Arabistan to me so I could go and become its governor. I did not accept and said I could not bear the weight of office but that if the person I suggest was appointed as governor I would guarantee the taxes and good order of 'Arabistan. He appointed Ihtisham al-Saltanah governor of 'Arabistan. He went by the Khurramabad road, and I came to Chaqakhur, having arranged for me to bring order and collect taxes in 'Arabistan after the month of Shavval.

Those Sagvand and the son of Asad Khan Bairanvand accompanied me from 'Arabistan. I gave them 600 tumans in cash for their expenses, and I brought them to Isfahan. In the Blessed Presence of His Highness I settled their affairs. I got them robes of honor, and I sent them to accompany Ihtisham al-Saltanah. They departed. I arranged that each year Ihtisham al-Saltanah would give those Sagvand 1,200 tumans salary.

When I was in Ahvaz, Hajji Ilbaigi and my children returned in perfect health from Mecca. Their expenses have amounted to 8,000 tumans. I spent a total of one month in Isfahan. H.H. Zill al-Sultan, may my soul be his sacrifice, went to Burujird; consequently I sent Isfandiyar and Hajji 'Ali Quli with 200 savars and Farajallah to accompany him there. I, when I left [Isfahan], came to Malamir. I ordered work on the qanats of Imam Riza this year. I sent for the Bavir who were at Susan to bring their households to the qanats and to cultivate.

Ja'far Khan Bahmah'i, Aqa Khan Bahmah'i, Mirza Aqa Khan, and Aqa Fath 'Ali were all in Malamir for 50 days. My dear brothers, Hajji Ilbaigi, arriving from Andakah, and Aqa Riza, from Ardal, came to Malamir for a while. H.H. Zill al-Sultan asked me to send Aqa Riza Quli to him in Tehran. This year [both] Aqa Riza Quli and Hajji 'Ali Quli went to Tehran.

[The events of] *The Year 1299.*[147]

At the end of winter, we migrated from Malamir and came to Murdafil, and in the evening snow fell. By morning the weather had turned good, and we moved to Kurkur and then to Shushtar, where we spent several nights with the Prince, Ihtisham al-Saltanah. I dispatched my beloved sons, Isfandiyar and Hajji Khusrau, with 200 savars to escort [and remain with] Ihtisham al-Saltanah in Ahvaz.

I came to Ab Bid and sent for the shaikhs of the Al Kasir. They were brought [before me]. Relations between Shaikh Farhan and Shaikh 'Ali were not good, but I brought about a reconciliation. I gave all of them robes of honor. Shaikh 'Ali brought a Vaznah horse and one mare as ta'aruf. The shaikh of the Kasir made a present (ta'aruf) of a two-year-old Jafizah mare. I bought a Kurand horse from the son of Chiragh 'Ali Khan for 200 tumans and took it for Zill al-Sultan.

Ten days after Aid[148] I mounted and rode to Ahvaz and to Ihtisham al-Saltanah. Shaikh Rahim Khan, Mir 'Abdallah, and Shaikh Jabarah all came. I settled their affairs and left. Nusrat al-Mulk died. I sent his son, Shaikh Muhammad Khan, to Tehran, [because] Shaikh Miz'al Khan, [another] son of Hajji Jabir Khan Nusrat al-Mulk, fought with Shaikh Muhammad Khan. Hajji Jabir Khan's power and wealth went to Shaikh Miz'al Khan, and the people gathered around him, too. He, on his part, generously gave money to them.

Ihtisham al-Saltanah went to Muhammarah with Isfandiyar and Hajji Khusrau. Shaikh Miz'al made a present (ta'aruf) of an 'Abayah Sharak mare and an 'Abayah 'Ajil mare to Isfandiyar. He also presented a gift (ta'aruf) to Ihtisham al-Saltanah of a Saglavi Jidran mare along with 1,000 tumans cash. Ihtisham al-Saltanah bestowed a Jidrani mare on Hajji Khusrau and a Vaznah mare on Isfandiyar. The rest of the shaikhs, also, have given horses to Isfandiyar as ta'aruf: 20 head in total.

During this year Khuda Karam Khan Buir Ahmad quarreled with his son Vali Khan, and they appeared before me in Shushtar so that I might mediate and reconcile them; then they could leave. I bestowed a good horse, a length of gabardine, a broadsword, a halter, and 100 tumans on Khuda Karam. I also gave a good horse to Vali Khan, his son, and they departed.

Letters came from Aqa Riza Quli and Hajji 'Ali Quli in Tehran saying they had been received by the Shah, who showed them great favor. The Shah had come to Zill al-Sultan's palace, and Aqa Riza Quli and Hajji 'Ali Quli gave the Shah pishkash of one good horse with 500 tumans cash. The Shah, too, honored Riza Quli with a flowered and jeweled sword.[149]

A letter from Zill al-Sultan arrived from Ahvaz calling Isfandiyar to Isfahan. I arranged with Ihtisham al-Saltanah that Hajji Khusrau should remain in 'Arabistan with 100 savars so Isfandiyar could go to Isfahan.

In this year Sipahsalar A'zam died in Khurasan.

I left Ahvaz for Andakah, where I stayed three nights in the house of Hajji Ilbaigi. Then I went toward yailaq accompanied by Chiragh 'Ali Khan and Iskandar Khan Bakhtiyarvand, until we reached Shimbar,[150] where Chiragh 'Ali Khan left to join his own tayafah, the Mahmud Salih, and Iskandar Khan remained with his own tents, too.

This year the important British merchant, McKenzie,[151] became friends with me. I ordered eight rifles, five double-barreled, three single-barreled, with one brace of pistols, and 10,000 rounds of ammunition from him to send to me. Their total value was 1,400 tumans. I paid him in Ahvaz from the taxes of 'Arabistan, because in Isfahan I could make up the money to the Divan.

In this year my beloved son, Amir Quli, went on pilgrimage to Najaf Ashraf with Zaman Khan, and all returned in perfect health.

Notes

Introduction

1 Colonel J.U. Bateman Champain, "On the Various Means of Communication between Central Persia and the Sea", *Proceedings of the Royal Geographical Society*, v, New Series (1883), pp. 133–4. Henry Blosse Lynch, "Across Luristan to Ispahan", *Proceedings of the Royal Geographical Society*, XII (1890), pp. 523–53. Major H.A. Sawyer, *Report: A Reconnaissance in the Bakhtiari Country, Southwest Persia* (Simla, 1891). Isabella L. Bird Bishop notes British strategic and commercial interest in the Bakhtiyari, and quotes a remark by Imam Quli Khan that "the English under the dress of the merchant often conceal the uniform of the soldier". She adds: "It is not wonderful, therefore, that many of the principal Khans, whose immemorial freedom has been encroached upon in many recent years by the Tihran Government, should look forward to a day when one of the Western powers will occupy south-west Persia, and give them security." Isabella L. Bird Bishop, *Journeys in Persia and Kurdistan* I (London, 1891), pp. 326–8.

Chapter I: A historical and theoretical survey

1 My thanks to my Dartmouth colleague, John Major, for his assistance in focusing and phrasing this hypothesis.
2 Hamdallah Mustaufi Qazvini, *Tarikh Guzidah*, edited by 'Abd al-Husain Nava'i (Tehran, 1339/1961), p. 540.
3 Amir Sharaf Khan Bidlisi, *Sharafnamah Tarikh Mufassil Kurdistan*, edited by Muhammad 'Abbasi (Tehran, 1343/1965). Sir John Chardin, *The Travels of Sir John Chardin into Persia and the East Indies. To Which is Added, the Coronation of this Present King of Persia, Solyman the Third* (London, 1686). Iskandar Baig Turkman [Munshi], *Tarikh 'Alam Ara 'Abbasi*, edited by Iraj Afshar, I, II (Tehran, 1334/1956). *Tadhkirat al-Muluk*, translated and edited by Vladimir Minorsky (London, 1943).
4 *Encyclopaedia of Islam*, 1st edn. S.v. "Lur", by Vladimir Minorsky.
5 Turkman, *Tarikh 'Alam Ara*, I, p. 503.
6 Chardin, *Travels*, p. 147.
7 John R. Perry, "Forced Migration in Iran during the Seventeenth and Eighteenth Centuries", *Iranian Studies*, VIII (1975), p. 212.

8 *Tadhkirat al-Muluk*, p. 44.

9 Jonas Hanway, *The Revolutions of Persia* (London, 1754), p. 238. Father Judasz Tadeusz Krusinski, *The History of the Revolution of Persia*, I (London, 1728), p. 97.

10 See Appendix II, Document 1.

11 See Appendix II.

12 See Appendix IIIb, Documents 1, 4.

13 I'timad al-Saltanah, *Ruznamah Khatirat I'timad al-Saltanah*, edited by Iraj Afshar (Tehran, 1345/1967), p. 197.

14 See Chapter VI, pp. 98–103.

15 See Chapter VI.

16 Jean-Pierre Digard, "De la Nécessité et des Inconvénients, pour un Baxtyâri, d'Être Baxtyâri. Communauté, Territoire et Inégalité chez des Pasteurs Nomades d'Iran", *Pastoral Production and Society* (Cambridge, 1979), p. 132.

17 Jean-Pierre Digard, personal communication.

18 Lois Grant Beck, "Economic Transformations among Qashqa'i Nomads, 1962–1978", in *Modern Iran: The Dialectics of Continuity and Change*, edited by Michael E. Bonine and Nikki R. Keddie (Albany, 1981), pp. 99–122.

19 See Chapter III, pp. 35–9. Also Digard, "De la Nécessité", p. 129.

20 Possibly the designations "bakhsh" or "buluk" date only from the 1930s, when the central government assumed direct administration of the Bakhtiyari. They are not to be found in earlier written sources. Also, these two terms may represent territorial, in addition to administrative, relationships as opposed to kin relationships.

21 Gene R. Garthwaite, "The Bakhtiyari Ilkhani: An Illusion of Unity", *International Journal of Middle East Studies*, VIII (1977), pp. 145–60.

22 Fasa'i records: "In that year [1234/1818], by mediation of Haji Mirza Reza Qoli Nava'i, vizier of Fars, the title 'Ilkhani' was bestowed upon Jani Khan-e Qashqa'i, ilbegi of Fars. His son Mohammad 'Ali he appointed ilbegi. Up to that year nobody in Fars had been called by the title 'Ilkhani'. The head of the tribes in Khorasan used to be called 'Ilkhani'." Hasan Fasa'i, *History of Persia under Qajar Rule (Farsnama Naseri)*, translated by Heribert Busse (New York, 1972), p. 160.

23 See Appendix IIIb, Document 4.

24 H.H. Gerth and C. Wright Mills, *From Max Weber* (New York, 1958), p. 78.

25 John R. Perry, *Karim Khan Zand: A History of Iran, 1747–1779* (Chicago, 1979).

26 Nikki R. Keddie, "The Iranian Power Structure and Social Change 1800–1969: An Overview", *International Journal of Middle East Studies*, II (1971), pp. 3–20.

Chapter II: The Bakhtiyari and nomadism

1 See Supplement and Appendix IV.

2 Major Sir Henry Rawlinson, "Notes on a March from Zohab through the

Province of Luristan to Kirmanshah in the Year 1836", *Journal of the Royal Geographical Society*, IX (1839), p. 103.

3 Isabella L. Bird Bishop, *Journeys in Persia and Kurdistan* (London, 1891), p. 295.

4 Fredrik Barth, *Nomads of South Persia: The Basseri Tribe of the Khamseh Confederation* (Oslo, London, and New York, 1964), p. 12. William Irons and Lois Grant Beck, personal communication.

5 *Encyclopaedia of Islam*, 1st edn. S.v. "Lur", by Vladimir Minorsky.

6 Pierre Oberling, *The Qashqa'i Nomads of Fars* (The Hague, 1974), p. 27.

7 Jean-Pierre Digard, "De la Nécessité et des Inconvénients, pour un Baxtyâri, d'Être Baxtyâri. Communauté, Territoire et Inégalité chez des Pasteurs Nomades d'Iran", *Pastoral Production and Society* (Cambridge, 1979), pp. 127–39.

8 Henry Field, *Contributions to the Anthropology of Iran* (Chicago, 1939), p. 185.

9 Mary Douglas, *Natural Symbols* (London, 1970), p. xi.

10 D.L.R. Lorimer, "The Popular Verse of the Bakhtiari of S.W. Persia, III: Further Specimens", *Bulletin of the School of Oriental and African Studies*, XXVI (1963), pp. 62–3.

11 Digard, "De la Nécessité", p. 135. Also C.A. Gault, "The Bakhtiari Tribe" (Isfahan, 1944), India Office Library, L/P&S/12/3546, pp. 6–7.

12 Digard, "De la Nécessité", p. 135.

13 Barth, *Nomads*, p. 6.

14 Frank Hole, "Ethnoarcheology of Nomadic Pastoralism: A Case Study", paper, Rice University (Houston, 1975), p. 45.

15 Jacques Berque, "Introduction", *International Social Science Journal*, XI (1959), p. 484.

16 Robert J. Braidwood, "The Earliest Village Communities of Southwestern Asia Reconsidered", paper, Atti del VI Congresso Internazionale delle Scienze Preistoriche e Protostoriche, I (Rome, 1962), p. 122. Kent V. Flannery, "The Ecology of Early Food Production in Mesopotomia", *Science*, CXLVII (1965), p. 1255. Jørgen Meldgaard, Peder Mortensen, and Henrik Thrane, *Excavations at Tepe Guran, Luristan* (Copenhagen, 1964), pp. 111, n. 15.

17 Owen Lattimore, *Inner Asian Frontiers of China* (Boston, 1962), p. 59.

18 Owen Lattimore, *Studies in Frontier History* (London and New York, 1962), p. 487.

19 Jean-Pierre Digard, "'Tsiganes' et Pasteurs Nomades dans le Sud-Ouest de l'Iran", in *Tsiganes et Nomades*, edited by Jean-Pierre Liegeois (Paris, 1978), pp. 43–53.

20 Neville Dyson-Hudson, "The Study of Nomads", *Journal of Asian and African Studies*, VII (1972), pp. 18–19.

21 Lattimore, *Studies*, p. 487.

22 Barth, *Nomads*, pp. 16–17.

23 Nikki R. Keddie, "The Iranian Village before and after Land Reform", *Journal of Contemporary History*, III (1968), p. 72.

24 Sir James Morier, "Some Accounts of the I'liyáts, or Wandering Tribes of

Persia, Obtained in the Years 1814 and 1815", *Journal of the Royal Geographical Society*, VII (1837), p. 239.

25 Patty Jo Watson, "Clues to Iranian Prehistory in Modern Village Life", *Expedition*, VIII (1966), p. 11; *Archeological Ethnography in Western Iran* (Tucson, 1979), pp. 94–6, 253, 280–1.

26 Barth, *Nomads*, p. 109.

27 John Kolars, "Locational Aspects of the Goat in Non-Western Agriculture", *Geographical Review*, LVI (1966), pp. 577–84.

28 'Abd al-Ghafar Najm al-Mulk, *Safarnamah Khuzistan*, edited by Muhammad Dabirsiyaqi (Tehran, 1341/1963), p. 171.

29 Robert McC. Adams, *Land behind Baghdad: A History of Settlement of the Diyala Plains* (Chicago, 1965), p. 114.

30 Xavier de Planhol, "Aspects of Mountain Life in Anatolia and Iran", in *Geography as Human Ecology*, edited by S.R. Eyre and G.R.J. Jones (London, 1966), pp. 292; "Caractères Généraux de la Vie Montagnarde dans le Proche-Orient et dans l'Afrique du Nord", *Annales de Géographie*, LXXI (1962), p. 124.

In a more recent analysis of this problem ("Geography of Settlement", in *The Cambridge History of Iran*, I: *The Land of Iran*, edited by W.B. Fisher, [Cambridge, 1968], pp. 409–67), de Planhol uses a fifteenth-century text (*Muntakhab al-Tavarikh Mu'ini*, edited by Jean Aubin [Tehran, 1335/1957], p. 44) as support for his thesis that the Mongol invasions forced peasants in many regions to abandon sedentary agriculture and turn to nomadism. There was possibly a shift from agriculture to a greater emphasis upon flocks, but foreign words (e.g., qishlaq and yailaq, Turkish for winter and summer pastures) may have been merely borrowed to describe indigenous and existing practices or institutions. In Bakhtiyari sources garmsir and sardsir, Persian words, are used interchangeably with their Turkish equivalents.

31 Werner Caskel, "The Bedouinization of Arabia", in *Studies in Islamic Cultural History*, edited by G.E. von Grunebaum (Menasha, Wisc., 1954), p. 41.

32 Ann K.S. Lambton, "The Evolution of the Iqta' in Medieval Iran", *Iran*, V (1967), pp. 41–50.

33 Marshall G.S. Hodgson, *The Venture of Islam*, II (Chicago, 1974), pp. 400–4.

34 William Irons, "Nomadism as a Political Adaptation: The Case of the Yomut Turkmen", *American Ethnologist*, I (1974), p. 635.

35 Barth, *Nomads*, p. 101.

Chapter III: The khans and the tribal structure

1 Jean-Pierre Digard, "De la Nécessité et des Inconvénients, pour un Baxtyâri, d'Être Baxtyâri. Communauté, Territoire et Inégalité chez des Pasteurs Nomades d'Iran", *Pastoral Production and Society* (Cambridge, 1979), pp. 127–39.

2 *Ibid.*

3 *Ibid.*, p. 129.

4 Western accounts identify pasture land with tayafahs and then tirahs. Captain
Robert P. Hand, "A Survey of the Tribes of Iran" (mimeographed, 22 July
1963), pp. 35–61. Sir Henry Layard, "A Description of the Province of
Khuzistan", *Journal of the Royal Geographical Society*, XVI (1846), pp. 102–5.

Layard also notes Muhammad Taqi Khan's ability to reassign pastures (p.
12). Husain Quli Khan Ilkhani, too, in his "Kitabchah", refers to pastures he
awarded to Darashuri khans who had fled from the Qashqa'i; presumably he
could do so without displacing Bakhtiyari tayafahs from traditional pastures,
but he may have accommodated the new groups at the expense of settled
agriculturalists. Barth notes:

. . . each oulad [roughly analogous to a Bakhtiyari tirah] is a division of one of the
named sections of the tribe, and thus has its defined place in the formal tribal
system. It constitutes a group with defined usufruct rights to pastures and a
designated headman, and is thus a product of the chief's administration. He
formally defines its membership, leadership, and estate. But in doing this he
merely recognizes and utilizes certain rules and groupings that are a part of the
Basseri social system. They are not his creations, though he gives them a formal
regularity and perhaps a field of relevance that they would otherwise lack.

The principle which the chief draws out and makes the basis for his recognition
of groups and allocation of rights is the patrilineal principle . . .

A man's rights in an oulad depend on his patrilineal descent . . .

. . . the members of [an oulad] have at any time, by allotment of the chief,
exclusive pasture rights in specified areas at specified times.

Frederik Barth, *Nomads of South Persia: The Basseri Tribe of the Khamseh
Confederation* (Oslo, London, and New York, 1964), pp. 55–6.

5 *Encyclopaedia of Islam*, 2nd edn. S.v. "Kalantar", by Ann K.S. Lambton.

6 Gene R. Garthwaite, "Two Persian Wills of Hajj 'Ali Quli Khan Sardar
As'ad", *Journal of the American Oriental Society*, XCV (1975), pp. 645–50.

7 Oliver Garrod, "The Qashqai Tribe of Fars", *Journal of the Royal Central
Asian Society*, XXXIII (1946), p. 301.

8 See Appendix I, Documents 4, 5.

9 Gene R. Garthwaite, "The Bakhtiyari Khans, the Government of Iran, and
the British, 1846–1915", *International Journal of Middle East Studies*, III
(1972), pp. 24–44; "The Bakhtiyari Ilkhani: An Illusion of Unity", *International Journal of Middle East Studies*, VIII (1977), pp. 145–60.

10 'Abd al-Ghafar Najm al-Mulk, *Safarnamah Khuzistan*, edited by Muhammad
Dabirsiyaqi (Tehran, 1341/1963), p. 30.

11 Layard, describing Muhammad Taqi Khan's wealth, writes:

His wealth, like that of other chiefs of these nomade [*sic*] tribes, consisted
principally in flocks and herds; actual specie they very seldom possess, and the
enormous sum that the Mo'tamid had represented to be in Mohammed Taki's
possession was such a ridiculous exaggeration as a Persian alone could credit.

Mohammed Taki's actual property might have consisted of 1500 buffaloes, 50 excellent Arab mares, some of which were valued at very high prices, and could have been sold for 500 tomans (250£) in Khuzistan; the same number of good Cha'b stallions, 500 broodmares, and 500 horses of Lur and mixed breeds, and about 10,000 sheep and goats. This I consider as having been about the whole amount of his property. Mohammed Taki, a despotic chief, had of course a certain power over the property of those who lived under his authority.

> Layard, "A Description", p. 15. Possibly these totals constitute the property of his tayafahs/tirahs rather than his personal holdings. Barth writes:

It is a characteristic feature of wealth in herds that its net productivity rate for the owner declines as the size of the herds increases. No effective means have been developed among the Basseri to protect the rights of the big herd-owner – the less the flocks are under the owner's constant supervision, the more he will be cheated out of his profits while made to carry real or fictitious losses . . .

What is more, the capital asset itself, the flock, is . . . subject to unpredictable fluctuations and severe losses from natural causes, averaging as much as 50 percent in some years . . .

As a herd-owner's wealth grows, there are thus growing economic incentives for him to transfer a part of his capital to another form than wealth in herds . . . The typical pattern for wealthy nomads is therefore to convert a fraction of their wealth in flocks into landed property.

> *Nomads*, pp. 103–4. Hole reaches similar conclusions and notes: "one seldom sees a rich nomad. The reason is that the potential for increase of herds is subject to great variation as a result of environmental, pathological, and economic factors." Frank Hole, "Ethnoarcheology of Nomadic Pastoralism: A Case Study", paper, Rice University (Houston, 1975), p. 42.

12 Elizabeth N. Macbean Ross, *A Lady Doctor in Bakhtiari Land*, pp. 97–108, 121.

13 Thomas R. Stauffer, "The Qashqai Nomads: A Contemporary Appraisal", *The Harvard Review* (Spring 1963), p. 33. Lois Grant Beck, personal communication.

14 See Chapter V, pp. 80–1.

Chapter IV: The Bakhtiyari and the state through the eighteenth century

1 Arnold J. Toynbee, *A Study of History* (New York and London, 1947), p. 168.

2 *Ibid.*, p. 169.

3 John MacDonald Kinneir, *A Geographical Memoir of the Persian Empire* (London, 1813), p. 44.

4 Sarhang Abu al-Fath Uzhan, *Tarikh Bakhtiyari* (Tehran, 1345/1967); Husain Pazhman, "Bakhtiyari dar Guzashtah Dur", *Vahid*, III, Nos. 2, 3, 4 (1344/1966).

5 Pazhman, *Vahid*, III, No. 2 (Bahman 1344/January 1966), p. 146.

6 "Bakht" comes into Persian from the Avestan "bag" (or in Sanskrit, "bhag"), which means to distribute a portion of a sacrifice, thus carrying with it the

connotation of good fortune (Christian Bartholomae, *Altiranische Wöterbuch* [Berlin, 1961], p. 921). "Yar" is derived from the Middle Persian "yavar", helper; hence, "Bakhtiyari" = helper, or friend, of luck, or good fortune. "Bactria" is the Greek for the Elamite "Ba-ak-ši-iš" (Roland G. Kent, *Old Persian* [New Haven, 1950], p. 199), and its root is most probably "bag".

7 Hajji Khusrau Khan Sardar Zafar, "Tarikh Bakhtiyari", (1329/1911–1333/1914), p. 3.

8 Hamdallah Mustaufi Qazvini, *Tarikh Guzidah*, edited by 'Abd al-Husain Nava'i (Tehran, 1339/1961), p. 540.

9 Kinneir, *Geographical Memoir*, pp. 138–9.

10 Sardar Zafar, "Tarikh Bakhtiyari", p. 3.

11 Hajji 'Ali Quli Khan Sardar As'ad, *Tarikh Bakhtiyari* (Tehran [?], 1333/1914), p. 42.

12 Qazvini, *Tarikh Guzidah*, p. 540. Minorsky adds: "Shihab al-Din al-'Umari ... mentions the existence of Lurs in Syria and Egypt and tells how Saladin ... alarmed by their dangerous ability to climb the steepest ramparts, had them massacred en masse. This anecdote throws light on the causes which produce the arrival (? return to) in Luristan about 600 AH of numerous Iranian tribes." *Encyclopaedia of Islam*, 1st edn. S.v. "Lur", by Vladimir Minorsky.

13 Muhammad Kazim, *Namah 'Alam Ara Nadiri*, facsimile, 3 vols. (Moscow, 1960–66).

14 Amir Sharaf Khan Bidlisi, *Sharafnamah Tarikh Mufassil Kurdistan*, edited by Muhammad 'Abbasi (Tehran, 1343/1965), p. 76.

15 Iskandar Baig Turkman [Munshi], *Tarikh 'Alam Ara 'Abbasi*, edited by Iraj Afshar, I (Tehran, 1334/1956), p. 503.

16 *Ibid.*, p. 908.

17 *Ibid.*, pp. 959–60.

18 Sardar Zafar, "Tarikh Bakhtiyari", p. 2.

19 Turkman, *Tarikh 'Alam Ara*, II, p. 1086.

20 Sir John Chardin, *The Travels of Sir John Chardin into Persia and the East Indies. To Which is Added, the Coronation of this Present King of Persia, Solyman the Third* (London, 1686), p. 147.

21 John R. Perry, "Forced Migration in Iran during the Seventeenth and Eighteenth Centuries", *Iranian Studies*, VIII (1975), p. 212.

22 *Tadhkirat al-Muluk*, translated and edited by Vladimir Minorsky (London, 1943), p. 44.

23 *Ibid.*, p. 104.

24 Xavier de Planhol, "Aspects of Mountain Life in Anatolia and Iran", in *Geography as Human Ecology*, edited by S.R. Eyre and G.R.J. Jones (London, 1966), p. 292.

25 Marshall G.S. Hodgson, *The Venture of Islam*, II (Chicago, 1974), pp. 400–4.

26 John R. Perry, "The Last Safavids, 1722–1773", *Iran*, IX (1971), pp. 59–62.

27 Roger M. Savory, *Iran Under the Safavids* (Cambridge, 1980), p. 27. Also Ann K.S. Lambton, "Quis Custodiet Custodes: Some Reflections on the Persian Theory of Government", *Studia Islamica*, VI (1956), p. 125.

28 Roger M. Savory, "The Principal Offices of the Safawid State during the Reign of Isma'il I (907–30/1501–24)", *Bulletin of the School of Oriental and African Studies*, XXIII (1960), p. 91.
29 See Appendix I, Document 1.
30 Lawrence Lockhart, *Nadir Shah: A Critical Study* (London, 1938), p. 99.
31 See Appendix I, Document 2.
32 See Appendix II, Document 2.
33 Sarhang Jahangir Qa'im Magami, "Muhrha va Tughraha Padishahan Iran", *Barrasiha Tarikhi*, IV, No. 4 (Mihr–Aban 1348/September–October 1969), p. 52. Although no impressions of 'Ali Mardan's seals have survived, an inscription has been copied along with one of his letters (see Appendix II, Document 1), and it has neither a Shi'i nor a Safavid sentiment.
34 Reginald Stuart Poole, *The Coins of the Shahs of Persia* (London, 1887), p. 102. Rabino notes, however, that Isma'il III's coins bore on the reverse: "Bandah-yi Shah-i Valayat-i Isma'il". H.L. Rabino di Borgomale, *Coins, Medals, and Seals of the Shahs of Iran, 1500–1941* (Algiers [?], 1945), p. 48.
35 *Encyclopaedia of Islam*, 2nd edn. S.v. "Karim Khan Zand", by A.H. Zarrinkoob.
36 Ahmad Kasravi, *Tarikh Pansad Salih Khuzistan* (Tehran, 1330/1952), pp. 20–1.
37 See Appendix I, Document 1.
38 Father Judasz Tadeusz Krusinski, *The History of the Revolution of Persia*, I (London, 1728), p. 97.
39 Kazim, *Namah 'Alam Ara*, I, pp. 177a–177b.
40 Muhammad Kazim, *Kitab Nadiri* (Institut Vostokove Leningrad, n.d.).
41 Lockhart, *Nadir Shah*, p. 65.
42 Jonas Hanway, *The Revolutions of Persia* (London, 1754), p. 419.
43 Kazim, *Namah 'Alam Ara*, II, pp. 21a–23a.
44 If coins were actually struck no reference to them is to be found in either Poole or Rabino.
45 Kazim, *Namah 'Alam Ara*, II, pp. 21a–23a.
46 *Ibid.*
47 See Appendix I, Document 2.
48 See Appendix I, Documents 3, 4, 5.
49 John R. Perry, *Karim Khan Zand: A History of Iran, 1747–1779* (Chicago, 1979), p. 27.
50 See Appendix II, Document 1.
51 See Appendix II, Document 2.
52 See Appendix II, Document 3.
53 See Appendix II, Documents 4, 5.
54 See Appendix II, Document 6.
55 See Appendix II, Document 7.
56 See Appendix II, Documents 8, 10, 11.
57 See Appendix II, Documents 8, 10, 11, 14.
58 Uzhan, *Tarikh Bakhtiyari*, I, pp. 12–15.

Chapter V: The Bakhtiyari and the nineteenth century

1 See Appendix IIIa, Documents 1–4, 6.
2 Sir Henry Layard, *Early Adventures in Persia, Susiana, and Babylonia* (New York, 1887).
3 Mas'ud Mirza Zill al-Sultan, *Tarikh Sar Guzasht Mas'udi* (?, 1325/1907).
4 *Ibid.*, pp. 287–8.
5 I'timad al-Saltanah, *Ruznamah Khatirat I'timad al-Saltanah*, edited by Iraj Afshar (Tehran, 1345/1967), p. 97.
6 Robert Grant Watson, *A History of Persia from the Beginning of the Nineteenth Century to the Year 1858* (London, 1866), p. 54.
7 Sir James Morier, "Some Accounts of the I'liyáts, or Wandering Tribes of Persia, Obtained in the Years 1814 and 1815", *Journal of the Royal Geographical Society*, VII (1837), p. 234.
8 Sir James Morier, *A Journey through Persia in the Years 1808 and 1809* (London, 1812), p. 110.
9 Sir John Malcolm, *The History of Persia from the Most Early Period to the Present Time*, II (London, 1815), p. 356.
10 Morier, "Some Accounts", pp. 237–8.
11 *Ibid.*, p. 234.
12 Major Sir Henry Rawlinson, "Notes on a March from Zohab through the Province of Luristan to Kirmanshah in the Year 1836", *Journal of the Royal Geographical Society*, IX (1839), pp. 102–3.
13 *Ibid.*
14 Morier, "Some Accounts", pp. 237–8.
15 Baron C.A. De Bode, *Travels in Luristan and Arabistan*, II (London, 1845), p. 88.
16 See Appendix IIIa, Document 5.
17 Sir James Morier, *A Second Journey through Persia* (London, 1818), p. 126.
18 Layard, *Early Adventures*, I and II.
19 *Ibid.*, I, p. 403.
20 *Ibid.*, II, p. 11.
21 *Ibid.*, I, p. 456.
22 Government of India, Foreign Department, Secret, No. 2, Captain S. Hennell, Resident, Persian Gulf to Colonel Sheil, Envoy and Minister, Erzerum, 8 February 1841.
23 See Chapter VI, pp. 103–4, 121–5.
24 Layard, *Early Adventures*, I, p. 287.
25 Rawlinson, "Notes on a March", p. 104.
26 Government of India, Foreign Department, Secret, No. 2, Captain S. Hennell, Resident, Persian Gulf to Colonel Sheil, Envoy and Minister, Erzerum, 8 February 1841.
27 See Supplement and Appendix IV.
28 See Appendix IIIa, Document 7.
29 See Appendix IIIa, Document 10.
30 Rawlinson, "Notes on a March", p. 104.

31 Hajji Khusrau Khan Sardar Zafar, "Tarikh Bakhtiyari" (1329/1911–1333/ 1914), p. 6.
32 Sarhang Abu al-Fath Uzhan, *Tarikh Bakhtiyari*, I (Tehran, 1345/1967), p. 58.
33 Sardar Zafar, "Tarikh Bakhtiyari", p. 12.
34 Layard, *Early Adventures*, II, p. 19.
35 Gene R. Garthwaite, "Two Persian Wills of Hajj 'Ali Quli Khan Sardar As'ad", *Journal of the American Oriental Society*, XCV (1975), pp. 645–50.
36 Uzhan, *Tarikh Bakhtiyari*, I, p. 82.
37 Genealogical data were primarily obtained from Sardar Zafar, "Tarikh Bakhtiyari", pp. 91–6; from Government of India, Foreign Department, Secret E, Proceedings 3–33, December 1912, No. 29, Major Percy Cox to Secretary, Government of India, Bushihr, 25 October 1912; and from C.A. Gault, "The Bakhtiari Tribe" (Isfahan, 1944), India Office Library, L/P&S/ 12/3546, pp. 42–50.
38 James A. Bill, "The Patterns of Elite Politics in Iran", in *Political Elites in the Middle East*, edited by George Lenczowski (Washington, D.C., 1975), pp. 32–6.
39 Garthwaite, "Two Persian Wills".
40 See Appendix IIIb, Documents 10, 13.
41 H.H. Gerth and C. Wright Mills, *From Max Weber* (New York, 1958), p. 78.
42 Sardar Zafar, "Tarikh Bakhtiyari", p. 84.
43 Sardar Zafar, "Tarikh Bakhtiyari", pp. 84–5.
44 Garthwaite, "Two Persian Wills".
45 See Appendix IIIb, Document 1.
46 See Appendix IIIb, Document 2.
47 See Appendix IIIb, Document 3.
48 See Appendix IIIb, Document 14.
49 See Appendix IIIb, Document 18.
50 Jean-Pierre Digard, personal communication. Also Asghar Karimi, "Nizam Mulkiyat Arzi dar Il Bakhtiyari", *Hunar va Mardum*, 189–90 (2537/1978), pp. 67–83.
51 Sawyer notes:

The same sites are always resorted to by the same families generation after generation, and the places where each family has had its tents for centuries can be seen marked out by large white stones of which there are many about. When a family becomes too large and the Ilyat site too small, a section or group removes to fresh pastures, forming a new habitation and circle. But such empty spaces are becoming scarce in this eastern part of the Bakhtiari country.

Major H.A. Sawyer, *Report: A Reconnaissance in the Bakhtiari Country, Southwest Persia* (Simla, 1891), p. 45.

52 See Appendix IIIb, Document 14.
53 Sir Arnold Talbot Wilson, *Military Report on S.W. Persia*, III: *Bakhtiari Country North of Karun River* (Simla, 1910), p. 26.
54 Sardar Zafar, "Tarikh Bakhtiyari", p. 3.

55 Hajji 'Ali Quli Khan Sardar As'ad, *Tarikh Bakhtiyari* (Tehran [?], 1333/1914), p. 198.
56 Government of India, Foreign Department, Proceeding 379, May 1882, No. 18, Ronald T. Thompson to Earl Granville, Tehran, 25 January 1882, transmission of a report made by Walter Baring of a journey in southern Iran, 27 October 1881 to January 1882, p. 5.
57 Great Britain, Foreign Office, No. 102, Inclosure, Sir Mortimer Durand, "Persia: Report by Consul J.R. Preece on a Journey through the Bakhtiari Country to Shuster", 26 December 1895, FO 248/548.
58 Wilson, *Military Report*, III, p. 26.
59 Sardar As'ad, *Tarikh Bakhtiyari*, p. 198.
60 Government of India, Foreign Department, Proceeding 379, May 1882, No. 18, Ronald T. Thompson to Earl Granville, Tehran, 25 January 1882, report by Walter Baring, p. 3.
61 De Bode, *Travels*, p. 82.
62 Government of India, Foreign Department, Proceeding 379, May 1882, No. 18, Ronald T. Thompson to Earl Granville, Tehran, 25 January 1882, report by Walter Baring, p. 5. Also Ann K.S. Lambton, *Landlord and Peasant in Persia* (London, 1953), p. 169.
63 Wilson, *Military Report*, III, p. 26.
64 See Supplement, p. 153.
65 See Appendix IIIb, Document 5.
66 Government of India, Foreign Department, Proceeding 379, May 1882, No. 18, Ronald T. Thompson to Earl Granville, Tehran, 25 January 1882, report by Walter Baring, p. 5.
67 'Abd al-Ghafar Najm al-Mulk, *Safarnamah Khuzistan*, edited by Muhammad Dabirsiyaqi (Tehran, 1341/1963), p. 53.
68 See Supplement and Appendix IV.
69 Najm al-Mulk, *Safarnamah Khuzistan*, p. 30.
70 Lambton, *Landlord and Peasant*, p. 170.
71 Isabella L. Bird Bishop, *Journeys in Persia and Kurdistan*, II (London, 1891), p. 11.
72 John Gordon Lorimer, *Gazetteer of the Persian Gulf, 'Oman, and Central Arabia* (Calcutta, 1915), pp. 1578–82.
73 *Ibid.*, p. 1576.
74 *Ibid.*, p. 1577.
75 *Ibid.*, p. 1576.
76 See Appendix IIIa, Document 2.
77 Uzhan, *Tarikh Bakhtiyari*, p. 87.
78 Najm al-Mulk, *Safarnamah Khuzistan*, p. 77.
79 See Supplement.
80 Great Britain, Foreign Office, No. 5991, Inclosure, Sir Henry Wolff to Lord Salisbury, Gulhak, 3 September 1890, "Memorandum" by Benam al-Mulk, p. 7.
81 Zill al-Sultan, *Tarikh Sar Guzasht*, p. 242.
82 I'timad al-Saltanah, *Ruznamah Khatirat*, p. 97.

83 *Ibid.*, p. 234.
84 Great Britain, Foreign Office, No. 5991, Inclosure, Sir Henry Wolff to Lord Salisbury, Gulhak, 3 September 1890, "Memorandum" by Benam al-Mulk, p. 7.
85 *Asnad Bar Guzidah az: Sipahsalar – Zill al-Sultan – Dabir al-Mulk*, edited by Ibrahim Safa'i (Tehran, 1350/1972), pp. 49–53.
86 Government of India, Foreign Department, Proceeding 379, May 1882, No. 18, Ronald T. Thompson to Earl Granville, Tehran, 25 January 1882, report by Walter Baring, p. 5.
87 *Ibid.*, p. 4.
88 Thanks to Henry Wright and to the Iranian Center for Archaeological Research for the photograph of Ilkhani's reservoir and its inscription.

Chapter VI: The post-1882 Bakhtiyari

1 Hajji Khusrau Khan Sardar Zafar, "Tarikh Bakhtiyari", 1329/1911–1333/1914, p. 84.
2 Gene R. Garthwaite, "The Bakhtiyari Khans, the Government of Iran, and the British, 1846–1915", *International Journal of Middle East Studies*, III (1972), pp. 24–44.
3 Sardar Zafar, "Tarikh Bakhtiyari", p. 84.
4 Great Britain, Foreign Office, No. 36, Inclosure 2, Consul P.J.C. Robertson to Colonel E.C. Ross, Basrah, 12 May 1888, FO 539/39.
5 Lord Curzon, *Persia and the Persian Question* (London, 1892), II, p. 295.
6 Government of India, Foreign Department, Secret E, July 1893, No. 315, Sir Frank Lascelles to the Earl of Rosebery, Secretary of State for Foreign Affairs, Tehran, 21 May 1893.
7 Curzon, *Persia*, II, p. 298.
8 Sardar Zafar, "Tarikh Bakhtiyari", pp. 84–5.
9 *Ibid.*
10 *Ibid.*
11 *Ibid.*
12 J.B. Kelly, *Britain and the Persian Gulf 1795–1880* (Oxford, 1968), pp. 483–4.
13 "Curzon's Analysis of British Policy and Interests in Persia and the Persian Gulf, 21 September 1899", in *Diplomacy in the Near and Middle East*, I, edited by J.C. Hurewitz (Princeton, 1958), pp. 224–5.
14 Firuz Kazemzadeh, *Russia and Britain in Persia, 1864–1914: A Study in Imperialism* (New Haven, 1968), p. 344.
15 Great Britain, Foreign Office, to and from Isfahan, Sir Frank Lascelles to Deputy Consul Agnoor, 4 May 1894, FO 248/572.
16 Great Britain, Foreign Office, No. 4, Inclosure, Sir Mortimer Durand to Lord Salisbury, Tehran, 17 January 1896, "Extracts from Consul Preece's Report on a Journey through the Bakhtiari Country to Shuster", Isfahan, 24 October 1895, FO 539/74.
17 *Ibid.*, No. 73, Inclosure 2, Sir Arthur Hardinge to Lord Salisbury, Tehran, 7 May 1897, FO 539/76.

18 *Ibid.*, No. 57, Inclosure 2, Sir Arthur Hardinge to Lord Salisbury, Tehran, 28 February 1898.
19 Government of India, Foreign Department, Secret E, Proceeding 9, No. 1901, Sir Arthur Hardinge to Lord Lansdowne, Gulhak, 26 June 1901.
20 *Ibid.*, Proceeding 10, No. 1901, Sir Arthur Hardinge to Lord Lansdowne, No. 186, Gulhak, 6 July 1901.
21 Great Britain, Foreign Office, No. 57, Inclosure 3, Sir Arthur Hardinge to Lord Salisbury, Tehran, 28 February 1898.
22 It will be seen in the following table that, except for dips in the toll and tonnage in 1903 and 1908, each year shows an increase.

Table of Annual Receipts

	1900	*1901*	*1902*	*1903*	*1904*
qirans	60,000	84,000		78,000	100,000
£	1,090	1,527	?	1,418	1,818
tons	102	549		409	753
	1905	*1906*	*1907*	*1908*	*1909*
qirans	130,000	132,000	170,000	140,000	200,000
£	2,362	2,400	3,100	2,545	3,636
tons	878	1,281	1,091	348	1,485

Government of India, Foreign Department, External B, Proceedings 103–4, February 1911, No. 103, Lynch Brothers to Foreign Office, 17 November 1910.

The tolls quoted above include the annual gallahdari of those tribes who used the routes on which the bridges were located for their migration as well as the tolls collected from the users of the Bakhtiyari road.
23 Great Britain, Foreign Office, Consul J.R. Preece to Sir Arthur Hardinge, 16 October 1901, FO 248/742.

It should be noted, too – regarding Lynch's complaints on the lack of transport animals – that tribesmen and their animals were following a pastoral nomadic life which did not free them for any length of time to participate regularly in carrying cargo; nor did such a task fit into their value system.
24 L.P. Elwell-Sutton, *Persian Oil: A Study in Power Politics* (London, 1955), pp. 17–19.
25 Government of India, Foreign Department, Secret E, Proceedings 612–42, May 1906, No. 617, Evelyn Grant Duff to Sir Edward Grey, Inclosure from Preece, 24 November 1905, Tehran, 20 December 1905.
26 *Ibid.*
27 "Translation of an Agreement between Messrs. W.K. D'Arcy and the Concession Syndicate Limited, with the Bakhtiari Khans Regarding the Right to Drill for Petroleum on the Lands of the Latter". 15 November 1905. (Author's personal collection.)
28 Government of India, Foreign Department, Secret E, Proceedings 616–42, May 1906, No. 636, Evelyn Grant Duff to Sir Edward Grey, No. 63, Tehran, 1 March 1906.

29 *Ibid.*, Proceeding 286, January 1907, Inclosure, Mushir al-Daulah to Evelyn Grant Duff, 26 July 1906.

30 *Ibid.*, Proceedings 650–68, No. 663, Cecil Spring-Rice to Sir Edward Grey, Tehran, 14 January 1907.

31 *Ibid.*, Proceedings 1–15, August 1907, No. 6, Inclosure, "Memo by M. Edouard Kitabji on the Affairs of the D'Arcy Oil Company", Tehran, 21 March 1907.

32 *Ibid.*, Proceedings 319–27, November 1907, No. 319, Percy Loraine to Cecil Spring-Rice, 20 May 1907.

33 *Ibid.*, No. 325, Inclosure, D.L.R. Lorimer to Cecil Spring-Rice, 20 June 1907.

34 *Ibid.*, Proceedings 206–38, January 1908, No. 222, D.L.R. Lorimer to Cecil Spring-Rice, January 1908.

35 Elwell-Sutton, *Persian Oil*, pp. 19–20.

36 Sir Arnold Talbot Wilson, *A Précis of the Relations of the British Government with the Tribes and Shaikhs of Arabistan* (Calcutta, 1912), p. 37.

37 Nikki R. Keddie, "The Origins of the Religious–Radical Alliance in Iran", *Past and Present*, XXXIV (1966), pp. 77–80.

38 Government of India, Foreign Department, Secret E, Proceedings 481–547, February 1910, No. 542, Sir George Barclay to Sir Edward Grey, Tehran, 4 October 1909.

39 *Ibid.*, External B, Proceedings 114–301, March 1912, No. 259, Sir Edward Grey to Sir George Buchanan, Foreign Office, 7 December 1911.

40 Nurullah Danishvar 'Alavi, *Tarikh Iran va Jumbish Vatan Partisan Isfahan va Bakhtiyari* (Tehran, 1335/1957), pp. 35–43.

41 *The Times* (London), 29 January 1909, p. 4. Curiously, at the turn of the century, the Bakhtiyari had strenuously objected to the British consul about a letter in *The Times* that slurred the Bakhtiyari road.

42 Mahdi Malikzadah, *Tarikh Inqilab Mashrutiyat Iran*, v (Tehran, 1328/1950), pp. 181–2.

43 Government of India, Foreign Department, Secret E, Proceedings 481–547, February 1910, No. 542, Sir George Barclay to Sir Edward Grey, Tehran, 4 October 1909.

44 E.G. Browne, *The Persian Revolution of 1905–1909* (London, 1910), p. 293.

45 Great Britain, Foreign Office, Note from A.T.W. [Arnold Talbot Wilson] to Major Percy Cox, 3 July 1909, FO 460/2, Section 14.

46 Government of India, Foreign Department, Secret E, Proceedings 308–575, October 1909, No. 380, Sir George Barclay to Sir Edward Grey, Tehran, 29 June 1909.

47 *The Times* (London), 3 July 1909, p. 5.

48 *Ibid.*, 14 July 1909, p. 5.

49 *Encyclopaedia of Islam*, 2nd edn. S.v. "Dustur", by Ann K.S. Lambton.

50 Government of India, Foreign Department, Secret E, Proceedings 362–408, April 1910, No. 404, Sir George Barclay to Sir Edward Grey, Tehran, 26 January 1910.

51 *Ibid.*, Proceedings 586–648, June 1910, No. 597, Political Resident, Persian Gulf to Secretary, Government of India, 12 April 1910.
52 *Ibid.*, No. 598, Political Resident, Persian Gulf to Secretary, Government of India, 12 April 1910.
53 *Ibid.*, Nos. 606–7, Political Resident, Persian Gulf to Secretary, Government of India, 17 April 1910.
54 Wilson, *Précis*, pp. 112–13.
55 Government of India, Foreign Department, Secret E, No. 331, Political Resident, Persian Gulf to Secretary, Government of India, 2 May 1910.
56 W. Morgan Shuster, *The Strangling of Persia* (New York, 1912), p. 93.
57 *Ibid.*, p. 116.
58 *Military Report on Persia, Compiled by the General Staff, 1911* (Simla, 1912), p. 244.
59 Peter Avery, *Modern Iran* (London, 1965), pp. 176–7.
60 Sir Percy M. Sykes, *A History of Persia* (London, 1930), p. 430.
61 Amin Banani, *The Modernization of Iran 1921–1941* (Stanford, 1961), p. 33.
62 Government of India, Foreign Department, External B, Proceeding 155, Sir George Barclay to Sir Edward Grey, Tehran, 21 November 1911.
63 Firuz Kazemzadeh, *Russia and Britain*, p. 638.
64 Government of India, Foreign Department, External B, Proceeding 170, Sir Edward Grey to Sir George Barclay, Foreign Office, 24 November 1911.
65 Kazemzadeh, *Russia and Britain*, p. 639.
66 Government of India, Foreign Department, External B, Proceeding 190, Sir George Barclay to Sir Edward Grey, Tehran, 28 November 1911.
67 Kazemzadeh, *Russia and Britain*, p. 638.
68 Government of India, Foreign Department, Proceeding 536, Sir George Barclay to Sir Edward Grey, Tehran, 7 December 1911.
69 *Ibid.*, Proceeding 259, Sir Edward Grey to Sir George Buchanan, Foreign Office, 7 December 1911.
70 Kazemzadeh, *Russia and Britain*, p. 639.
71 *Ibid.*
72 Government of India, Foreign Department, Proceeding 605, Sir George Barclay to Sir Edward Grey, Tehran, 24 December 1911.
73 Shuster, *Strangling of Persia*, p. 215.
74 *The Times* (London), 27 January 1912, p. 5.
75 Hajji Mirza Yahya Daulatabadi, *Hayat Yahya*, III (Tehran, 1330/1952), pp. 215–16.
76 Kazemzadeh, *Russia and Britain*, pp. 670–1.
77 Government of India, Foreign Department, Secret E, Proceedings 481–547, February 1910, No. 542, Sir George Barclay to Sir Edward Grey, Tehran, 4 October 1909.
78 *Ibid.*
79 Sardar Zafar, "Tarikh Bakhtiyari", p. 95.
80 Dr M.Y. Young, "Memorandum: The Governorship of Bakhtiaristan", August 1912. (Author's personal collection.)

81 "Copy of Agreement Given to Sardar Jang". 10 July 1912. (Author's personal collection.)

82 Government of India, Foreign Department, Secret E, Proceedings 487–522, August 1905, No. 503, Captain A.P. Trevor to Secretary, Government of India, Bushihr, 27 May 1905, and No. 519, Inclosure, Confidential Diary No. 20 by Major W.P. Morton, Ahvaz, 19 July 1905.

83 *Ibid.*, Proceedings 427–50, January 1906, No. 427, Inclosure, Confidential Diary No. 21 by Major W.P. Morton, 2 August 1905.

84 *Ibid.*, Proceedings 799–800, No. 799, Inclosure, Mushir al-Daulah to Evelyn Grant Duff, 15 March 1906.

85 Garthwaite, "Bakhtiyari Khans", pp. 24–44.

86 Great Britain, Foreign Office, Lynch Brothers to Evelyn Grant Duff, Tehran, 18 May 1906.

87 Government of India, Foreign Department, Secret E, Proceedings 307–21, June 1906, No. 308, Inclosure, Lynch Brothers to Persian Transport Co., Isfahan, 20 January 1906.

88 Government of India, Foreign Department, External B, Proceedings 180–98, December 1912, No. 181, Sir Walter Townley to Sir Edward Grey, Tehran, 6 August 1912.

89 Great Britain, India Office Library, Miscellaneous Lists 20, Political and Secret Files, Vol. 50, 1914, 3516, pt 12, No. 22, "[B]akhtiari Affairs", Sir Walter Townley to Sir Edward Grey, Tehran, 17 January 1915.

90 *Ibid.*, Register No. 1505, "Minute Paper", 19 and 20 April 1915.

91 *Ibid.*, Register No. 817, Viceroy to London Office, 2 March 1915.

92 *Ibid.*, Register No. 94, Sir Walter Townley to Sir Edward Grey, Tehran, 12 March 1915.

93 *Ibid.*, Vol. 11, 1917, 469, pt 1, Register No. 1082B, "Persia: Bakhtiari Affairs", Sir Percy Cox to Foreign Office, Tehran, and India Office, 10 May 1915.

94 *Ibid.*

95 *Ibid.*, Vol. 50, 1914, 3516, pt 12, Register No. 1748, "Minute Paper", 10 and 12 May 1915.

96 *Ibid.*

97 Hurewitz, *Diplomacy*, II p. 11.

98 Government of India, Foreign Department, Secret War, Proceeding 45, March 1916, No. 386F, British Minister to Secretary, Government of India, Foreign and Political Department, Tehran, 7 October 1915.

99 *Ibid.*, Proceeding 286, British Minister to Secretary, Government of India, Foreign and Political Department, Tehran, 23 September 1915.

100 Great Britain, India Office Library, Miscellaneous Lists 20, Political and Secret Files, Vol. 50, 1914, 3516, pt 12, Register No. 2218, "[B]akhtiari Affairs", Sir Percy Cox to Foreign Office, Tehran, and Secretary of State, India, Basrah, 27 May 1915.

101 Government of India, Foreign Department, Secret War, Proceeding 222, May 1916, No. 3031B, Political Resident, Persian Gulf to Secretary, Government of India, Foreign and Political Department, Basrah, 15 December 1915.

102 *Ibid.*, Proceeding 29, August 1916, Inclosure, C.M. Marling to Sir Edward Grey, Tehran, 17 February 1916.
103 *Ibid.*, Proceeding 60, October 1916, Inclosure 2, Sir Percy Cox to British Minister, No. 2476, Basrah, 26 May 1916.
104 *Ibid.*
105 C.A. Gault, "The Bakhtiari Tribe" (Isfahan, 1944), India Office Library, L/P&S/12/3546.
106 Donald N. Wilber, *Riza Shah Pahlavi: The Resurrection and Reconstruction of Iran* (Hicksville, N.Y., 1975), p. 100.
107 Great Britain, India Office Library, Political and Secret Files, External Collection 28, File 7, No. 341, "Persia: Internal Affairs", Mr Mallet to Sir John Simon, Tehran, 14 July 1933.
108 Gault, "Bakhtiari Tribe", p. 25.
109 Jean-Pierre Digard, personal communication.
110 Personal communication.
111 Fredrik Barth, "Father's Brother's Daughter Marriage in Kurdistan", *South-western Journal of Anthropology*, X (1954), p. 171.
112 Ann K.S. Lambton, *Landlord and Peasant in Persia* (London, 1953), p. 140.

Supplement: "Kitabchah" (translation)

1 *The Year of the Cock, 1290.* Ilkhani uses both the Turkic calendar, or twelve-year cycle in which each year is given the name of an animal and each begins with the vernal equinox, and the Hijri calendar, which is, of course, lunar.

2 Bani 'Abd al-Khan. A major division of the Arab confederation of the Bani Lam, whose tribesmen, in the nineteenth century, were known as notorious robbers, and who occupied the region of 'Amarah (in present-day Iraq) east of the Karkhah river in Iran and south to the vicinity of Havizah.

3 Aqa Susan, the brother of Aqa Bandar. Ilkhani's bastagan?

4 Aqa Parviz. Ilkhani's most important munshi (agent–secretary) and a Babadi.

5 Sharak. A subbranch of the 'Abayan, one of the five noble bloodlines of the Arab horse.

6 Mirza 'Ali Baz. Another of Ilkhani's munshis.

7 'Ali Quli. The fourth of Ilkhani's six sons, born (*c.* 1856) to Hajjiyah Bibi Mihrijan, daughter of Ilyas Khan of the Zarasvand, Ilkhani's own tayafah. Isfandiyar, the eldest son, and 'Ali Quli, the eldest son of the noblest mother, were Ilkhani's favorites. 'Ali Quli was later entitled Sardar As'ad (II).

8 Bibi Sanam, the daughter of Khajah Khalil. Khalil was the khan of the 'Abdalvand of the Mugu'i, an important Chahar Lang tayafah.

9 Gumbadan. Misspelled?

10 Ganduman. A major town 55 miles southwest of Isfahan and *c.* 45 miles southeast of Shahr Kurd, renowned for its pastures.

11 The Shah . . . Europe. Nasir al-Din Shah's first trip to Europe.

12 Isfandiyar. Ilkhani's eldest son, born (*c.* 1851) to Bibi Khanum of the Khadir

Surkh of the Zarasvand of the Duraki. Later entitled Samsam al-Saltanah and then Sardar As'ad (I).

13 Hajjivand. A Chahar Lang tayafah.

14 Shahi. A Zarasvand tirah.

15 Malamir. Ilkhani's winter headquarters and an important town *c.* 65 miles east of Shushtar in the Bakhtiyari garmsir.

16 Aqa Riza Quli. Ilkhani's younger half-brother, born to Mihr Banu of the Dinarani, a Haft Lang bab. During Ilkhani's lifetime he functioned as his fiscal agent and representative in Chahar Mahall. After Ilkhani's death he became known by his title as Ilbaigi. (See Chapter VI, pp. 98–101.)

17 Bahmah'i. A pastoral nomadic tribe from Kuhgiluyah, immediately south of the Bakhtiyari.

18 The upper fortress. Qal'ah A'la. A Bahmah'i fortress on a branch of the Jirrahi river *c.* 40 miles northeast of Ram Hurmuz.

19 Mann. Unit of weight, here probably Tabriz mann, *c.* 6½ lbs.

20 Muhammad Husain Khan, the son of Khuda Karam Khan. Buir Ahmadi Khans. (See Appendix IIIb, Documents 12 and 14.)

21 Falard. A town located *c.* 24 miles west of Samirum on the boundary between the Bakhtiyari and Qashqa'i summer pastures. Its taxes were paid to the governor of Fars and were a bone of contention between him (Farhad Mirza) and Ilkhani. (See Appendix IIIb, Document 14.)

22 Chaqakhur. A well-watered plain *c.* 30 miles south of Shahr Kurd, the center of Duraki power and their yailaq, where Ilkhani had a fortified headquarters.

23 Hajji Muhammad Karim. Probably an Isfahan artisan.

24 Karbala Mu'ala. Karbala the Exalted, a major shrine city south of Baghdad and the burial place of Husain, the third Imam.

25 Gulgir. A well-watered agricultural village located on the western side of Kuh Asmari, *c.* 53 miles southeast of Shushtar.

26 Kuh Asmari. A small range of sandstone mountains that reaches its highest elevation above Gulgir and known as a hunting site, especially for wild boar.

27 *The Year of the Dog, 1291.* Began with the vernal equinox, 1874.

28 'Ali Riza Khan. Nephew of Muhammad Taqi Khan, a major Kiyanursi (Chahar Lang) khan, and father of one of Ilkhani's wives.

29 Aqa Riza Mustaufi. Kadkhuda (headman) of Dizful?

30 Saglavi. One of the five noble Arab bloodlines.

31 Husam al-Saltanah. Sultan Murad Mirza, third son of 'Abbas Mirza, thus Nasir al-Din Shah's paternal uncle, and the governor of Fars.

32 Suhrab Khan Qashqa'i. An important Qashqa'i khan whose father had fought Ilkhani.

33 Revenue list. Tafriqah. (See Appendix II, Documents 2 and 14.)

34 Day, 1291. Tenth month of the solar year, *c.* December 1874–January 1875.

35 Sudanjan. Surishjan, a large village *c.* 6 miles west of Shahr Kurd.

36 Sirak. A small village south of Shahr Kurd. 2 *dangs* are the equivalent of one-third ownership, 6 dangs being full ownership.

37 Charmini. Residents of a village in the district of Linjan west of Isfahan.

38 Zill al-Sultan. Mas'ud Mirza, Nasir al-Din Shah's eldest son. (See Chapter V, pp. 91–3 and Chapter VI, pp. 98–103.

39 Farman. Tehran, 1292.

40 Mizdij. One of the four districts of Chahar Mahall, south and to the west of Shahr Kurd, where Ilkhani had a number of villages and held a tuyul.

41 Aqa Imam Quli. Ilkhani's younger and only full brother, thus born to Bibi Shahpasand (of the Bakhtiyarvand) and Ja'far Quli Khan. Imam Quli was known as Ilbaigi during Ilkani's lifetime, when he served his brother as second in command, and after Ilkhani's death he served as ilkhani and became known subsequently as Hajji Ilkhani.

42 Shaikh 'Abd al-Rashid, son of Shaikh Sultan. Ka'b shaikhs?

43 Aqa Fath 'Ali, son of 'Ali Riza Khan. Kiyanursi khans.

44 Andakah. The villages of Malamir, present-day Izah, *c.* 42 miles east of Masjid Sulaiman.

45 *The Year of the Hog, 1292.* Began with the vernal equinox, 1875.

46 Najaf Quli. Ilkhani's second son, born (*c.* 1846) to Bibi Khanum, hence full brother to Isfandiyar Khan.

47 Mamivand. A Chahar Lang bab.

48 Fuladvand. A Chahar Lang tayafah.

49 Ahmad Khusravi. A Duraki tirah, closely allied with Ilkhani, and a number of whose men were bastagan to the khans.

50 Bahmah'i Lajmir Aurak. Bahmah'i, see n. 17. The Lajmir Aurak are listed by both Sardar Zafar and Sardar As'ad as a Dinarani tirah. Possibly the Bahmah'i group was a splinter from the Bakhtiyari, or had come into the Bakhtiyari after this time.

51 Kahkash. A Kiyanursi tirah listed by Sardar Zafar but not by Sardar As'ad.

52 Hishmat al-Daulah. Hamza Mirza, fourth son of 'Abbas Mirza, Nasir al-Din Shah's paternal uncle, and the governor of 'Arabistan. (See Appendix IIIb, Document 14.)

53 Cha'b (colloquial pronunciation, but correctly spelled as Ka'b). The largest of the Arab tribes, centered at Fallahiyah, east–northeast of Muhammarah.

54 'Abayah Sharak. 'Abayah, most likely 'Abayan, the third of the five noble Arab breeds. Sharak, see n. 5. (The dam is listed first, followed by the sire, and then the owner.)

55 Kuhalan. The first of the five noble Arab bloodlines.

56 Nimah. "Halves", a type of agreement used by the Bakhtiyari whereby an owner of an animal – and with Ilkhani apparently only horses – gives the animal to someone to care for and raise in return for half the offspring. If the owner wishes to sell or present the animal owned nimah to a third party, he must pay the keeper for the loss of half the offspring.

57 Mu'izz al-Daulah. Bahram Mirza, the second son of 'Abbas Mirza and the governor of 'Arabistan.

58 Chahar Mahall. The major agricultural districts bordering the Bakhtiyari summer pastures and comprising Lar, Kiyar, Mizdij, and Ganduman.

59 Kharvar. The equivalent of 100 Tabriz manns, or *c.* 655 lbs.

60 Pishkash. Either a gift given in lieu of dues or a gift from an inferior to a superior.

61 Hamdani. The fourth of the five noble Arab bloodlines.

62 Janiki. A Haft Lang bab, with a predominantly agricultural membership, located at the southern border of Bakhtiyari.

63 Darashuri. A large Qashqa'i tribe whose summer pastures adjoined the Duraki summer pastures at Falard.

64 Babadi Kashah ('Akashah). A Babadi tayafah, hence Haft Lang.

65 Sartip. Brigadier.

66 Saham al-Daulah. Sulaiman Khan Armani, nephew of Manuchihr Khan, Mu'tamid al-Daulah.

67 Shaikh Miz'al. Son of Hajji Jabir Khan, and after his death paramount shaikh of the Ka'b and the governor of Muhammarah.

68 Hajji Jabir Khan. Shaikh of the Muhaisin Arabs and later paramount shaikh of the Ka'b; died 1881.

69 Khusrau. Ilkhani's youngest son by Hajjiyah Bibi Mihrijan, hence full brother to 'Ali Quli Khan. Later Khusrau was entitled Salar Arfa' and then Sardar Zafar.

70 Darab Khan Qashqa'i. Ilkhani of the Qashqa'i.

71 Ab Bid. Ilkhani's agricultural estate of some 160 houses (1910), *c.* 35 miles north of Shushtar.

72 Paradumbah. A large village of some 1,000 houses (1910), 6 miles west of Burujin, where Ilkhani built his first permanent dwelling.

73 25th of the month of Shavval. 24 November 1875.

74 *The Year of the Mouse, 1293.* Began vernal equinox 1876.

75 Muhammad Husain. Eldest son of Imam Quli Khan, future rival to Ilkhani's leadership. (See Chapter v, pp. 91–2.)

76 Mirza Aqa. Son of 'Ali Riza Khan Chahar Lang, and Ilkhani's son-in-law.

77 Ardal. A village in Pusht Kuh, *c.* 25 miles due southwest of Shahr Kurd on the Bakhtiyari road.

78 'Ali Quli Khan Qashqa'i. Born *c.* 1815, son of Murtaza Quli Khan and cousin of his rival Darab.

79 Aqa Zaman. A Bakhtiyari hero, one of Ilkhani's munshis or bastagan.

80 Bazuft. A river, fortress, and valley, *c.* 45 miles due west of Chahar Mahall and 135 miles northeast of Shushtar.

81 Daupulan. A village on the Karun and Sabz Kuh rivers; hence the name, "Two Bridges", one of which was built by Ilkhani. *C.* 6 miles southwest of Ardal on the Bakhtiyari road to 'Arabistan.

82 Mu'tamid al-Daulah. Farhad Mirza, 'Abbas Mirza's sixth son, the Shah's paternal uncle, and Ilkhani's major Qajar rival. (See Chapter v, pp. 89–90.)

83 Vali'ahd. Muzaffar al-Din Mirza, heir to Nasir al-Din Shah, and the governor of Azerbaijan. This gift is acknowledged in a letter sent by the Vali'ahd dated Sha'ban 1294.

84 Burburud. A district of some 16 villages in the Burujird province, and adjacent to one of the Chahar Lang yailaqs.

85 Amir Quli. Ilkhani's youngest (?) and least important son.

86 Ramazan. September 1876.

87 H.I.M. the Shah. The actual Persian is *Qiblah 'Alam*, the "Center of the World".

88 Mushir al-Mulk. Mirza Abu al-Hasan, son-in-law of the governor of Fars until Hashmat al-Daulah's appointment in 1293/1876.

89 4th of the month of Zi al-Qa'dah. 21 November 1876.

90 2nd of the month of Zi al-Qa'dah. 19 November 1876.

91 Bani Turuf. An Arab tribe of *c.* 20,000, predominantly agriculturalist, in Havizah in southern 'Arabistan.

92 'Alafchah. Pastures tax, primarily for camps that utilized pastures other than their own.

93 *The Year 1294.* 1877.

94 Gutvand. A large village of some 1,000 households (1910), *c.* 12 miles north of Shushtar; its incomes were attached to the office of the ilkhani.

95 As'ad Khan Bakhtiyari. The notorious Bakhtiyarvand khan and robber of the early nineteenth century.

96 Ta'aruf. A complimentary gift – in contrast to pishkash, where an obligation is attached (see n. 60).

97 We shall see what God's will is. See Chapter v, p. 89 and Appendix IIIb, Document 14.

98 Farman. Tehran, Zi al-Qa'dah 1294/November 1877.

99 Taxes . . . Mugu'i. Similar to Appendix IIIb, Document 7.

100 2nd of the month of Shavval in the year 1294. 10 October 1877.

101 2nd of the month of Zi al-Qa'dah. 8 November 1877.

102 Dih Kurd. Today Shahr Kurd, largest town and capital of Chahar Mahall.

103 Farman. Isfahan (?), Zi al-Qa'dah 1294/November 1877.

104 Al Khamis. A small Arab tribe in the districts of Ram Hurmuz and Fallahiyah.

105 Gabardine sardari. A frock coat with a raised, clerical-like collar. (See photograph of the Ilkhani, Hajji Ilkhani, and Ilbaigi khans.)

106 Isfahan gaz. A nougat-like candy made in Isfahan.

107 Dasht Gul. A Bakhtiyari winter pasture camp site where Ilkhani was making capital investment in irrgation systems and orchards. *C.* 42 miles from Qal'ah Bazuft on the Shushtar road.

108 1st of the month of Muharram 1295. 5 January 1878.

109 Charah. A cable-suspended basket used as transport across rivers and chasms.

110 'Abbas Quli. Imam Quli Khan's fourth son, born to Hajjiyah Bibi Zainab, daughter of Abdal Khan.

111 Babadi Raki. A Babadi tayafah.

112 Shar' authority. Religious, legal authority.

113 2,500 tumans cash. According to "Administration Report of the Persian Gulf Residency", 1878–9, p. 8 (*Selections from the Records of the Government of India*, No. 165), Ilkhani refused to turn over the recovered property and was fined 30,000 tumans by the government.

114 Sipahsalar A'zam. Mirza Husain Khan.

115 Khajahs. Equivalent to khans, or chiefs.
116 Kashkuli. A major Qashqa'i component.
117 Shah 'Abd al-'Azim. A shrine in the city of Rai, just to the south of Tehran.
118 Ab sar. Lit. "starling water", an unidentified elixir that supposedly attracted starlings that would then devour the locusts.
119 *The Year 1296.* 1879.
120 Plunder. See n. 113.
121 Vali'ahd. Muhammad Husain's assignment to the Vali'ahd at this time may have given the Qajars the opportunity to undercut Ilkhani's power within his own family.
122 Sagvand. Faili Lurs numbering *c.* 40,000 families (1910), living to the north of the Bakhtiyari.
123 Burujin. A large community *c.* 30 miles west of Shah Riza at the border of Chahar Mahall.
124 Raqam. No longer extant?
125 8th of the month of Zi al-Hijjah. 23 November 1879.
126 Aid Qurban. 25 November 1879.
127 Shams al-'Amarat. A palace built by Nasir al-Din Shah in the Gulistan complex in Tehran.
128 Ashrafis. 1 ashrafi = *c.* 1 tuman.
129 Jajrud. A hunting area east of Tehran.
130 Dushan Tapah. A community at Tehran's eastern border.
131 Kursis. Low, blanket-draped tables under which braziers of coals are placed for heat.
132 Namaz. Prayers.
133 Naz shust. Here, gift in exchange of, or honoring, the hunt's trophy.
134 Safar. January–February 1880.
135 *The Year 1297.* 1880.
136 Qahfarukh. (Today Farukh Shahr.) A large village of some 2,500 (1910) in Chahar Mahall on its border with Linjan, *c.* 8 miles south of Shahr Kurd.
137 Naghan. A large village of some 1,200 (1910), 8 miles from Daupulan on the way to Chaqakhur.
138 27th of Jumadi II. 7 June 1880.
139 Bagh Malik. A large village *c.* 6 miles south of Qal'ah Tul, or *c.* 20 miles south of Izah.
140 Ramazan. August 1880.
141 23rd of Shavval. 29 September 1880.
142 Kashah. Babadi 'Akashah (see n. 64).
143 Sarhad. Border, frontier, and here the border of the Bakhtiyari and Qashqa'i summer pastures in the Falard area.
144 *The Year 1298.* 1881.
145 Ja'far Quli Khan. Zill al-Sultan's 'Arabistan agent, who charged that it was Ilkhani's name that was feared there and not Zill al-Sultan's.
146 Aqa Zaman Zarasvand. Aqa Zaman (see n. 79).
147 *The Year 1299.* 1882.
148 Ten days after Aid. Aid [the festival of] Nau Ruz, the vernal equinox.

149 Riza Quli . . . sword. Riza Quli Khan's visit to Tehran at the Shah's behest sealed Ilkhani's fate. (See Chapter v, pp. 92–3.

150 Shimbar. A valley in central Bakhtiyari famed for its pastures and beauty.

151 McKenzie. G.S. McKenzie, of Grey, Paul and Co., who twice visited Ilkhani from his Bushihr base.

Further reading

The two decades preceding the 1979 Revolution and formation of the Islamic Republic of Iran, when access to research and field work was curtailed, now stand as something of a golden age for the study of the tribes and pastoral nomadic peoples of Iran. Moreover, the social sciences generally were greatly expanded during the 1950s and 1960s, and linked with development theory. The importance of Iran's tribes had long been recognized by historians, if in a general way, but in those two decades, anthropologists would take the lead through their field work. One monograph, in particular, Fredrik Barth, *Nomads of South Persia: The Basseri Tribe of the Khamseh Confederacy* (Oslo/London, 1964) provided both inspiration and a model for that new generation of research.

Similarly, within Iran, universities and government centres recognized the need for data and studies of rural society and leadership and valuable support was exercised in this endeavour by scholars such as Dr Nader Afshar-Naderi. Also of critical importance was the establishment of the British Institute of Persian Studies in Tehran. Its director, David Stronach, and library became central for all scholars working in Iran, particularly in archaeology and anthropology. Too few monographs resulted from the extensive research across Iran during those two decades but would include notable contributions such as: Richard Tapper, *Pasture and Politics: Economics, Conflict and Ritual among Shahsevan Nomads of Northwestern Iran* (London, 1979) and then his *Frontier Nomads of Iran: A Political and Social History of the Shahsevan* (Cambridge, 1997); William Irons, *The Yomut Turkmen: A Study of Social Organization among a Central Asian Turkic-Speaking Population* (Ann Arbor, 1975); and Lois Beck, *The Qashqa'i of Iran* (New Haven, 1986). Research of the late 1960s and early 1970s would subsequently be published by Jacob Black-Michaud, *Sheep & Land: The Economics of Power in a Tribal Society* (Cambridge, 1986); Daniel Bradburd, *Ambiguous Relations: Kin, Class, and Conflict among Komanchi Pastoralists* (Washington, DC, 1990); and Philip Carl Salzman, *Black Tents of Baluchistan* (Washington DC, 2000).

Both Tapper and Beck included significant historical backgrounds and contexts in their publications. Significantly, Stephanie Cronin's *Tribal Politics in Iran: Rural Conflict and the New State, 1921–1941* (London, 2007) and Arash Khazeni's forthcoming book, "The Open Land: Tribes and Empire on the Margins of Qajar Iran, 1800–1911" (Washington University Press) added, or will add, important and larger historical contexts for understanding the pastoral nomadic peoples of Iran. Other histories, too, have been published ranging from the thirteenth to fourteenth centuries in John E. Woods' *The Aqquyunlu: Clan Confederation, Empire Revised and Expanded* (Salt Lake City, 1999) to Pierre Oberling's *The Qashqa'i Nomads of Fars* (The Hague, 1974) that focuses especially on the nineteenth and twentieth centuries.

The absence of monographs by Western scholars of pastoral nomadic peoples in Iran's late Pahlavi or Islamic Republican periods reflects political obstacles, while Iranians have continued research and publications. Fars Province has received considerable attention, and Beck has continued research there after the revolution and published *Nomad: A Year in the Life of a Qashqa'i Tribesman in Iran* (Berkeley, 1991). Significantly, Iranian Kurdistan continues to be understudied, but has been included in more general works on the Kurds, such as Martin van Bruinessen's *Agha, Shaikh, and State: The Social and Political Structures of Kurdistan* (1978; London, 1992). Importantly, Kurds and Kurdistan represent daunting complexities in terms of pastoral nomadism, tribal organization, and interaction within large social and political contexts.

Women are central in pastoral nomadic societies, and their roles in them are analysed in important articles by Lois Beck, Erika Friedl, and Nancy Tapper/Nancy Lindisfarne included in collected essays such as Lois Beck and Nikki Keddie's pioneering *Women in the Muslim World* (Cambridge, MA, 1978). Religious practice of pastoral nomadic peoples is also under-represented in monographs, while receiving mention in individual studies, or again as articles, for example Ziba Mir-Hosseini's on the Ahl-i Haqq of Kurdistan. Similarly, popular culture has received scant attention, but for Sekandar Amanolahi and W.M. Thackston, *Tales from Luristan: Tales, Fables and Folk Poetry from the Lur of Bala-Gariva* (Cambridge, MA, 1986) or similar works in Persian. Amanolahi has numerous Persian publications on the tribes of Luristan and Fars, as do his students.

The study of Bakhtiyari material culture was pioneered in Jean-Pierre Digard's *Technique des nomads baxtyâri d'Iran* (Cambridge1981) and Bakhtiyari carpets and carpet-making has received splendid treatment in Peter Willborg's coffee-table-sized *Chahar Mahal va Bakhtiari: Village, Workshop & Nomadic Rugs of Western Persia* (Stockholm, 2002).

Equally over-sized but an invaluable overview of Iran's nomadic peoples would be *The Nomadic Peoples of Iran* (London, 2002) edited by Richard

Tapper and Jon Thompson with its fine photographs by Nasrollah Kasrarian and the most up-to-date bibliography on Iran's nomads, in all languages, including many Ph.D. dissertations, otherwise difficult to locate. Here, too, *Nomadic Peoples of Iran* covers the major regions and peoples – often, not represented by monographs – in essays written by leading contemporary scholars, including a too brief sample of the late David Brooks' extensive field work and analysis of the Bakhtiyari.

Given the range of economies and social and political organization represented in works cited above has given pause as to what is meant by pastoral nomadism and tribalism and how such organization expressed itself in history, especially in relation to the state. And these concerns have been explored at conferences and in publications that focus on both theory and practice, notably in Richard Tapper, ed. *The Conflict of Tribe and State in Iran and Afghanistan* (London, 1983); Philip S. Khoury and Joseph Kostiner, eds, *Tribes and State Formation in the Middle East* (Berkeley, 1990); and at the 'International Conference on Nomadism & Development: Survival Strategies & Development Policies', Shahr-i Kurd, Chahar Mahal, Iran, 1–6 September 1992. Only a limited number of the papers from this conference have been published, but this conference sponsored by Dr 'Ali Ghanbari, Deputy Minister and Director of the Organization for the Nomadic Peoples of Iran brings us back a half century ago to the renaissance in study of Iran's nomadic peoples of the 1960s and 1970s and its relationship of research to development and where we began.

Bibliography

Archival Sources (not otherwise noted by author's name)

British Museum, London
  Sir Arnold Wilson's Papers and Correspondence
  Sir Henry Layard's Papers
India Office, London
  India Office Papers, Miscellaneous Lists
  Political and Secret Department Files
  Political and Secret Memoranda
National Archives of India, New Delhi
  Foreign and Political Department Proceedings 1830–1916
Public Record Office, London
  Foreign Office – Persia/Iran
    FO 60 General Correspondence 1897–1905
    FO 248 Embassy and Consular Archives Correspondence 1807–1922
    FO 371 General Correspondence, Political 1906–22
    FO 416 Confidential Prints, Persia 1899–1922
    FO 460 Files, Vice Consulate at Mohammerah
    FO 539 Confidential Prints, Central Asia 1834–1911
University of London, Library of the School of Oriental and African Studies
  Lorimer Papers, MS 181247

Primary Sources

'Abd al-Ghafar Najm al-Mulk. *Safarnamah Khuzistan.* Edited by Muhammad Dabirsiyaqi. Tehran, 1341/1963.
'Abu al-Hasan b. Muhammad Amin Gulistanah. *Mujmal al-Tavarikh Afshariyah va Zandiyah.* Edited by Mudaris Razavi. Tehran, 1344/1966.
'Ala al-Din 'Ata-Malik. *The History of the World-Conqueror.* Translated by John A. Boyle. Cambridge, Mass., 1958.
Amir Sharaf Khan Bidlisi. *Sharafnamah Tarikh Mufassil Kurdistan.* Edited by Muhammad 'Abbasi. Tehran, 1343/1965.
Amiri, Mihrab. *Zindigi Siyasi: Atabak A'zam.* Tehran, 1346/1968.
Asnad Bar Guzidah az: Sipahsalar – Zill al-Sultan – Dabir al-Mulk. Edited by Ibrahim Safa'i. Tehran, 1350/1972.

Bamdad, Mihdi. *Tarikh Rijal Iran*. Tehran, 1347/1969.

Daulatabadi, Hajji Mirza Yahya. *Hayat Yahya*. Tehran, 1330/1952.

Fasa'i, Hasan. *History of Persia under Qajar Rule (Farsnama Naseri)*. Translated by Heribert Busse. New York, 1972.

Hajji 'Ali Quli Khan Sardar As'ad. *Tarikh Bakhtiyari*. Tehran (?), 1333/1914.

Hajji Khusrau Khan Sardar Zafar. "Tarikh Bakhtiyari". 1329/1911–1333/1914 [but also including entries up to the time of his death in 1933].

"Kitab Ruzanah". 1302/1924–1303/1925.

"Kitabchah Yadashtha Ruzanah". n.d.

Iskandar Baig Turkman [Munshi]. *Tarikh 'Alam Ara 'Abbasi*. Edited by Iraj Afshar. Tehran, 1334/1956.

I'timad al-Saltanah. *Ruznamah Khatirat I'timad al-Saltanah*. Edited by Iraj Afshar. Tehran, 1345/1967.

Kazim, Muhammad. *Namah 'Alam Ara Nadiri*. Facsimile, 3 vols. Moscow, 1960–66.

Kitab Nadiri. Institut Vostokove Leningrad, n.d.

Mas'ud Mirza Zill al-Sultan. *Tarikh Sar Guzasht Mas'udi*. ?, 1325/1907.

Muntakhab al-Tavarikh Mu'ini. Edited by Jean Aubin. Tehran, 1335/1957.

Mustaufi, 'Abdallah. *Tarikh Ijtima'i va Idari Daurah Qajariyah*. Tehran, 1343/1965.

Mustaufi, Hamdallah. *The Geographical Part of the Nuzhat al-Qulub*. Translated by Guy Le Strange. London, 1919.

Qa'im Magami, Sarhang Jahangir. "Muhrha va Tughraha Padishahan Iran". *Barrasiha Tarikhi*, IV (1348/1969).

Qazvini, Hamdallah Mustaufi. *Tarikh Guzidah*. Edited by 'Abd al-Husain Nava'i. Tehran, 1339/1961.

Razmara, Husain 'Ali. *Farhang Jughrafiya Iran: Ustan Shish, Khuzistan va Luristan*. Tehran, 1330/1952.

Farhang Jughrafiya Iran: Ustan Dihum, Isfahan. Tehran, 1332/1954.

Ruzbah, Amir 'Ali. "Tarikh Bakhtiyari". n.d. (*c.* 1333/1955–1343/1965).

Tadhkirat al-Muluk. Translated and edited by Vladimir Minorsky. London, 1943.

Zaigham al-Daulah, Iskandar Khan. "Haz Kitab Famil Babadi 'Akashah va Tavayif Haft Lang Bakhtiyari". n.d.

Contemporary Travel and Military Reports

Abbott, K.E. "Notes Taken on a Journey Eastwards from Shiraz in 1850". *Journal of the Royal Geographical Society*, XXVII (1857): 149–85.

Aucher-Eloy, Remi. *Relations de Voyages en Orient de 1830 à 1838*. Paris, 1843.

Baring, Walter. "Report on a Journey to Shuster, Dizful, Behbehan, and Shiraz". October–January 1882. India Office Library, L/P&S C.38/18.

Bell, Colonel Mark S. *Military Report on S.W. Persia Including the Provinces of Khuzistan, Luristan, and Parts of Fars*. Simla, 1885.

"A Visit to the Karun River and Kum [*sic*]". *Blackwood's Magazine*, CXLV (1889): 453–81.

Bishop, Isabella L. Bird. *Journeys in Persia and Kurdistan*. London, 1891.

Blunt, Lady Anne. *Bedouin Tribes of the Euphrates*. New York, 1879.

A Pilgrimage to Nejd. London, 1881.

Brydges, Sir Harford Jones. *The Dynasty of the Kajars*. London, 1833; reprinted New York, 1973.

Burn, R. "The Bakhtiari Hills, an Itinerary of the Road from Isfahan to Shustar". *Journal of the Asiatic Society of Bengal*, LXVI (1897): 170–9.

Champain, Colonel J.U. Bateman. "On the Various Means of Communication between Central Persia and the Sea". *Proceedings of the Royal Geographical Society*, V, New Series (1883): 121–38.

Chardin, Sir John. *The Travels of Sir John Chardin into Persia and the East Indies. To Which is Added, the Coronation of this Present King of Persia, Solyman the Third*. London, 1686.

Christian, Captain A.J. *The Tribes of Fars*. Simla (?), 1918.

A Chronicle of the Carmelites in Persia and the Papal Missions of the XVIIth and XVIIIth Centuries. London, 1939.

Curzon, Lord. "The Karun River and the Commercial Geography of S.W. Persia". *Proceedings of the Royal Geographical Society*, XII (1890): 509–32.

"Leaves from a Diary on the Karun River". *Fortnightly Review*, XXVI (1890): 479–98, 694–715.

Persia and the Persian Question. London, 1892.

D'Allemagne, H.R. *Du Khorassan au Pays des Bakhtiaris*. Paris, 1909.

De Bode, Baron C.A. "Extracts from a Journey Kept while Traveling in January 1841 through the Country of the Mamásení and Khógilú". *Journal of the Royal Geographical Society*, XII (1842): 75–109.

Travels in Luristan and Arabistan. London, 1845.

Dupré, Adrian. *Voyage en Perse Fait dans les Années 1807, 1808, et 1809*. Paris, 1819.

Durand, E.R. *An Autumn Tour in Western Persia*. London, 1902.

Edmonds, C.J. "Luristan: Pish-i Kuh and Bala Garivah". *Geographical Journal*, LIX (1922): 335–56.

Notes on Luristan 1917. Anglo-Persian Oil Co., 1922.

Fraser, James. *The History of Nadir Shah*. London, 1742.

Gault, C.A. "The Bakhtiari Tribe". Isfahan, 1944. India Office Library, L/P&S/ 12/3546.

Hand, Captain Robert P. "A Survey of the Tribes of Iran". Mimeographed, 22 July 1963.

Hanway, Jonas. *An Historical Account of the British Trade over the Caspian Sea*. London, 1753.

The Revolutions of Persia. London, 1754.

Harrison, J.V. "The Bakhtiyari Country, South-Western Persia". *Geographical Journal*, LXXX (1932): 193–210.

Kinneir, John MacDonald. *A Geographical Memoir of the Persian Empire*. London, 1813.

Krusinski, Father Judasz Tadeusz. *The History of the Revolution of Persia*. London, 1728.

199

Layard, Sir Henry. "A Description of the Province of Khuzistan". *Journal of the Royal Geographical Society*, XVI (1846): 1–105.
　Early Adventures in Persia, Susiana, and Babylonia. New York, 1887.
Lorimer, D.L.R. *A Report on Pusht-i Kuh*. Simla, 1908.
Lorimer, John Gordon. *Gazetteer of the Persian Gulf, 'Oman, and Central Arabia*. Calcutta, 1915.
Lynch, Henry Blosse. "Across Luristan to Ispahan". *Proceedings of the Royal Geographical Society*, XII (1890): 523–53.
Military Report on Persia, Compiled by the General Staff, 1911. Simla, 1912.
Morier, Sir James. *A Journey through Persia in the Years 1808 and 1809*. London, 1812.
　A Second Journey through Persia. London, 1818.
　"Some Accounts of the I'liyáts, or Wandering Tribes of Persia, Obtained in the Years 1814 and 1815". *Journal of the Royal Geographical Society*, VII (1837): 230–42.
Napier, Captain G.S.F. *Military Report on South Persia*. Simla, 1900.
Norden, Hermann. *Under Persian Skies: A Record of Travel by the Old Caravan Routes of Western Persia*. London, 1928.
Polo, Marco. *The Book of Ser Marco Polo*. Translated and edited by Henry Yule. London, 1871.
Rawlinson, Major Sir Henry. "Notes on a March from Zohab through the Province of Luristan to Kirmanshah in the Year 1836". *Journal of the Royal Geographical Society*, IX (1839): 26–116.
Ross, Elizabeth N. Macbean. *A Lady Doctor in Bakhtiari Land*. London, 1921.
Sawyer, Major H.A. "The Bakhtiyari Mountains and Upper Elam". *Geographical Journal*, IV (1894): 481–505.
　Report: A Reconnaissance in the Bakhtiari Country, Southwest Persia. Simla, 1891.
Sheil, Mary Lenora. *Glimpses of Life and Manners in Persia*. London, 1856.
Stark, Freya. "The Pusht-i-Kuh". *Geographical Journal*, LXXXII (1933): 247–59.
Stocqueler, J.H. *Fifteen Months Pilgrimage through Untrodden Tracts of Khuzistan and Persia*. London, 1832.
Waring, Edward Scott. *A Tour of Sheeraz*. London, 1807; reprinted New York, 1973.
Wells, Captain H.L. "Surveying Tours in Southern Persia". *Proceedings of the Royal Geographical Society*, V, New Series (1883): 138–63.
Wilson, Sir Arnold Talbot. "The Bakhtiaris". *Journal of the Royal Central Asian Society*, XIII (1926): 205–25.
　Loyalties: Mesopotamia 1914–1917. London, 1930.
　Mesopotamia 1917–1920: A Clash of Loyalties. London, 1931.
　Military Report on S.W. Persia, I: *Bakhtiyari Garmsir*. Simla, 1909.
　Military Report on S.W. Persia, II: *Arabistan*. Simla, 1912.
　Military Report on S.W. Persia, III: *Bakhtiari Country North of Karun River*. Simla, 1910.
　Military Report on S.W. Persia, IV: *Kuhgelu Country*. Simla, 1909.
　Military Report on S.W. Persia, V: *Luristan*. Simla, n.d.
　The Persian Gulf. Oxford, 1928.

A Précis of the Relations of the British Government with the Tribes and Shaikhs of Arabistan. Calcutta, 1912.
Report on Fars. Simla, 1916.
Southwest Persia: A Political Officer's Diary, 1907–1914. Oxford, 1941.

Secondary Sources

Adams, Robert McC. *Land behind Baghdad: A History of Settlement of the Diyala Plains.* Chicago, 1965.
'Alavi, Nurullah Danishvar. *Tarikh Iran va Jumbish Vatan Partisan Isfahan va Bakhtiyari.* Tehran, 1335/1957.
Ansari, Mustafa. "Internal and External Politics of the Ka'b Confederation of Southwest Iran ca. 1870–1900". Paper, American Oriental Society, Washington, D.C., 20–22 March 1973.
  "Land and the Fiscal Organization of Late Qajar Iran: 1880–1925". Paper, Research Seminar on the Economic History of the Near East, Princeton, 1974.
Arfa, General Hasan. *Under Five Shahs.* London, 1964.
Avery, Peter. *Modern Iran.* London, 1965.
Bacon, Elizabeth. "A Preliminary Attempt to Determine the Cultural Areas of Asia". *Southwestern Journal of Anthropology*, II (1946): 117–32.
  "Types of Pastoral Nomadism in Central and Southwest Asia". *Southwestern Journal of Anthropology*, X (1954): 44–68.
Bakhash, Alfred. "The Bakhtiari Migration". *Kayhan International* (13, 15, 19, 21 June 1966).
Bakhash, Shaul. "The Evolution of Qajar Bureaucracy: 1779–1879". *Middle Eastern Studies*, VII (1971): 139–68.
  Iran: Monarchy, Bureaucracy and Reform under the Qajars: 1858–1896. London, 1978.
Balfour, J.M. *Recent Happenings in Persia.* London, 1922.
Banani, Amin. *The Modernization of Iran, 1921–1941.* Stanford, 1961.
Barth, Fredrik. "Capital, Investment and the Social Structure of a Pastoral Nomad Group in South Persia". In *Capital, Savings and Credit in Peasant Societies*, pp. 69–81. Edited by Raymond Firth and B.S. Yamey, Chicago, 1964.
  "Descent and Marriage Reconsidered". In *The Character of Kinship*, pp. 3–19. Edited by Jack Goody, London, 1973.
  "Father's Brother's Daughter Marriage in Kurdistan". *Southwestern Journal of Anthropology*, X (1954): 164–71.
  "The Land Use Pattern of Migratory Tribes of South Persia". *Norsk Geografisk Tidsskrift*, XVII (1959–60): 1–11.
  Models of Social Organization. London, 1966.
  "Nomadism in the Mountain and Plateau Areas of South West Asia". *Arid Zone Research*, XVIII (1962): 341–55.
  Nomads of South Persia: The Basseri Tribe of the Khamseh Confederation. Oslo, London, and New York, 1964.
  Principles of Social Organization in South Kurdistan. Oslo, 1953.

Bartholomae, Christian. *Altiranische Wöterbuch*. Berlin, 1961.

Bates, Daniel G. "The Role of the State in Peasant–Nomad Mutualism". *Anthropological Quarterly*, XLIV (1971): 109–31.

Bavar, Mahmud. *Kuhgiluyah va Ilat An*. Gach Saran, 1324/1946.

Beck, Lois Grant. "Economic Transformations among Qashqa'i Nomads, 1962–1978". In *Modern Iran: The Dialectics of Continuity and Change*, pp. 99–122. Edited by Michael E. Bonine and Nikki R. Keddie. Albany, 1981.

"Herd Owners and Shepherds: The Qashqa'i of Iran". *Ethnology*, XIX (1980): 329–51.

"Iran and the Qashqa'i Tribal Confederacy". In *Tribe and State in Afghanistan and Iran, 1800–1980*. Edited by Richard Tapper. Paper in preparation.

"Local Organization in Nomadic Societies: Qashqa'i Pastoralists of Iran". Paper, American Anthropological Association, San Francisco, 2–6 December 1975.

"Nomads and Urbanites, Involuntary Hosts and Uninvited Guests". *Middle Eastern Studies* (forthcoming 1983).

"Revolutionary Iran and Its Tribal Peoples". *Middle East Research and Information Project Reports*, 10 (4) (1980): 14–20.

"Tribe and State in Revolutionary Iran: The Return of the Qashqa'i Khans". In *Perspectives on the Iranian Revolution*. Edited by Farhad Kazemi. *Iranian Studies*, XIII (1980): 215–55.

"Woman among Qashqa'i Nomadic Pastoralists in Iran". In *Women in the Muslim World*, pp. 351–73. Edited by Lois Beck and Nikki Keddie. Cambridge and London, 1978.

Beck, Sam. "Sedentarization among the Pastoral Nomadic Qashqa'i". Mimeographed, December 1976.

Benjamin, S.G.W. *Persia and the Persians*. Boston, 1887.

Berque, Jacques. "Introduction". *International Social Science Journal*, XI (1959): 481–98.

Bill, James A. "The Patterns of Elite Politics in Iran". In *Political Elites in the Middle East*, pp. 17–40. Edited by George Lenczowski. Washington, D.C., 1975.

Binder, Leonard. *Iran: Political Development in a Changing Society*. Berkeley and Los Angeles, 1962.

Black, Jacob, "Tyranny as a Strategy for Survival in an 'Egalitarian' Society: Luri Facts versus an Anthropological Mystique". *Man*, VII, New Series, (1972): 614–34.

Black-Michau, Jacob. "An Ethnographic and Ecological Survey of Luristan, Western Persia: Modernization in a Nomadic Pastoral Society". *Middle Eastern Studies*, X (1974): 210–20.

Bobek, Hans. "The Main Stages in Socio-Economic Evolution from a Geographical Point of View". In *Readings in Cultural Geography*, pp. 218–247. Edited by Philip L. Wagner and Marvin W. Mikesell. Chicago, 1962.

Boyle, John A. "Dynastic and Political History of the Il-Khans". In *The Cambridge History of Iran*, V: *The Saljuq and Mongol Periods*, pp. 303–421. Edited by John A. Boyle. Cambridge, 1968.

Braidwood, Robert J. "The Earliest Village Communities of Southwestern Asia Reconsidered". Paper, Atti del VI Congresso Internazionale delle Scienze Preistoriche e Protostoriche, I, Rome, 1962.

Bromberger, Christian and Jean-Pierre Digard. "Pourquoi, Comment des Cartes Ethnographiques de l'Iran?" *Objets et Mondes*, XV (1975): 7–24.

Brooks, David. "Bakhtiari: Iran". In *Peoples of the Earth: Western and Central Asia*, XV, pp. 58–67. Edited by André Singer. New York (?), 1973.

Browne, E.G. *The Persian Revolution of 1905–1909*. London, 1910.

van Bruinessen, M.M. *Agha, Shaikh and State*. Utrecht, 1978.

Bruk, S.I. "The Ethnic Composition of the Countries of W. Asia". *Sovietskaia Ethnografiia*, II (1965): 66–81.

Busk, H.G. "The Shimbar Valley Landslip Dam, Bakhtiari Country, South Persia". *Geographical Magazine*, LXIII (1926): 355–9.

Busse, Heribert. "Persische Diplomatik im Überlick: Ergebnisse unde Probleme". *Der Islam*, XXXVII (1961): 202–45.

Untersuchungen zum Islamischen Kanzleiwesen: An Hand Turkmenischer und Safawidischer Urkunden. Cairo, 1959.

Caskel, Werner, "The Bedouinization of Arabia". In *Studies in Islamic Cultural History*, pp. 36–46. Edited by G.E. von Grunebaum. Menasha, Wisc. 1954.

Chirol, Valentine. *The Middle Eastern Question*. New York, 1903.

Coon, Carleton S. *Caravan: The Story of the Middle East*. New York, 1951.

Cooper, M.G. *Grass*. New York, 1925.

Coulson, N.J. *Succession in the Muslim Family*. Cambridge, 1971.

Cressey, George B. *Crossroads*. New York, 1960.

Demorgny, G. *Essai sur l'Administration de la Perse*. Paris, 1913.

Digard, Jean-Pierre. "Campements Baxtyâri: Observations d'un Ethnologue sur des Matériaux Intéressant l'Archéologue". *Studia Iranica*, IV (1975): 117–29.

"Histoire et Anthropologie des Sociétés Nomades: Le Cas d'une Tribu d'Iran". *Annales*, VI (1973): 1423–35.

"De la Nécessité et des Inconvénients, pour un Baxtyâri, d'Être Baxtyâri. Communauté, Territoire et Inégalité chez des Pasteurs Nomades d'Iran". *Pastoral Production and Society* (Cambridge, 1979): 127–39.

"Les Nomades et l'Etat Central en Iran: Quelques Enseignments d'un Long Passe d'Hostilité Réglementée". *Peuples Méditerranéens*, VII (1979): 37–53.

"La Parure chez les Baxtyâri". *Objects et Mondes*, XI (1971): 117–32.

"Le Système Segmentaire: Modèle Indigène ou Construction d'Anthropologue? – Discussion d'un Exemple Iranien". Unpublished paper, IXe Congrès International des Sciences Anthropologiques et Ethnologiques, Chicago, 1973.

"Techniques et Cultures des Nomades Baxtyâri d'Iran". Thesis, Université René Descartes, Paris, 1973.

"'Tsiganes' et Pasteurs Nomades dans le Sud-Ouest de l'Iran". In *Tsiganes et Nomades*, pp. 43–53. Edited by Jean-Pierre Liegeois. Paris, 1978.

Douglas, Mary. *Natural Symbols*. London, 1970.

DuHousset, E. *Etudes sur les Populations de la Perse et Pays Limitrophe pendant Trois Années de Séjour en Asie*. Paris, 1863.

Dyson-Hudson, Neville. "The Study of Nomads". *Journal of Asian and African Studies*, VII (1972): 2–29.

Eberhard, Wolfram. "Nomads and Farmers in Southeastern Turkey: Problems of Settlement". *Oriens*, VI (1953): 32–49.

Ehmann, D. *Bahtiyaren – Persische Bergnomaden in Wandel der Zeit*. Wiesbaden, 1975.

Eickelman, Dale F. *The Middle East: An Anthropological Approach*. Englewood Cliffs, N.J., 1981.

Elwell-Sutton, L.P. *Persian Oil: A Study in Power Politics*. London, 1955.

Encyclopaedia of Islam, 1st edn. S.v. "Lur", by Vladimir Minorsky.

    2nd edn. S.v. "Diplomatic", by Heribert Busse.

    2nd edn. S.v. "Dustur", by Ann K.S. Lambton.

    2nd edn. S.v. "Ilat", by Ann K.S. Lambton.

    2nd edn. S.v. "Kadjar", by Ann K.S. Lambton.

    2nd edn. S.v. "Kalantar", by Ann K.S. Lambton.

    2nd edn. S.v. "Karim Khan Zand", by A.H. Zarrinkoob.

English, Paul Ward. *City and Village in Iran*. Madison, 1966.

Falcon, N.L. "The Bakhtiari Mountains of S.W. Persia". *The Alpine Journal*, XLVI (1943): 351–9.

Farman-Farma, Hafez. "The Last Phase of the Qajar Monarchy: A Study of the Political and Diplomatic History of the Persian People, 1914–1925". Thesis, Georgetown University, Washington, D.C., 1953.

Fazel, G. Reza. "The Economic Bases of Political Leadership among Pastoral Nomads: The Case of the Boyr Ahmad Tribe of Southwest Iran". Paper, American Anthropological Association, Mexico City, 1974.

    "The Encapsulation of Nomadic Societies in Iran". In *The Desert and the Sown*, pp. 130–42. Edited by Cynthia Nelson. Berkeley, 1973.

Feilberg, C.G. *Les Papis*. Copenhagen, 1952.

Field, Henry. *An Anthropological Reconnaissance in the Near East*. Cambridge, Mass., 1956.

    Contributions to the Anthropology of Iran. Chicago, 1939.

Fisher, W.B. *The Middle East: A Physical, Social, and Regional Geography*. New York, 1961.

Flannery, Kent V. "The Ecology of Early Food Production in Mesopotamia". *Science*, CXLVII (1965): 1247–56.

Floor, W.M. "The Office of Kalantar in Qajar Persia". *Journal of the Economic and Social History of the Orient*, XIV (1971): 253–68.

Fox, Robin. *Kinship and Marriage: An Anthropological Perspective*. Baltimore, 1967.

Fraser, David. *Persia and Turkey in Revolt*. London, 1910.

Garrod, Oliver. "The Nomadic Tribes of Persia Today". *Journal of the Royal Central Asian Society*, XXXIII (1946): 32–44.

    "The Qashqai Tribe of Fars". *Journal of the Royal Central Asian Society*, XXXIII (1946): 293–305.

Garthwaite, Gene R. "The Bakhtiari Ilkhani: An Illusion of Unity". *International Journal of Middle East Studies*, VIII (1977): 145–60.

"The Bakhtiyari Khans, the Government of Iran, and the British, 1846–1915". *International Journal of Middle East Studies*, III (1972): 24–44.

"Two Persian Wills of Hajj 'Ali Quli Khan Sardar As'ad". *Journal of the American Oriental Society*, XCV (1975): 645–50.

Gashgai, Abdollah. "The Gashgai in Iran". *Land Reborn*, V (1954): 6–7.

Gerth, H.H. and C. Wright Mills. *From Max Weber*. New York, 1958.

Greenfield, James. *Die Verfassung des Persischen Staates*. Berlin, 1904.

Gulliver, P.H. "Introduction". In *Tradition and Transition in East Africa*, pp. 5–35. Edited by P.H. Gulliver. London, 1969.

Haas, William S. "The Transformation of the Nomadism of the Iranian Tribes into Sedentary Life". *Proceedings of the International Congress of Anthropological and Ethnological Sciences*, II (1939): 238–9.

Hakken, David, "Marxism and Ethnology: A Comparison of Terray and Sahlins". In *Ethnology: Traditional Africa*. Edited by A. Vilakazi. Forthcoming.

Helfgott, Leonard. "Tribalism as a Socio-Economic Formation in Iranian History". Paper, Middle East Studies Association, Boston, 7–9 November 1974.

Herzfeld, Ernst. "Eine Reise durch Luristan, Arabistan, und Fars". *Petermanns Mitteilungen*, LIII (1907): 49–63, 73–90.

Hodgson, Marshall G.S. *The Venture of Islam*. Chicago, 1974.

Hole, Frank. "Ethnoarcheology of Nomadic Pastoralism: A Case Study". Paper, Rice University, Houston, 1975.

Hurewitz, J.C., ed. *Diplomacy in the Near and Middle East*. Princeton, 1958.

Irons, William. "Nomadism as a Political Adaptation: The Case of the Yomut Turkmen". *American Ethnologist*, I (1974): 635–58.

"Political Stratification among Pastoral Nomads". *Pastoral Production and Society* (Cambridge, 1979): 361–79.

"The Turkmen Nomads". *Natural History*, LXXVII (1968): 44–51.

"Variation in Political Stratification among the Yomut Turkmen". *Anthropological Quarterly*, XLIV (1971): 143–56.

The Yomut Turkmen: A Study of Social Organization among a Central Asian Turkic-Speaking Population. Ann Arbor, 1975.

Johnson, Douglas L. *The Nature of Nomadism*. Chicago, 1969.

Karimi, Asghar. "Nizam Mulkiyat Arzi dar Il Bakhtiyari". *Hunar va Mardum*, 189–90 (2537/1978): 67–83.

Kasravi, Ahmad. *Tarikh Mashrutah Iran*. Tehran, 1340/1962.

Tarikh Pansad Salih Khuzistan. Tehran, 1330/1952.

Kazemzadeh, Firuz. *Russia and Britain in Persia, 1864–1914: A Study in Imperialism*. New Haven, 1968.

Keddie, Nikki R. "The Iranian Power Structure and Social Change 1800–1969: An Overview". *International Journal of Middle East Studies*, II (1971): 3–20.

"The Iranian Village before and after Land Reform". *Journal of Contemporary History*, III (1968): 69–91.

"The Origins of the Religious–Radical Alliance in Iran". *Past and Present*, XXXIV (1966): 77–80.

Kelly, J.B. *Britain and the Persian Gulf 1795–1880*. Oxford, 1968.

Kent, Roland G. *Old Persian*. New Haven, 1950.

de Khanikoff, Nicolas. *Mémoire sur l'Ethnographie de la Perse*. Paris, 1866.

Kolars, John. "Locational Aspects of the Goat in Non-Western Agriculture". *Geographical Review*, LVI (1966): 577–84.

Krader, Lawrence. "Ecology of Central Asian Pastoralism". *Southwestern Journal of Anthropology*, XI (1955): 301–26.

"The Ecology of Nomadic Pastoralism". *International Social Science Journal*, XI (1959): 499–510.

"Principles and Structures in the Organization of the Asiatic Steppe-Pastoralists". *Southwestern Journal of Anthropology*, XI (1955): 67–92.

Kroeber, A.L. "Culture Groupings in Asia". *Southwestern Journal of Anthropology*, III (1947): 322–30.

La Fontaine, J.S. "Tribalism among the Gisu". In *Tradition and Transition in East Africa*, pp. 177–92. Edited by P.H. Gulliver. London, 1969.

Lamb, Harold. "Mountain Tribes of Iran and Iraq". *National Geographic Magazine* (March 1946): 385–408.

Lambton, Ann K.S. "The Administration of Sanjar's Empire as Illustrated in the 'Atabat al-Kataba". *Bulletin of the School of Oriental and African Studies*, XX (1957): 367–80.

"Aspects of Saljuq–Ghuzz Settlement in Persia". In *Islamic Civilization, 950–1150*, pp. 105–25. Edited by D.S. Richards. London, 1973.

"The Evolution of the Iqta' in Medieval Iran". *Iran*, V (1967): 41–50.

"Justice in the Medieval Persian Theory of Kingship". *Studia Islamica*, XVII (1962): 91–119.

Landlord and Peasant in Persia. London, 1953.

"The Office of Kalantar under the Safawids and Afshars". In *Mélanges d'Orientalisme Offers à Henri Masse à l'Occasion de son 75 ème Anniversaire*, pp. 206–18. Tehran, 1342/1963.

"Persian Society under the Qajars". *Journal of the Royal Central Asian Society*, XLVIII (1961): 123–39.

"Quis Custodiet Custodes: Some Reflections on the Persian Theory of Government". *Studia Islamica*, V (1956): 125–48 and VI (1956): 125–46.

"The Tribal Resurgence and the Decline of the Bureaucracy in the Eighteenth Century". In *Studies in Eighteenth Century Islamic History*, pp. 108–29. Edited by Thomas Naff and Roger Owen. London, 1977.

"Two Safavid Soyurghals". *Bulletin of the School of Oriental and African Studies*, XIV (1952). 44–54.

Lattimore, Owen. *Inner Asian Frontiers of China*. Boston, 1962.

Studies in Frontier History. London and New York, 1962.

Leach, E.R. *Social and Economic Organization of the Rowanduz Kurds*. London, 1940.

Lockhart, Lawrence. *The Fall of the Safavi Dynasty and the Afghan Occupation of Persia*. Cambridge, 1958.

Nadir Shah: A Critical Study. London, 1938.

Loffler, Reinhold. "From Tribal Order to Bureaucracy: The Transformation of Political Society in Buir Ahmad, S. Iran". Paper, n.d.

Lorimer, D.L.R. "The Bakhtiari of S.W. Persia". *Man*, XLV (1945): 87.

The Phonology of the Bakhtiari, Badakhshani, and Madaglashti Dialects of Modern Persia. London, 1922.

"The Popular Verse of the Bakhtiari of S.W. Persia, I". *Bulletin of the School of Oriental and African Studies*, XVI (1954): 542–55.

"The Popular Verse of the Bakhtiari of S.W. Persia, II: Specimens of Bakhtiari Verse". *Bulletin of the School of Oriental and African Studies*, XVII (1955): 92–110.

"The Popular Verse of the Bakhtiari of S.W. Persia, III: Further Specimens". *Bulletin of the School of Oriental and African Studies*, XXVI (1963): 55–68.

Malcolm. Sir John. *The History of Persia from the Most Early Period to the Present Time.* London, 1815.

Malikzadah, Mahdi. *Tarikh Inqilab Mashrutiyat Iran.* Tehran, 1328/1950.

Matley, Ian M. "Transhumance in Bosnia and Herzegovina". *Geographical Review*, LVIII (1968): 231–61.

Mazzaoui, Michel M. *The Origins of the Safawids.* Wiesbaden, 1972.

Meldgaard, Jørgen, Peder Mortensen, ar. I Henrik Thrane. *Excavations at Tepe Guran, Luristan.* Copenhagen, 1964.

Miller, William Green. "Hosseinabad: A Persian Village". *The Middle East Journal*, XVIII (1964): 483–98.

Millspaugh, Arthur C. *The American Task in Persia.* New York, 1925.

Monteil, Vincent. *Les Tribus du Fârs et la Sédentarisation des Nomades.* Paris, 1966.

Murphy, Robert F. and Leonard Kasdan. "The Structure of Parallel Cousin Marriage". *American Anthropologist*, LXI (1959): 17–29.

Myres, John L. "Nomadism". *Journal of the Royal Anthropological Institute of Great Britain and Ireland*, LXXI (1941): 19–42.

van Nieuwenhuijze, C.A.O. *Social Stratification and the Middle East: An Interpretation.* Leiden, 1965.

Oberlander, Theodore. *The Zagros Streams.* Syracuse, 1965.

Oberling, Pierre. *The Qashqa'i Nomads of Fars.* The Hague, 1974.

Patai, Raphael. *Golden River to Golden Road.* Philadelphia, 1962.

Pazhman, Husain. "Bakhtiyari dar Guzashtah Dur". *Vahid*, III, Nos. 2, 3, 4 (1344/1966).

Perry, John R. "The Banu Ka'b. An Ambitious Brigand State in Khuzistan". *Le Monde Iranien et l'Islam*, I (1971): 131–52.

"Forced Migration in Iran during the Seventeenth and Eighteenth Centuries". *Iranian Studies*, VIII (1975): 199–215.

Karim Khan Zand: A History of Iran, 1747–1779. Chicago, 1979.

"The Last Safavids, 1722–1773". *Iran*, IX (1971): 59–69.

de Planhol, Xavier. "Aspects of Mountain Life in Anatolia and Iran". In *Geography as Human Ecology*, pp. 291–308. Edited by S.R. Eyre and G.R.J. Jones. London, 1966.

"Caractères Généraux de la Vie Montagnarde dans le Proche-Orient et dans l'Afrique du Nord". *Annales de Géographie*, LXXI (1962): 113–29.

"Geography of Settlement". In *The Cambridge History of Iran*, I: *The Land of Iran*, pp. 409–67. Edited by W.B. Fisher. Cambridge, 1968.

"Nomades et Pasteurs, IV". *Revue Géographique de l'Est*, IV (1964): 315–28.

"Traits Généraux de l'Utilisation du Sol en Perse". In *Land Use in Semi-Arid Mediterranean Climates*, pp. 95–9. Paris, 1964.

Poole, Reginald Stuart. *The Coins of the Shahs of Persia*. London, 1887.

Rabino di Borgomale, H.L. *Album of Coins, Medals, and Seals of The Shahs of Iran*. Oxford, 1951.

Coins, Medals, and Seals of the Shahs of Iran, 1500–1941. Algiers (?), 1945.

Rice, C. Colliver. *Persian Women and Their Ways*. Philadelphia, 1923.

Rochefort, Régina. "Les Effets du Milieu sur les Communautés Humaines des Régions Arides". *Arid Zone Research*, VIII (1957): 11–42.

Rosman, Abraham and Paula G. Rubel. "Nomad–Sedentary Interethnic Relations in Iran and Afghanistan". *International Journal of Middle East Studies*, VII (1976): 545–70.

Rowton, M.B. "Autonomy and Nomadism in Western Asia". *Orientalia*, XLII, New Series (1973): 247–58.

"Enclosed Nomadism". *Journal of the Economic and Social History of the Orient*, XVII (1974): 1–30.

"Urban Autonomy in a Nomadic Environment". *Journal of Near Eastern Studies*, XXXII (1973): 201–15.

Sahlins, Marshall D. "The Segmentary Lineage: An Organization of Predatory Expansion". In *Comparative Political Systems*, pp. 89–119. Edited by Ronald Cohen and John Middleton. New York, 1967.

Tribesmen. Englewood Cliffs, N.J., 1968.

Salzman, Philip Carl. "Continuity and Change in Baluchi Tribal Leadership". *International Journal of Middle East Studies*, IV (1973): 428–39.

"Movement and Resource Extraction among Pastoral Nomads: The Case of the Shah Nawzi Baluch". *Anthropological Quarterly*, XLIV (1971): 185–97.

"National Integration of the Tribes in Modern Iran". *The Middle East Journal* (1971): 325–36.

"Political Organization among Nomadic People". *Proceedings of the American Philosophical Society*, III (1967): 115–31.

"The Study of Complex Society in the Middle East: A Review Essay". Mimeographed, June 1975.

"Tribal Chiefs as Middlemen: The Politics of Encapsulation in the Middle East". *Anthropological Quarterly*, XLVII (1974): 203–10.

Savory, Roger M. *Iran Under the Safavids*. Cambridge, 1980.

"The Principal Offices of the Safawid State during the Reign of Isma'il I (907–30/1501–24)". *Bulletin of the School of Oriental and African Studies*, XXIII (1960): 91–105.

"The Principal Offices of the Safawid State during the Reign of Tahmasp I (930–84/1524–76)". *Bulletin of the School of Oriental and African Studies*, XXIV (1961): 65–85.

Schurmann, Franz. "The Nomads of the World". Unpublished manuscript, 1956–7.

Shuster, W. Morgan. *The Strangling of Persia*. New York, 1912.

Smith, John Masson. "Mongol Manpower and Persian Population". *Journal of the Economic and Social History of the Orient*, XVIII (1975): 271–99.

"Mongol and Nomadic Taxation". *Harvard Journal of Asiatic Studies*, XXX (1970): 46–85.
Southall, Aidan W. "The Illusion of Tribe". *Journal of Asian and African Studies*, V (1970): 28–50.
Spooner, Brian. *The Cultural Ecology of Pastoral Nomads*. Addison–Wesley Module in Anthropology No. 45, Reading, Mass. 1973.
Stack, Edward. *Six Months in Persia*. New York, 1882.
Stauffer, Thomas R. "The Economics of Nomadism". *The Middle East Journal*, XIX (1965): 284–302.
"The Qashqai Nomads: A Contemporary Appraisal". *The Harvard Review* (Spring 1963): 28–39.
Sunderland, E. "Pastoralism, Nomadism and the Social Anthropology of Iran". In *The Cambridge History of Iran*, I: *The Land of Iran*, pp. 611–83. Edited by W.B. Fisher. Cambridge, 1968.
Sykes, Christopher. *Wassmuss: The German Lawrence*. London, 1936.
Sykes, Sir Percy M. "Anthropological Notes on South Persia". *Journal of the Royal Anthropological Institute of Great Britain and Ireland*, XXXII (1902): 339–52.
A History of Persia. London, 1930.
"South Persia and the Great War". *Geographical Journal*, LVIII (1921): 101–19.
Tapper, Richard. "The Organization of Nomadic Communities in Pastoral Societies of the Middle East". *Pastoral Production and Society* (Cambridge, 1979): 43–66.
Pasture and Politics: Economics, Conflict and Ritual among Shahsevan Nomads of Northwestern Iran. London, 1979.
"The Tribes in 18th and 19th Century Iran". Unpublished paper, 1976.
Toynbee, Arnold J. *A Study of History*. New York and London, 1947.
Tursunbayev, A. and A. Potapov. "Some Aspects of the Socio-Economic and Cultural Developments of Nomads in the U.S.S.R". *International Social Science Journal*, XI (1959): 511–24.
Uzhan, Sarhang Abu al-Fath. *Tarikh Bakhtiyari*. Tehran, 1345/1967.
Tarikhchah Dau Qarn Akhir Shu'ra va 'Urafa Chahar Mahall va Bakhtiyari. Tehran, 1332/1954.
Walther, R. "Note sur la Tribu des Bakhtiaris en Iran". *La Géographie*, LXX (1938): 133–41.
Watson, Patty Jo. *Archeological Ethnography in Western Iran*. Tucson, 1979.
"Clues to Iranian Prehistory in Modern Village Life". *Expedition*, VIII (1966): 9–19.
Watson, Robert Grant. *A History of Persia from the Beginning of the Nineteenth Century to the Year 1858*. London, 1866.
Whyte, R.O. "Evolution of Land Use in South-Western Asia". *Arid Zone Research*, XVII (1961): 57–118.
Wilber, Donald N. *Riza Shah Pahlavi: The Resurrection and Reconstruction of Iran*. Hicksville, N.Y., 1975.
Woods, John E. *The AqQuyunlu: Clan, Confederation, Empire*. Chicago, 1976.

Index

'Abbas I, Shah, 5, 7, 51, 52, 53
'Abbas II, Shah, 5, 7, 52
'Abbas III, Shah, 53, 56
'Abbas Mirza, 73, 142
'Abbas Quli, 157, 165, 190 n. 110
'Abd al-Khalil, 56, 57, 60, 80
Abdal Khan, 8, 56, 59, 60, 63, 64, 75, 77
Adams, Robert McC., 31
'Adil Shah ('Ali Riza Mirza), 68, 69
Afghanistan, 68, 94, 103, 135
Afghans, 34, 52, 54
Afshars, 7, 8, 34, 53, 54, 55, 56, 59, 60, 61,
    67, 74
Ahmad Khusravi, 48, 76, 80, 81, 84, 149,
    150, 188 n. 49
Ahmad Shah (Sultan Ahmad Mirza), 10, 119
Ahvaz, 20, 134, 149, 153, 154, 161, 165,
    167, 168, 169
'Ali Asghar Khan, Amin al-Sultan, Atabak
    (Atabaig) A'zam, 91, 98–102, 106, 109,
    111, 114, 131, 132
'Ali Mardan Khan (Bakhtiyari), 5, 8, 53–5,
    59, 60, 67, 69, 177 n. 33
'Ali Murad (Chahar Lang), 57–8
'Ali Naqi Khan (Chahar Lang), 68, 70
'Ali Quli Khan, Hajji, Sardar As'ad (II), 10,
    44, 48, 63, 75–102, 104, 105–10,
    114–27, 129–31, 134, 145, 147, 149–52,
    159, 161, 167, 168, 186 n. 7
'Ali Riza Khan (Chahar Lang), 70, 71
'Ali Salih Khan, 8, 39, 56–8, 59, 63
Amir Mufakham. See Lutf 'Ali
Amir Quli, 152, 169, 190 n. 85
Amir Sharaf Khan Bidlisi, 49
Andakah, 149, 150, 188 n. 44
Anglo-Russian Convention (1907), 116, 124,
    135
Aq Quyunlu, 34, 52
'Arabistan, 7, 9, 19, 21, 30, 40, 51, 56, 63,
    66–9, 71, 79, 86–105, 120, 129, 132,
    134, 137–9, 149, 151, 160, 163–9. See
    also Khuzistan
Arabs, 18, 66, 70, 98, 129, 147, 150, 153,

157, 164, 166, 168; shaikhs, 15, 40, 44,
    71, 147–69 passim
Ardal, 151, 152, 155, 161, 167, 189 n. 77
As'ad Khan (Bakhtiyarvand), 64, 66, 154,
    190 n. 95
Atabak A'zam. See 'Ali Asghar Khan
Azad Khan Afghan, 54, 60, 61
Azerbaijan, 53, 57, 60, 133

Babadi, 36, 61, 64, 65, 75, 76, 158, 165
Bahmah'i, 74, 78, 148, 164, 167, 187 n. 17
Bakhtiar, Shahpour (Shapur), 1, 140
Bakhtiyar, Aqa Khan, 140
Bakhtiyar, Timur, 140
Bakhtiyari
    agreements: of 1894, 9, 97, 110, 117, 125,
        142; of 1909 (Secret), 117, 125–7; of
        1912, 127–33; of 1915
        (Anglo-Bakhtiyari), 136–8
    dialects, 2, 6, 18, 48
    districts, 5–6, 17–19, 24
    economy: agriculture, 18–33; comparative
        pastoral nomadism, 24–33, 47, 173 n.
        30; dual base of khans in, 13–14, 17–18,
        34–6, 38–41, 43, 58–61, 86–9, 142–4;
        relation of khans to, 35, 38, 39, 40–4,
        81–9
    ethnic composition, 18
    factions: Hajji Ilkhani, 9, 11, 48, 74, 81,
        88, 93, 97, 98, 101, 102, 109, 113, 114,
        124, 125, 127, 128, 131, 140, 141, 142;
        Ilbaigi, 9, 74, 95, 97, 98, 102, 126, 127;
        Ilkhani, 9, 11, 48, 74, 81, 88, 93, 97,
        98, 101, 102, 109, 113–33, 130, 141,
        142
    flock size, 22–3, 28–9, 40, 74, 84, 174–5
        n. 11
    lineage/descent, 9, 38–40, 61, 74, 142
    marriage: great khan, 52, 63, 74–80, 142;
        parallel-cousin, 74–9
    migration, 21–4
    offices: ilkhani, 6, 9, 17, 37, 81–2, 139,
        146; ilbaigi, 64, 139; kadkhuda, 8, 36,

210